THE DEAD STAGE

A GUIDE TO WRITING FOR THEATRE

DAN WEATHERER

Let the world know:
#IGotMyCLPBook!

Crystal Lake Publishing
www.CrystalLakePub.com

Copyright 2018 Crystal Lake Publishing

All Rights Reserved

ISBN: 978-1-64467-969-2

Cover Design:
Ben Baldwin—http://www.benbaldwin.co.uk/

Interior Layout:
Lori Michelle—www.theauthorsalley.com

Proofread by:
Paula Limbaugh
Nancy Scuri
Tere Fredericks

No part of this publication may be reproduced, stored in a retrieval system, or transmitted in any form or by any means, without the prior permission in writing of the publisher, nor be otherwise circulated in any form of binding or cover than that in which it is published and without a similar condition including this condition being imposed on the subsequent purchaser.

WELCOME TO ANOTHER CRYSTAL LAKE PUBLISHING CREATION.

Thank you for supporting independent publishing and small presses. You rock, and hopefully you'll quickly realize why we've become one of the world's leading publishers of Dark and Speculative Fiction. We have some of the world's best fans for a reason, and hopefully we'll be able to add you to that list really soon. Be sure to sign up for our newsletter to receive two free eBooks, as well as info on new releases, special offers, and so much more. To follow us behind the scenes while supporting independent publishing and our authors, be sure to follow us on Patreon.

Welcome to Crystal Lake Publishing—Tales from the Darkest Depths.

OTHER NON FICTION TITLES BY CRYSTAL LAKE PUBLISHING

Where Nightmares Come From, edited by Eugene Johnson and Joe Mynhardt

Horror 201: The Silver Scream Vol.1 & Vol.2

Horror 101: The Way Forward

Modern Mythmakers: 35 interviews with Horror and Science Fiction Writers and Filmmakers by Michael McCarty

Writers On Writing: An Author's Guide, edited by Joe Mynhardt

Or check out other Crystal Lake Publishing books for more Tales from the Darkest Depths.

*For Bethany & Nathan
(Budding actors, the pair of them!)*

COPYRIGHT ACKNOWLEDGEMENTS

Strictly for personal use only. Performance rights can be attained by contacting:

Beige, The Haul, A Brother Born and *The Holding* are published by Heartland Plays, and performance rights for these pieces are available via www.heartlandplays.com.

The Release of Theodore Marlow is published via Off The Wall Plays, and performance rights can be obtained via www.offthewallpays.com.

All other performance rights are available by emailing the author direct at danweatherer@fatherdarkness.com, or by visiting www.fatherdarkness.com and using the contact form

CONTENTS

Introduction 1

Place the Play 4

Industry Insights:
   Deborah McAndrew 15
      Actor/Playwright/Creative Director
   Matthew Spencer 21
      Actor
   Kate Danbury 26
      Producer, London Horror Festival
   Catherine Lord 32
      Writer/Director
   Ellie Pitkin 42
      Creative Lead, Blackshaw Theatre
   Andrew Crane 47
      Technician. Blackshaw Theatre
   Jill Young 51
      Drama Tutor, Actor and Director
   Tom Slatter 56
      Actor

Stage Plays:
   Beige 65
   A Question of Authorship 85
   Crippen 98
   Eloise 221

Killing Gary	228
One for the Road	242
Parents	254
Penkhull Paranormal	276
Points	310
The March of the Pagan King	321
A Brother Born	326
The Release of Theodore Marlow	371
Tuesday of the Dead	453
The Haul	466
The Holding	476
Friends like Us	513
About the Author	555

INTRODUCTION

YOU MIGHT SAY that I started to write plays to prove a point. Now admittedly, that probably sounds like an awful reason to write any piece, but allow me to explain my reasoning; you will see it was a point worth proving.

My first published short story *The Legend of the Chained Oak*, through a lot of hard work on all parts, eventually became a successful short film. Together, a group of first-time filmmakers, actors, etc. produced an award-winning short on a budget of £500, the success of which got me to thinking that maybe my future was in films.

OK, I admit that I was naïve as to the complications of the film industry at the time but high from the success of the short, I believed that anything was possible.

So, I sat down and wrote three of four full-length screenplays, submitted them to anyone and everyone whom I thought might be interested in my efforts, sat back, and waited for the offers to flood in.

Only that never happened.

They didn't even so much as drip in.

Never one to take rejection to heart (a trait that is imperative if you are to forge a career for yourself in the creative arts), I digested whatever feedback came my way and decided to reevaluate my career goals.

I forget who said it to me, but one piece of advice stands out in my mind with regards to screenplays, and what directors/producers are drawn to:

"Producers like a script with a lot of white spaces."

Upon first hearing this I admit to being taken aback. Some of my favourite movies were talkies, my own preference leaning towards an intelligent script over impressive special effects, etc.

However, on reflection, the weight of their words began to sink in. Film is a visual medium, whereby a story is told predominantly with images, and my scripts were weighed down with extensive (but in part, half decent) dialogue.

Unless I altered my approach to writing, the chances of a career in film looked slim at best.

The stage seemed to be the natural outlet for my work.

Now, I'm not going to call myself any kind of authority on theatre, and when I began to write for the stage, I was more than a little wet behind the ears. The book that follows this introduction will elaborate more on the mistakes that I made, and the tips that I picked up from other playwrights during my limited experience as a playwright.

What I will say is that I enjoyed the challenge of writing for the stage, and that so long as you do so, then any obstacle you may encounter on your journey will not be so nearly as disheartening as it could initially appear.

My first, full-length piece was met with a degree of negative feedback, feedback that came from those in

DEAD STAGE

the industry that I both trusted and respected. It would have been easy to dwell on their advice and call it a day, instead choosing to focus on writing books. Theatre was the most difficult medium to break into, as you are always competing with the established, timeless works of Shakespeare, Miller, and Wilde. There is little money supporting new writing, and it can take years to get a piece to stage.

Daunting words that I did not take lightly; words that only increased my desire to write for the stage.

If there is one thing that you take from this book, it is the simple message that it IS possible to get work onto the stage. I enjoy my work, and actors/directors and audiences seem to do so also. Why? I have no idea, but I like to believe that my enjoyment of the art shows in the scripts that I produce.

Dan Weatherer
27th, September, 2016

PLACE THE PLAY

This essay first appeared in the Horror Writers Association Writing Tips section of their website.

SO YOU HAVE penned your theatrical debut and it is a masterpiece, but what now? How do you get your freshly completed stage play from your hard drive and onto the stage?

Believe it or not, this is not as daunting or as complicated a process as it might sound. While there is no 100% sure-fire way to ensure your piece gets to be performed on stage, I will share a few useful tips that will save you a lot of time when it comes to submitting material, and help manage your expectations of what you can expect to experience during the process. Again, I must stress that this is in no way, shape or form the ONLY way to get your work onto the stage, but as of writing this I have only been writing as a playwright for eighteen months, and I have already had several pieces of work staged/aired in the UK/USA, and have successfully landed representation as a playwright. What has worked for me may work for you.

OK, so let's dive in with what I have learned during my short stint as a playwright:

DEAD STAGE

First, some truths as regards to theatre and new writing (most of what I will discuss is born of my experience with the UK theatre scene, but I imagine some of it will ring true wherever you are in the world). New writing is seen as a gamble, more so than with regard to traditional book publishing. Many believe that theatre is the toughest nut to crack when compared to film and book industries. The aim of the theatre is to make money by filling seats. The sad truth is that new writers are not often seen as seat fillers, and theatre companies are reluctant to take a risk on any piece, regardless of its merit, if they feel the name of the author is not enough of a draw to cover their overheads and make a profit.

However, don't despair! There are many theatres that DO encourage new writing, and they often post submission calls detailing exactly the kind of work that they are looking for. I use the Play Submission Helper and the London Playwrights Blog. Check them often and I guarantee you will eventually come across a theatre/group that will be willing to read your work. From then, it is a case of following their submission guidelines and waiting patiently for a response (please bear in mind that response times vary considerably, and as with any submission, decisions are based a multitude of factors, and feedback is rarely provided with a rejection).

Before You Submit:

Proof it.

How many times have you looked over your work,

confident that it reads perfectly well, submitted it, then later found a glaring typo?

Proofreading a script is just as important as proofreading a manuscript. Shabby submissions rarely get to the stage. Remember, you might be submitting alongside countless other playwrights; you may as well give your work the best chance of acceptance possible by submitting a watertight script to begin with.

Further, if you can get a group of people together to read your script aloud before submitting, you will immediately hear if your dialogue is in need of further work. Hearing others speak your material will highlight any clunkiness of dialogue, or other shortfalls (such as the flow of the piece, plot holes, etc.). I would also advise listening to what your readers/performers have to say with regards to your characters. For example, not everybody speaks in full sentences, and your readers may highlight lines that feel awkward when spoken aloud. Properly written dialogue can be wooden and unbelievable. Listen to how it is performed and amend accordingly. You will be surprised at how different a line is heard as to read inside your head. However, taking into account their feedback is entirely up to you (not every piece of advice you will be given need be followed, after all: you are the architect of the piece), but sometimes they may be able to highlight issues that you may have overlooked. All of this effort can help fine-tune a script and make it 'pop' from the page, improving your chances of success.

Leave meat on the bone for the actors/director.

DEAD STAGE

This tip is born of both personal experience and preference.

When providing a character breakdown, I find that supplying the character's name/age is more than sufficient. Let me explain why: Theatre scripts differ from novels etc. in that you are handing over your work to be interpreted by others. Directors/actors like to delve into your words and present/interpret them in their own way. The more they have to play with, the more likely the project will appeal to them. Sometimes you can dictate far too much; for instance, a character may have had a string of one-night stands, a failed marriage, a drinking problem, no regular income, and once saw a Heron, but the strength of your writing SHOULD convey all of that in the way the character acts/speaks, if it is relevant to the piece. There is no need to explain every nuance of their personality in the character breakdown. Less in this instance is indeed more. Think of it as you handing over a recipe; the key ingredients are there (and will always be yours) but the way the meal is prepared and served, is up to the chef.

The same can be said for stage directions. Specify any important gestures/actions that you feel are integral to the action, but allow the directors/actors to add and amend any they see fit, as they explore the possibilities of the scene. I can't stress enough how (in my experience) it is important to trust the director/actors with your work. They will keep you in the loop and may suggest amendments (ones you can of course refuse), but they may uncover new and exciting angles to your work that transfer better to the medium of the stage.

Types of Performance:

In my experience, the kind of submission calls most commonly found online involve either a rehearsed reading or a full performance.

Rehearsed Reading:

A rehearsed reading is just that: actors (with script in hand) read aloud your work while in character. Usually, there are no set/props on stage. Actors may sit, and any stage directions are usually described using the text in the script. Occasionally, there will be audience feedback sessions. These types of events are great for testing new writing on both actors and audience alike. Excerpts of larger works can also be performed; the benefit of this is that you can road test a project without needing to have completed it first.

Full Performance:

In this instance, your work will be rehearsed beforehand, and a full performance by actors in full costume, and props/sets will be involved This may be a one-off event or part of a longer run.

The Small Print:

A quick note on contracts: read them thoroughly before signing. There are a myriad of ways a Playwright may attain royalties. Be sure to fully understand what you are entitled (and that you are happy with the agreement) before signing. Remember:

DEAD STAGE

If there is something in the contract you do not like or are unsure of, ask to discuss it further.

How to Maximise the Chances of Getting Your Work onto the Stage:

The length of a piece:

You may have written an epic, five-act period drama, spanning two hours and featuring a cast of hundreds (which is great), but bear in mind that such a bold offering is unlikely to be considered by all but the most adventurous of theatres.

There are several reasons for this, but the most important is cost. Such a production would require a huge budget, a budget that (unless you are a major player on the theatre scene) you are unlikely to secure. Competitions are sometimes receptive of longer pieces from new writers (more on those later).

I have written full-length productions but have not placed them as of yet. Theatre is timeless; anything written can be stockpiled until the day theatres come knocking at your door, begging for your work (I have amassed quite the collection already!).

You will find that there are plenty of theatre groups looking for short pieces. Short is cheap. Short is good. You can still tell a story in five pages (if it is written well) and you will find theatres much more receptive to reading short pieces for that very reason (I have had some of my best results with pieces no more than fifteen minutes long).

Remember, as a general rule of thumb: One page

of typed script equates to one and a half minutes' performance time.

Characters and Scenery:

Again, the simpler, the better. The types of theatres/groups that are looking to stage new writing often have little to no budget, and a stable numbering only a handful of dedicated actors. Often you will see submission calls for pieces containing no more than two characters. If you can write a tight script with only a few characters and a minimal setting, you make your work far more appealing to would-be theatre producers. Ease of production goes a long way to selling your work.

If you can write and be mindful that the piece can be easily performed, you will be at a distinct advantage when it comes to selection.

Fringe and Competitions:

I have had the majority of my success submitting to fringe events in the UK/US. While there has been little in the way of financial reward, seeing your piece interpreted and brought to life by others is often reward itself. There is no greater feeling than seeing an audience respond to your words the way you imagined they would. Further, I have built up a network of actors/directors/producers who work tirelessly in various theatre scenes around the world. Indeed, my agent came by way of a recommendation from an actress who starred in one of my pieces! Theatre is very much a *people* industry. This is something to bear in mind when speaking to actors/directors who have shown an interest in your work. If they like you, they will usually support you to the hilt!

You will also see plenty of submission calls for competition writing. Some of these have entry fees attached, but many do not. Again, if you feel you have something that might fit the submission criteria, then consider submitting. Competition wins (or final placings) look great on the résumé.

One final tip:

Start with a bang. If you catch your audience early, it's easier to keep them interested than to build slowly towards the crux of your story. *Beige* begins right after one of the main characters is murdered. *Crippen/The Release of Theodore Marlow* begins with relationships already strained. This serves to get people asking questions as to your characters/story from the off. There's no need for a slow burning build up (especially in shorter pieces) unless the narrative demands it.

Again, I must remind you that these tips are all based on the journey that I have undertaken during the past year and a half, and that they are in no way a guarantee of success. However, I have built an impressive portfolio of work, and sport a resume that lists several international performances/final placings, all in the space of eighteen months. Yes, the theatre is tough, but the point of this book is to highlight that there are ways to get your work performed in front of an audience. It worked for me (and yes, there is still a long way for me to go, but it got me where I am today), and it can also work for you; just don't forget to invite me to opening night!

INDUSTRY INSIGHTS

The following section contains interviews from various professionals that I have met on my journey as a playwright.

Each has a wealth of experience within the industry, and I am forever grateful for their contributions with regards to this book.

What follows is a brief insight into their theatre backgrounds, opinions on the state of the current theatre scene, as well as advice for aspiring playwrights.

Theatre is family.

I hope you find their words helpful and inspiring.

DEBORAH McANDREW
PLAYWRIGHT ACTOR DIRECTOR

How did you initially become involved with the theatre industry?

I grew up in a normal, non-showbiz house in Yorkshire, but fell in love with the theatre at an early age. I was good at English and planned to study this at University, but then I found out you could do Drama at degree level. I wasn't sure I wanted to be an actor, and I couldn't imagine going to Drama School. In those days, there weren't many degree courses in Drama. Manchester was one of the few, and I got in, in 1986. I was the first in my family ever to go to University.

At University, I did quite a bit of acting and caught the eye of a casting director at Granada TV. However, at the end of my undergraduate years, I still wasn't sure I could be an actor and didn't go on to post-grad at Drama School, as my tutors advised, but went to Teacher Training College instead. After a difficult year, I got my PGCE but realised I needed to give showbiz a go. I got my Equity Card through singing with a jazz band (you needed one then to work), got back in touch with the University Drama Department, and things snowballed quite quickly. I got an acting agent through

DAN WEATHERER

my tutor's recommendation (I'm still with that same agent), and then an audition came in for Coronation St. I got the job, which was a three-month contract. This was extended and extended, and I ended up staying as a regular in the show for three years—at which point I left to go into the theatre where I really wanted to be.

After eleven years as an actor, working constantly in theatre and radio, my daughter was born. At this point, I focused back on my first love—writing. I'd been writing all through my acting years, but too busy to give it the time and focus that it takes to be any good. Sixteen years on from that point and I make a living as a playwright. I still work as an actor on radio and do voice overs, too. I haven't been in a play on stage for ten years. I have three agents—a Literary, Acting, and Voice Over.

What does a Creative Director do?

When I founded my theatre company, Claybody Theatre, three years ago I called myself Creative Director because I make all the key creative choices, and am the main driving force behind the company. I write the plays (obviously), but I also do most of the outreach work and marketing too, to build our audience and our connection to the community we serve. It's fundamentally my vision to create work that grows directly from the unique people and experience of North Staffordshire (specifically Stoke). Conrad Nelson is Artistic Director—and he directs the shows, and has gradually become more involved in funding applications, etc. . . .

DEAD STAGE

What qualities do you look for in a script? Does this differ depending on if you are approaching the script as an actor, or as a Creative Director? If so, how?

I'm looking for a script that fits the brief—whatever that might be. I've written for many different companies, and they all want different things. Northern Broadsides is different to Mikron, which is in turn very different to a Christmas show for Bolton. It's quite rare that I find myself just writing what I want to write. I get commissioned, and it's my job to give the buyer what they want. I'm a working writer. It's mostly not about me. I do like to write the stories that just come to me, but this is a luxury.

But whatever the piece, I'm always looking for key ingredients in my own work and that of others: a strong narrative, clear story telling (including a solid structure), good dialogue, and characterisation. I'm looking for a lean script—without fat or flabbiness. Something that is thoroughly worked to make every line count—multitasking wherever possible to provide character, plot, and subtext all at once.

As an actor, writer or director I'm looking for the same things. A good script is a good script.

Does your experience as an actor influence your approach to writing? If so, how?

My work as an actor is inextricably linked to my writing. Both are rooted in the same place in my imagination—the part that is very interested in what it feels like to be other people. When I have written something I work with it as an actor as well as a writer, saying it out loud and feeling the rhythms and the narrative from that perspective. I like to think that my lines are 'sayable' for actors. In everything I do I am rigorous and disciplined.

Do you feel experience in theatre/drama at an academic level is necessary for a playwright? If so, how?

I don't think it's necessary, but it's been my experience, and I can't imagine being without it. I do think that writing plays is a very muscular intellectual activity, and so a high level of education is needed, but this may be gained in other ways—or through the process of writing itself.

In your experience, is the theatre industry accepting of new writing? If so/not—how?

The theatre doesn't eat up new writing the way TV, film, and radio do. Theatres do a lot of adaptations, as they are generally constrained financially and need a 'title' they can sell. Audiences are quite risk averse and therefore so are theatres. It takes a lot of trust in a writer or a company for an audience to book in large numbers for a new and untested work. However, there is an appetite for this, which can be cultivated. There are theatres specifically dedicated to new writing—though these tend to be in London, Manchester, Liverpool, Birmingham, Leeds, etc. . . . Many of the big publicly funded theatres in major cities employ a literary manager to sift through scripts and work on developing new writers and new writing.

DEAD STAGE

What one piece of advice would you offer to aspiring playwrights?

It's very difficult to break in, but as an actor you're in a much bigger pool than as a writer. There are far fewer writers out there, as it's really hard—and even fewer good ones. If you've got ability and you persevere and learn your craft you're in with a shout. Also—see anything and everything and learn from others. It's possible to learn as much (if not more) from a bad play as from a good one.

Websites:
http://deborahmcandrew.com
http://claybodytheatre.com

Bio:
Current Commissions include: *Cyrano* for Northern Broadsides and New Vic Theatre (touring Spring 2017); *The Tenant of Wildfell Hall* for Octagon Theatre Bolton and York Theatre Royal (March/April 2017); *Anna of the Five Towns* for New Vic Theatre (May/June 2017); *The Chester Mysteries* 2018.

Deborah's moving 1st World War drama *An August Bank Holiday Lark* for Northern Broadsides and New Vic Theatre won both UK Theatre Award and Manchester Theatre Award for Best New Play 2014. This play is published by Methuen.

Credits include: *The Grand Gesture* (2013) *A Government Inspector* (2012), published by Methuen; *Accidental Death Of An Anarchist* (2008); *Vacuum* (2006) and *The Bells* (2004) all for Northern Broadsides Theatre Company; *Digging In* (2015) and

DAN WEATHERER

Ugly Duck (2013) for Claybody Theatre; *One of Each* (2015), *Till The Cows Come Home* (2014), *Beyond The Veil* (2013) and *Losing The Plot* (2012), Mikron Theatre; *David Copperfield* (2010) and *Oliver Twist* (2009), Octagon Theatre, Bolton; *King Macbeth* (2010), Reveal Theatre Company and *Flamingoland* (2008), New Vic Theatre, published by Nick Hern Books.

In her acting career, Deborah has worked extensively in television, radio, and theatre—including appearing in productions for Northern Broadsides. She is best known for her role as *Coronation Street* regular, Angie Freeman, in the 1990s.

MATTHEW SPENCER
ACTOR, CURRENTLY TOURING WITH *THE WOMAN IN BLACK*.

How did you originally become involved in the theatre industry?

I first became involved in the theatre when I was growing up doing amateur dramatics with local drama groups and then studying GCSE Drama and then A-Level Theatre Studies at school, but I didn't know that I wanted to be involved in it as a career until getting into Drama School. I had always enjoyed it as a hobby but hadn't really considered the idea that it could become a career. Over 2000 people audition for 24-30 places at the Drama Schools that I was applying to so I never really thought that that would happen. But once I was offered a place at the age of 18 I knew I had to take it, and I knew that that was what I wanted to do.

My first job as an actor was in a Moliere play, 'Tartuffe.' This was a production for the Watermill Theatre in Newbury and then a twelve-week tour. These jobs are the bread and butter for actors so I suppose, looking back, this was exactly the right job to have first to introduce me to the world of theatre and being an actor.

As an actor, when presented with a script, what captures your interest? What is it about the script that makes you want to audition for the role?

When you first graduate and start out, you'll audition for anything. You're just happy to be offered the opportunity to work. Obviously, you still want to play interesting parts and parts that have as much stage time as possible. For me now, I've had the opportunity to play some fantastic parts in the last three—four years. So, it means that you can be more particular with regards as to what you want to go in for.

When I first read the first draft of Robert Icke's and Duncan Macmillan's '1984', I was so excited at the prospect of being involved with that project. Their ideas of how to put that story theatrically on stage were so exciting; I knew I wanted to be involved. And then getting the opportunity to play Winston Smith in it was amazing. Looking at that script, and indeed any script, when the character has an interesting and challenging arc, then that is always exciting for me. If he gets to go through many emotions and settings, you know that you will have creative fulfilment. That was the case with Winston, and with '1984' as a whole.

When you secure a part, how much input do you have with regards to amending lines/dialogue? Do you feel this is often necessary? If so, do you feel this is due in part

DEAD STAGE

to mistakes made by the playwright, or is this a natural result of working with the script, and finding alternative ways of delivering a line?

This is an interesting question. Most plays that I've been involved with have been scripts that are set in stone, by playwrights who are either long dead or very strict about their lines of dialogue. So, the job of an actor is really to take what's been given to you and make it live and real. Quite often there will be lines that feel very awkward to say at first as they are very different from how you'd normally portray them, but with rehearsals and understanding it often becomes apparent that this is the right way to say the line. Just because it feels weird to begin with shouldn't mean it needs re-writing.

However, when you are involved in new writing and maybe have the playwright there in the room with you, that's absolutely a time when those dialogue changes can happen. Sometimes with rehearsal, you can discover things as an actor that even the writer hasn't thought about. In my experience, if you have open communication with the actors and writers, then an actor might say, "This doesn't quite feel right, can I change this word, etc." and the writer will just say "Sure," or maybe, "No, I put it that way because . . . ." Either way, it is important to reach an agreement where both parties are happy.

In your experience, is the theatre industry accepting of new writing? If so/not—how?

I'd say it's harder for new writing to be put on, simply

because it's not tried and tested and theatres don't know whether people are going to come and see it. Especially now, after all the cuts to the Arts, it seems to be an industry leaning more towards the commercial sector than ever before, and new writing isn't a commercial venture. So, you look to the large theatres like The National to put on new work because they have a massive audience base already. New writing from established playwrights often makes it to the stage, but new writers have it the toughest.

What one piece of advice would you offer to aspiring playwrights?

The most important thing for me working in the creative arts I think is to be brave, and this can be applied to writers, directors, designers, and actors alike. Be brave, be bold, pursue stories and ideas you think are important or you have a connection with or interest you. The biggest mistake anyone can make is to try to please someone creatively. Do the work you love, and your passion and your message will show in your writing.

Bio:
Theatre: Valère in *Tartuffe* (Watermill Theatre Newbury); SS Officer in *Bent* (Trafalgar Studios); Mr Pike in *Nicholas Nickleby* (on tour, Gielgud Theatre and Toronto); Captain Nicholls in *War Horse* (New London Theatre); Laertes in *Hamlet 1603* (White Bear, Kennington); Reg in *This Happy Breed* (Theatre Royal, Bath); B in *Atman* (Finborough Theatre); The Prince in *Romeo and Juliet* (Headlong Theatre/Tour);

DEAD STAGE

Sir George Airy in *The Busy Body* (Southwark Playhouse), Milo in *Sleuth* (Watermill, Newbury), Macbeth in *Macbeth* (Orange Tree Theatre).

Matthew created the role of Syme in Robert Icke's original Headlong production of *1984* which played at Nottingham, on tour, at the Almeida Theatre and the Playhouse Theatre. He played Winston in the 2014 tour.

TV: *My Family*

Film: *Alice* (Directed by Marianne Elliott for Ruby Films) and *The Runner* (Emperor's New Films) which won the People's choice Award and Best Short Film at the 2013 Reed Film Festival.

KATE DANBURY
DIRECTOR OF THE LONDON
HORROR FESTIVAL.

How did you originally become involved with the theatre industry?

Theatre has always been a part of my life. I began my performance career as a toddler ballerina and trained in a variety of dance disciplines throughout my childhood, performing in both amateur and professional shows and competitions, before joining the Stagecoach Theatre School. When I was seventeen, I took a playwriting course at the Northcott Theatre in Exeter and managed to get my first short play staged there. I went on to write a number of plays—some long-listed, some short-listed and one a finalist—for various playwriting competitions and had my work staged in a number of venues in different cities around the UK. I volunteered for Arts Council England throughout my late teens and early twenties, liaising with arts professionals and attending and running workshops, conferences, debates, and projects based around creating more theatre provisions to encourage young people into a future career in the sector.

DEAD STAGE

From a young age, I grappled with the jargon, tight budgets, and funding cuts until eventually my projects no longer had the funds to continue (Young People's Participatory Theatre and Find Your Talent). I have since worked in a number of areas in the theatre sector, including an Archiving internship (I set up the Young Vic Theatre's archive at the V&A Museum's Theatre Department), studying clowning, performing for children, and at a number of immersive and site-specific theatre events, directing, venue management, and acting for both stage and screen. Eventually, I fell into Theatre Producing and worked my way into co-producing the London Horror Festival. I took over the running of the LHF in 2016.

What are the key differences between a producer and a director?

A director must be artistically creative, but a producer must be creatively strategic. Every producer is different and will bring their own unique skills to this ever-changing role, which is why it is important to discuss the details in advance of a project determining exactly what is required. For example, some companies might already have funding in place before they recruit a producer, whereas other companies might want you to contribute to the process of securing funds. Overall a producer must be aware of every aspect of the production, whereas the Director can simply focus on what's happening on the stage.

When I'm producing a show, I find it helps that I have an active understanding of other roles within the industry as this gives me the ability to see a project from the perspective of an actor, director, venue manager, and stage manager. This makes it easier to anticipate everyone's needs and concerns and foresee certain areas where issues may arise. Not to say that you should have taken on all these roles before becoming a producer, but I feel that having this additional knowledge and experience makes my job as a producer easier and my role in a new project more flexible.

As a producer, when presented with a script, what captures your interest? What is it about the script that seals the deal and makes you want to produce the piece?

It has to be unique, fresh, and well-written with a captivating story and fully fleshed-out characters. I have a personal taste for the strange and macabre, but that is preferable, not essential! It is imperative to have a producer on board who is passionate about the play. Otherwise they're not going to market it well or target the right audience.

Does producing pieces for the stage influence how you approach your own writing? If so, how?

Absolutely. Especially in the fringe. You have to be very economical with what you can do regarding action. I have been in the position where I have been the producer, director, writer, and actor of the same show. You soon learn in rehearsals what isn't going to work and you need to be flexible with the space you're in.

DEAD STAGE

Normally a director will inform the writer before taking on a piece if there are any aspects they struggle to envision working well on the stage. You need to have an understanding of the medium you are writing for and at what level you can expect it to be produced. If you have never written for the stage before then, you might not realise a certain sequence of actions/stage directions will not translate well to the stage until the director tells you. It sounds obvious, but if you have written a play with a West End Theatre in mind and suddenly need your character to float up into the sky, well, that's not going to work at fringe level.

As a producer, what are the most common restrictions placed upon you, in terms of staging a piece of work?

As I produce at Fringe level, I often encounter many restrictions in just one project. The budget is your biggest restriction. Closely followed by tight schedules and limited get-in/get-out times at venues. Then there's storage. You don't normally have space or time, let alone budget, to construct a big, complicated set. You will normally be sharing the space with another show performing either straight before or after you. Especially if you're at a festival.

Never, ever run over into another company's time slot—it's seriously poor form. Work within your means and keep props, costume, and cast numbers to a minimum. If you haven't managed to secure any kind of funding for your project, you must be prepared to be very economical with rehearsal space and time. You can choose to work on a profit share, but this does not guarantee an income for anyone and these projects tend to be short-term. I will go for a profit share if I am presented with a great piece of writing and have an ideal venue/festival to showcase it at.

In your experience, is the theatre industry accepting of new writing? If so/not—how?

Unfortunately, this is an ongoing issue for programming venues and emerging writers. It is very hard to sell new writing from an unknown playwright. Once you start to get a reputation in the industry and a few awards under your belt—a great producer with strong marketing skills is also a plus—it becomes infinitely easier. Sometimes you can seemingly do all the right things regarding marketing—posters, flyers, social media, sponsored posters, etc.—but if you fail to market the unique selling point of your play, then you're less likely to capture a potential audience.

I love receiving new writing submissions, and if I think the script is great and the company can pull it off I will always programme it in the festival—but a top creative team sadly doesn't guarantee bums-on-seats. If a company applies with an adaptation of a classic author's work, i.e. H. P. Lovecraft, Edgar Allan Poe, Shakespeare, Marlowe, it is much more likely to sell-out than a brand new play, no matter who the creative team is behind it.

What one piece of advice would you offer to aspiring playwrights?

It sounds cliché but write what interests you. Commit

DEAD STAGE

to your story and characters and let them guide the play. Don't sell them out for a forced ending. If it doesn't work then, your audience will leave unsatisfied and frustrated.

Enter as many writing competitions and bursaries as you can and if you're lucky to receive feedback take it on board and use it to better your next work. Read writing briefs carefully and don't submit if your script doesn't fit the criteria. They're not going to change the brief just for you; they have created it for a reason. If you think altering your script to fit the bill will work then do it—but remember not to sacrifice your story or characters!

Bio:
Kate Danbury is a freelance Actor and Theatre Producer and currently runs the London Horror Festival, the UK's original and largest festival of horror in the live performing arts. She is also the Assistant Manager of the Etcetera Theatre, one of London's best-loved fringe venues, where the Camden Fringe Festival began life ten years ago. Kate graduated top of her class at the Lincoln School of Performing Arts, leaving with a First-Class Honours degree and the Drama Award for Best Overall Achievement, then gained her Masters degree in Theatre Studies (Performance and the City) at the Royal Central School of Speech and Drama. You can keep up-to-date with Kate's latest projects by following her on Twitter @katyloudanbury and @LndnHorrorFest.

CATHERINE LORD
WRITER/DIRECTOR

How did you initially become involved with the theatre industry?

As a student actor at Cambridge, I acted in one to two plays each term for the first two years. One was the role of Mrs Toynbee in *Love of a Good Man* by Howard Barker, produced at the ADC. As a darkly comedic anti-war play set in 1920 on the detritus of a World War I battlefield, where I got to play the British version of Mother Courage with a Ouija board, I had my first, physical experience of channelling a theatrical language which raises political questions. In my twenties, I was meeting those tough questions which recur endlessly around urgent matters of class difference, suffering, and death.

I was part of a company, *The Cambridge Theatre Group*, which premiered at the Edinburgh Fringe; the director-writer Nick Ward adapted a D.H. Lawrence short story about a miner killed in an accident. This play was a double bill with Kafka's *Metamorphosis*. As a group, we got a double fringe first, which bemused me. Themes of war and class where entangling themselves into my youthful neurology. As a third play

DEAD STAGE

in the Edinburgh production, we did an improvised feminist play called *Bint*. Matters of feminism, class and race were weaving themselves into my theatrical concerns.

After a break of ten years from theatre when I lived abroad, I worked on a BFI screenplay commission that had war and feminism as its central themes. I was working with a veteran of the Gay Sweatshop, actor and visionary director Nancy Diuguid, and the screenwriting experience very sadly ended when Nancy became ill. That project too had feminism, history, and class at its heart. With alchemy, keep the magic of the drama in full flight.

During this period working on the BFI commission, I was living a life between London and Amsterdam. When I was in Amsterdam, I became the co-founder of a theatre company specialising in improvised comedy, *Off Your Head*.

You might ask which of these points has been the 'beginning.' I would say without question: some beginnings have grown into specific projects, which then lead to new projects, which for me, feel like yet another challenging beginning.

It is because of my politics and my experience as an actor and an emerging writer that I have turned to directing. Directing and acting in Caryl Churchill's *Seagulls*, in a recent production, threw me yet again in the frays of class and feminism. Neoliberalism infused with another 'magical' if not metaphorical dimension regarding the protagonist's career as a telekinetic show woman.

The new writing I have directed in the last two years carries its freight of politics. So much so, that the play I am writing for the Royal Court Playwright's programme 2017, is speculative fiction, feminist, and deals with what I will explore as a neoliberalism which exploits the ecological aspects of poverty and disenfranchisement.

As a director, when presented with a script, what captures your interest? What is it about the script that seals the deal and makes you want to direct the piece?

The characters I can relate to and a story which captures my joys and terrors. Recently, I directed a piece by Sian Rowland about the Sisters Romanov, the daughters of the Czar moving from prison to prison, in various houses that became increasingly divested of any light or comfort. I was fascinated by the massive journey from wealth to poverty, and the daily acts of courage they adopted to survive. Something similar happened when I was an assistant director on a piece about a women's refuge, and an intercultural friendship between a white woman and an Indian woman. I was fascinated by the humour that they brought to address the pain.

I am not hidebound by particular stories. I would love to direct *Anthony and Cleopatra*, Arthur Miller's less well-known plays, Lucy Kirkwood's work, and revive *Blasted*. I do like theatre where the text is still central, though I learn all the time from movement-based work. I have always loved anything that *Theatre de Complicité* do.

DEAD STAGE

Does directing pieces for the stage influence how you approach your writing? If so, how?

I feel I can write best if I am also directing. There is one fundamental to text analysis, and actors do it instinctively. Directors must know how to experience this process, and that is, breaking up the text into sections. This is sometimes called 'actioning' the text or 'finding the shifts,' and thanks to Katie Mitchel's work and the book which has gone with it, finding 'events' in the play is now part of the grammar of both directors and many actors. That sense of 'how long does this section take and need' is deeply intuitive for me as a writer, but I think that my writer's intuition is guided by the spirits of good writing, as the wonderful writer knows where these shifts and movements must happen. When I am the fish in the sea, often in my precarity, trying to find my way, the great writers particularly seem to know the currents.

The important thing about directing modern classics (I experienced this with Caryl Churchill), is that you have a sense of how far you might venture upstream, take risks and not hold back on saying what might be unsayable. I am an emerging playwright, so when it comes to opportunities to direct classics, I am in the privileged position of accessing and channelling writers who have covered immense ground.

Do you feel your background as a director is an asset when writing? If so, how?

Oddly, I think that many talented, great or able writers can direct if they need to, but they don't need to be good directors to write. In fact, I often hear playwrights and dramatists say that the writer is an actor who wishes to remain physically invisible, and after all, you get to play all the parts. You actually have to improvise dialogue. So yes, I believe there is a certain amount of 'acting' involved, but not the type of acting that you dare talk about with working actors, who know all too well, the dues paid in that challenging game. So strangely, maybe there is more acting going on in writing than in directing.

Each year I do make sure I do at least one acting gig, even if it is a short film. I have often done acting roles that I improvised. The craft of improvising feeds back into writing drama.

Then how does the director in me appear again in the process?

I often cannot help visualising the result, and smell, light, and size up the location. I write down somewhere how I want it to look. The orthodox way of writing TV and screenplays is to obey the rule that you are responsible for the story, dialogue locations, but not the look. In playwriting, I break that rule. I am writing the whole thing. Perhaps I should consider directing my work, and perhaps I might write something that demands that I do not, under any circumstances direct it?

I think many more playwrights would direct their work if they pursued the director's skill set. But the fact is that there is only so much time.

As a director, what are the most common restrictions placed upon you, regarding staging a piece of work?

DEAD STAGE

What many people might regard as restrictions on the freedoms of the artists making the piece together, I see as essential to the creative process. A play is a text to be honoured: that is the restriction. Within the constraints of the text which carries its array of meanings, are the limitations of what you can do. I would never set *Julius Caesar* in a mental asylum. That would override the horizon of the meanings that Shakespeare's text makes possible. It is a play depicting a political world in civic and political life. A different play would be the inmates of a prison or a mental asylum performing the play, either as a revolt or as part of their therapy. Even as a 'mind-game' film or theatre piece where the narrators or story-world is held to be unreliable, a Shakespeare play would have to be a play-within-the-play.

Then there are the restrictions on the size of the space and the lighting grid. But then any director makes sure that the 'horse for the course' is the first consideration in staging a play. Recently, in a production run by a cutting-edge company called *Doughnuts*, I had to stage a play in an immersive setting where the actors could walk in a square around the audience, work at the corners of the quadrangle and along the lines of the cross which cut the audience space into four sectors. At first, it was mind-boggling to consider the possibilities. Yet it was humbling because you realised that there is only so much you can do. Just as actors need to be cast and casting is essential to the success of the entire work, so, too, must you cast the play to the space: never the other way around.

Then there can be the limitations of staging new

writing when, with the help of the playwright, you realise that the writing cannot quite cover the task the story has set itself. You realise some more development is needed. Saying this, I want to make clear that I agree with Christopher Hampton on this topic, new writing can be developed to death. What I am referring to is taking a play at the stage of production and you know it has flaws. The point is to respect the text and try to make good with the collaborative task of storytelling as a way of respecting the play. The flaws will not go away. They need to be treated with respect. They need to be the cracks that let the light through.

In your experience, is the theatre industry accepting of new writing? If so/not—how?

Which sector of the industry supports new writing? Perhaps the word 'industry' itself is always problematic unless you consider theatre the factory floor of the human soul where the industrial equipment no longer exists, and we are using a warehouse to recover our means of soul 'production.'

Effectively, the most daring new writing comes through the Fringe. It often comes to birth on no money whatsoever. I am doing the Royal Court Playwright's programme from January 2017, and however much everyone there would dream of having their play produced at the Royal Court itself, good work will emerge when people take their plays to directors and producers on the Fringe, where the tremendous work can emerge or, like myself, I may have to face the daunting task of directing my own play.

DEAD STAGE

It would seem that outside the Fringe, British theatre is still the 'ecological' space for new writing and yes, I would say this is true, broadly speaking. Though many will, and quite rightly, strongly disagree with me, as the funding for new writing has been cut over the years. No one earns a living with playwriting these days unless they have many other jobs. There is a whole area of industry research needed to be done to consider which feature film writers and television writers still write plays, whether these are done on the basis of commission or spec. This would be a very rich area of research. For me, I have always longed for there to be more of a connection between new writing in theatre and, for instance, new writing in television. The idea that the Royal Court could be given a Sky classics season—that would be a dream. I think this is a dream worth dreaming, and even with the ferocity of certain global, political events, this dream needs to be turned into reality. There are audiences who cannot always get to a theatre and would relish new writing. There is too much condescension towards different groups of people and generations that assume they will measure out their life on social media and reality TV. There *are* audiences, they are there, and perhaps social media can be used more effectively to bring the new writing and the audiences together and to create a TV product that would excite audiences about a theatre production. It could be a multimedia experiment. One would see if you could only get the resolution to an episode of *Black Mirror* by turning up to your local theatre. Would this work?

DAN WEATHERER

What one piece of advice would you offer to aspiring playwrights?

The obvious advice is this: write as much as possible and don't leave too many gaps in between.

Every writer is different, but I have to hear people's voices. I have to sit on buses, in latte shops, sometimes in places I can't bear supporting, but places where people will say things to one another that you could never make up. Then there is the protection of your imagination. There are day jobs, and there are day jobs. Avoid what hurts your brain chemistry. Don't close yourself off in an elite group of people but protect yourself from those who will be bad for your art, who deride you for the steep path and who secretly die inside without admitting this to themselves or you, and all because you have the guts to be on the artistic path at all.

Unfortunately, this can happen in families. I call it 'If you are not writing *Downton Abbey* or *Dr Who*, then you don't exist as an artist." It is the 1 or 0 solution, and people who do this have no imaginative resource to the idea of a 'quantum computing' between the 1 and the 0. And in fact, in my view, between the black and the white extremes of full-time success, or zero success, the myriad colours in between is where the real innovations take place. Because there is more at stake than writing through practising one's craft is the goal. Listening to people, their intentions, and their humanity and having immense compassion for this humanity and being able to observe it without allowing the toxic fall-out from this humanity to contaminate your soul and artistic craft—mandatory. Look at *Death of a Salesman*.

DEAD STAGE

Throw yourself into the flow of writing even though you have no idea what to write next. When you feel like falling asleep, that is a fight-flight-fold mechanism attempting to intervene. That means you are onto something and therefore write through it.

I can never say write as 'fast as possible' or as 'slowly as possible.' In fact, I would tell playwrights to go to the theatre, to understand how theatre is made. Because if you are a filmmaker and you don't have a sense of film grammar from understanding film history and the corpus of work, you will be weaker in your efforts. Yet, having said that, for any writer, so much comes from the unconscious. The other crucial advice is: NEVER GIVE UP.

What does the future have in store for you and your work?

My future projects I am keeping secret, except to say that ecology and our survival as a species need to be treated with wit, comedy, and elegance. I would never do a theatre adaptation of *The Road*. I am keeping things secret because when something is brewing in the alchemy chamber, you keep the doors shut and let the spiritual chemicals bubble away. But I want to blend directing new writing and producing my writing with projects which involve directing classics in the sense of nineteenth-century novels and Shakespeare, but also from the 1980s and 1990s repertoires. It is all a tall order—but why not?

For more information about Catherine and her work, visit: **www.Catherinelordmaker.com**

ELLIE PITKIN
ARTISTIC DIRECTOR OF
BLACKSHAW THEATRE, LONDON.

How did you originally become involved with the theatre industry?

I studied drama and theatre at the Royal Holloway University, graduating in 2008. I was told that was the worst year to graduate due to the ongoing financial crisis, so I decided to set about creating theatre with no money. That's where new writing came in. In difficult times, art thrives. There was so much for people to draw upon, and a lot of the bigger theatres were not looking at the work new writers were producing. I was ideally placed, able to come together with people I had graduated with, and in 2010 we set up Blackshaw, the aim of which was to create our own artistic opportunities, with similar likeminded individuals.

I'd worked freelance as a stage manager a couple of years prior to the formation of Blackshaw, but as funding dried up, so did the projects. This meant that I could move away from producing pieces that I was not necessarily 100% about, and move more towards the types of pieces that I wanted to develop and stage. Blackshaw further allowed me to do this.

I carry out much of Blackshaw's day to day admin, manage our army of volunteers, and report to our core team. I oversee the running of the company and ensure that everyone is pulling in the same direction.

As a director, when presented with a script, what captures your interest? What is it about the script that seals the deal and makes you want to direct the piece?

For me personally the two things I look for most in a script are character and comedy. I'm looking for characters that have a solid base that I can build something brilliant on, or I'll look for a situation (comic or otherwise) that I feel would be great to build on, having the potential to further develop the existing characters. I'm not saying that I only prefer comedies. I feel that it is important to have an aspect of comedy in theatre, it appears in other genres, and I feel it is a great tool for engaging an audience and helps to make them care about your characters.

The script doesn't have to be this amazing, ground breaking story. It can be smaller than that; it can be just something as simple as an interesting character that captures my interest.

As a director, what are the most common restrictions placed upon you, in terms of staging a piece of work?

So much! We've being discussing this question

between ourselves recently, and one view was that the most successful companies seem to be those that have the most limitations placed upon them, because they strive to make things work by becoming more innovative. So, we try to see our limitations as a positive.

We are forever battling financial limitations. Arts funding is incredibly difficult to secure. We have had some success with regards to local councils etc. but not anything major in the grand scheme of things. We always place an emphasis on paying people, at least covering their costs, including those who design sets/props for us etc. as they are able to create wonderful things from not a lot.

We are also limited by what the venue can offer. As a fringe company, we could be working in the back room of a pub, to bigger, more established venues such as The Pleasance. So, The Pleasance for instance would have a full lighting set up, sound booth, raised seating and a back-stage area, whereas you won't have that in other venues that aren't theatre spaces. Here you can face all manner of complications; we've had to work around fixed desks, no lights, glass roofs that need blanking out, listed buildings that won't allow us to attach anything to the wall. All of this can throw up lots of logistical challenges that we don't get when using a theatre space.

In your experience, is the theatre industry accepting of new writing? If so/not—how?

An interesting one. I think fringe theatre is far more accepting than the big theatre. There's a trend in the

DEAD STAGE

West End to only put on shows that they know will sell (such as *The Lion King*); it's an easy thing to put on because producers know it will sell.

Blackshaw thinks that a good way of getting more new writing into some of the more established theatres would be to get celebrities involved in performing them. A known name is a way of guaranteeing seat sales, and a producer might be more inclined to put on a piece of new writing.

New writing is essentially high risk. Producers are not sure a new piece will make money, whereas theatre fringe, with its low cost/low risk approach, is far more likely to be accepting of new writers and their work. It can also be mutually beneficial, in that we at Blackshaw pay writers at a rate agreeable to both us and the writer, but we also work with them to help further develop the script and the writer. This is something fringe can offer that higher-level theatre may not be able to.

We are starting to see more mid-tier theatres take an interest in new writing, but it's a difficult one because the risk remains, and it's all about what is sellable.

What one piece of advice would you offer to aspiring playwrights?

Show your work to someone! Don't hide it away! We've come across this quite a lot, where we've liked a piece, asked the writer if they have more, and they have and they've been too afraid to show anyone.

There are plenty of new writers' nights out there now; get submitting. Or, if that seems beyond you at this stage, get your friends to read your work aloud. It makes such a difference hearing it aloud as opposed to just reading it yourself. There's an abundance of actors out there up for workshopping with writers. The more collaborative you can be the better. Be confident in your work.

ANDREW CRANE
BLACKSHAW THEATRE TECHNICIAN.

What are the main constraints that a playwright should bear in mind with regards to the technical requirements when writing for the stage?

Andrew: I graduated in 2012 with a drama degree. I got into tech after realising I wasn't good enough to be an actor, and saw that everyone needed tech. I like to get involved in a show, and tech was my way in. I'm a sound and lighting designer.

What does your role entail?

Andrew: My duties depend on what the venue has or hasn't got. Most of my job involves pre-programming sound and light cues into the laptop, ready for the performance. Most of my duties on the day involve making sure everything is where is should be, works, and is ready to go.

What are the main constraints that a playwright should bear in mind with regards to the technical requirements when writing for the stage?

Andrew: I'd say don't think about them, because as a tech person I enjoy figuring out how to get around those things. Trying to solve these problems is one of the fun parts of the job. Trying to think about these things will constrain the piece.

Ellie: Write what you want, and we'll try and interpret what you wrote. Just lower your expectations. There are things that won't' happen.

Andrew: We'll always make the best of what we've got.

Ellie: Fringe theatres don't have the highest spec equipment. Lighting is probably where fringe theatre is most limited.

Has there ever been an example of a script that you wanted to stage, but for technical reasons found impossible?

Andrew: I don't think so. As I said, we'll always find a way. With new writing, especially, we feel that we can bend a script to what we want and need to work.

Ellie: We'll turn down scripts with large cast sizes as there's just no room to accommodate large cast sizes in a fringe venue. Usually, we can open a discussion, where we'd tell the writer what we can't do, and suggest alternatives. The active relationship between us and the writer enables us to confront any potential difficulties.

DEAD STAGE

About Blackshaw Theatre

A theatre production company working in London and the surrounding areas, Blackshaw champions new writing and adaptations, but above all, strives to produce quality theatre which inspires an audience. Alongside their main productions, Blackshaw runs regular new writing nights, from which their annual Showcase Award was born.

Blackshaw's talented members and associates form an extensive network of writers, directors, actors, designers, and technicians; all of whom see the value in embracing a wide range of disciplines, sharing knowledge, and supporting fellow practitioners to create great work.

Founded in 2010, Blackshaw's productions include new works; *Staying Alive* (Pleasance Theatre 10-29 Nov 2015) by Kat Roberts, *Audience with the Ghost Finder* (May & Oct 2013—Selkirk Upstairs & Etcetera Theatre) by M. J. Starling, and *Character* by Florence Vincent (May 2014 & March 2015—Selkirk Upstairs & Tristan Bates Theatre); as well as adaptations of Gormenghast: *Titus Groan* by Mervyn Peake (Apr 2012—The Actors' Church, Covent Garden) and *Alice in Wonderland* by Lewis Carrol (May 2014, May 2015 & July 2015—Selkirk Upstairs, Battersea Library & The British Home).

Taken from www.blackshawonline.com

Blackshaw Theatre can be found online at:
   www.Blackshawonline.com
   @BlackshawUpdate (Twitter)

DAN WEATHERER

BlackshawTheatre (Facebook)
The Blackshaw Theatre podcast is also available on ITUNES

JILL YOUNG
ACTOR/DRAMA TUTOR/DIRECTOR.

My name is Jill Young, and I have been involved in performance arts all my life; firstly, following vocational training, as a dancer, then after ongoing study as a singer and actress. I have worked in many genres, from circus, fashion, TV, commercial and repertory theatre, and the small screen. I continue to perform when possible, and I am passionate about the life enhancing skills that can be obtained through involvement in performance arts.

As such, I facilitate in all areas of theatre. I also direct, write, and educate as a living history actor. Freelance availability gives me the freedom I love to be able to drop in and out of schools, communities and groups, delivering sessions to all ages and abilities. I specialise in working with those who have learning and/or physical disabilities.

How did you originally become involved with the theatre industry?

I originally became involved in theatre having danced from the age of 4 within my mother's dance school. My grandfather directed widely in the Staffordshire and

DAN WEATHERER

Cheshire area (primarily Musical Comedy and straight plays), and having left school, I was undecided about the path I wanted to take and was taken on a trial basis at a vocational college in Manchester. The principal was a very formidable character, who delighted in telling me that at 5'11" I was far too tall to dance, and encouraged me to study singing and drama, as well as become an advanced dancer and fully qualified teacher.

I have a lot to thank her for.

Four years later, and between performance contracts, I was on the staff—so much for a trial!

What makes a good teaching script?

A good script for teaching drama has one of two things (depending on the age of whom you are teaching and the reason for doing so); either complete imaginative fiction, or one hundred per cent graspable fact.

The first gives rise to let the students fly with their imagination and creativity—anything is possible, there are no restrictions. The second, although more issue based, is something that they can relate to, but equally, enables them to *become* a character. Therefore, characters are immensely important.

What I don't want as a teacher is for a student to '*be themselves in a piece,*' (or a student appearing in costume). They need to be able to get into the role of the character, and de-role at the end of a session or performance. Indeed, they might identify with a character and take something away from the study, but that character should not *be* them.

This is especially important in dark issue based

DEAD STAGE

projects which can affect the student mentally after the end of a rehearsal. The writing needs to provoke thought, but not invade the mind-set of the performer to their detriment.

Is there a need for new writing with regards to presenting material to teach? If so, why?

There is always need for new writing! Not only as an opportunity for the exploration of new ideas and issues, but to freshen and maintain standards for the future. The old playwrights are to be commended, and those whose brilliance has transcended centuries are of course still vital for study and shouldn't be underestimated in teaching or performing. In the study of these established works the student can learn so much about that era of history, the lifestyle lived, the problems faced by humanity, and the stories that were passed down through the generations.

Should new work not be written, then where are the stories of our time to come from? Writers and performers are simply story tellers after all! Fictional work is always developing as the future becomes the present, and the present becomes the past; innovation is limitless, and the imagination can (and should) run riot.

Does directing pieces for the stage influence how you approach your own writing? If so, how?

Directing influences my writing as I always have a vision of how a work would be portrayed in a performance space. For example: how does an audience perceive a character when they are not speaking? In a book, when there is no dialogue from a character, then they aren't *present*, but on stage they are constantly being assessed by the audience even if the focus of the scene is no longer upon them.

As such, I write thinking *where in the picture* the other characters are, and if they are not visible to an audience, then how did they leave the space, and for what reason? This can be applied to why/when they re-enter etc.

Every action has an impulse driving it, and a reaction produced by it. Back stories are also vital for realism, whether on paper or explored in the script. It is especially important to share this back story with the actor playing the part of the character.

In your experience, is the theatre industry accepting of new writing? If so/not—how?

Good question. The answer to this one must be that it is entirely dependent (in my experience) on where you are based geographically. How radical are you prepared to be? Will you create the waves needed to be noticed, and how much control do you wish to retain with your writing once it is accepted? I have seen pieces go to script development, and come out the other side almost unrecognisable; bent to suit a director's idea of casting etc.

The time and finance required to make the waves is often hard to find, and the industry is a closed shop in many ways for writers who are either too niche, or too isolated in their genre as writers.

DEAD STAGE

What one piece of advice would you offer to aspiring playwrights?

Just one piece of advice? I'm not sure that I am qualified to give advice, but if I was to do so it would be to write about what you have a passion for. Believe in the subject, and visualise how you want the piece to be appreciated, on paper, stage or screen.

TOM SLATTER
ACTOR.

How did you initially become involved with the theatre industry?

I started acting at school. I was lucky to have a reasonably active English teacher who would direct a play every term, and I tried to get involved in that. I also did GCSE Drama, then went on to do Theatre Studies A-Level, and then on to study a GNVQ in Performing Arts. It was here that I found what I was looking for. The course is all-encompassing and teaches you all aspects of theatre-making, and the Faculty of Jenny Lingham and Maggie Etheridge are real pioneers in showing young adults how to work as a professional, highlighting the standard required to be taken seriously.

I went on from there to do a degree in Drama at Goldsmiths College, which was wonderful, but it was terrible at teaching you what to do when you graduate, and I became disheartened after graduating. I set up my own business for three years and after that and much soul-searching, I decided to come back to acting and went to Drama School, which I now believe is what I should have done in the first place.

DEAD STAGE

I trained at The Poor School and graduated in 2010. Since graduating I have worked in Film, Theatre, Voice over, and TV.

When I was fifteen, I was taken to see *Death of a Salesman* with my school. This is now one of my favourite plays and Arthur Miller is one of my favourite playwrights. When I saw this play for the first time, I had never read it and wasn't studying it, and it blew me away. It had Alun Armstrong as Willy Loman, Mark Strong as Biff, and it was a National Theatre Production. This was when I knew I wanted to be an actor.

As an actor, when presented with a script what captures your interest? What is it about the script that seals the deal and makes you want to audition for the role?

There are many things that I look for in a script. Not all of them need to be there, but some of them need to be there to make it an exciting or compelling script. I like to work on plays that have a unique universe, or something that makes me see the world differently. We can see this in the works of playwrights such as Harold Pinter, Philip Ridley, Martin McDonagh, or Steven Berkoff. I love issue-based drama, like plays by David Hare, Alan Bennett, Michael Frayn, or Carol Churchill. I also like farce and dark comedies by playwrights Richard Bean (*One Man, Two Guvnors*) or Anthony Nielson (*Realism*).

The reason why I would want to be part of plays like this would have to be because the character excites me, and the work would have something important to say. When I read a script, I ask: *Is the voice saying something to me? Is there something I recognise, and how important is it that this voice is heard right now?*

Often when you read plays you read lines, and they speak to you. I have the perfect example of it from a wonderful playwright, Alan Bennett from his play *The History of Boys*. The Main Character Hector says to his class of students:

'The best moments in reading are when you come across something—a thought, a feeling, a way of looking at things—that you'd thought special, particular to you. And here it is, set down by someone else, a person you've never met, maybe even someone long dead. And it's as if a hand has come out, and taken yours.'

Dialogue is critical. You can have wonderful pictures and important things to say, but poor dialogue will sink a play. If you read your plays and the feedback you're getting is they are clunky, slow or boring, then you need to edit them. The best play will be one where nothing is wasted. Every line is important and serves the purpose of the story, the characters and the meaning.

When you secure a part, how much input do you have with regards to amending lines/dialogue? Do you feel this is often necessary? If so, do you feel this is due in part to mistakes made by the playwright, or is this a natural result of working the script aloud, and finding alternative ways of delivering a line?

DEAD STAGE

Personally speaking, I believe that I am not here to change the writing: I am here to honour it. I have not slaved away for months, even years in some cases, to create this piece of work. I do not profess to know better than the writer and I think it is arrogant of the actor to think that you should. If the writing is good, then the actor can do a good job because it sparks the imagination and allows an actor to be free. If an actor is struggling with the writing, it is maybe because the actor is still trying to work out what they need to do, or it may be because they need to develop how to make a line work.

There is a reason why something is written in a specific way, and it is my responsibility to find out why. In rehearsal, I must speak to the writer or director and come to an understanding. It is important to remember that just because a line doesn't work for me, that doesn't mean it wouldn't work for someone else. A director told me once, 'If one actor struggles with a line—it is the actor. If a hundred actors struggle with the line. It is the line.' I believe this is correct.

Often the most enlightening part of rehearsals can be when an actor talks with the writer and discovers things that they had not seen, realised or understood and vice versa for the writer because they do not always think of everything when they write. Often writers can have stories that aren't in the play but are about a character or even scenes that have been omitted before you have read the play. Essentially the rehearsal process is how everyone in all aspects of the production discovers what the play will become.

DAN WEATHERER

In your experience, is the theatre industry accepting of new writing? If so/not—how?

The industry could not survive without new writing. New writing is the future, and for me the most exciting work. It is difficult for writers because it is often the case that, to be able to write full-time and earn a living as a playwright, you must have some recognition from an established venue that is willing to develop your work.

This is the challenge because in order to do this your work must be seen by those working in the state-funded sector of the industry, mainly the venues such as the Royal Court, Live Theatre Newcastle, Manchester Royal Exchange, Hull Truck, The Bush, The National Theatre, Soho Theatre, or work with state-funded companies such as Paines Plough, Tamasha Theatre Company, Out Of Joint, or Papatango Theatre Company. These companies/theatres will be able to offer help, support, and guidance to make your work the best work it can be.

There are also fringe venues that will do the same, such as The Finborough Theatre and Theatre503, but these Theatres will not be able to help you financially while you write.

What advice would you offer to aspiring playwrights?

Write about what is important to you. Find what matters most to you and write about that. You will create something far more interesting for the audience and the cast if we can see what you wish to say.

DEAD STAGE

Never be afraid to fail or write something that you don't think is very good, because it can and often will become good later. A director friend of mine said, 'There are no ideas that don't work, only ideas that don't work *yet*.' Don't be the critic of your own work.

Get other people who you like and trust to be honest, to read your work and give you feedback. Also, try and get actors to read your work out loud so that you can start to hear whether something works and to get feedback.

Remember that everyone has an opinion, so if one person doesn't like your work then that is just their taste and not a reflection on how good your writing is.

Always ask people for advice. You don't have to take it but the more people you ask the more you might hear certain pieces of advice, and this might tell you something important. Being a writer can be a very solitary job, and so it can mean you don't often get to hear that other people struggle the same way you do: remember, a problem shared is a problem halved. Go to every contact you have, ask for 10 minutes of their time, buy them a coffee and remember that you must do this for others, too.

There are no rules about writing. No one can tell you how to write well or what is good; if they could then you would only have good work now. Be faithful to your ideas and have integrity. Do not be unbending and do not compromise unnecessarily.

Tom Slatter has written/produced a 2 minute short film, is currently writing a Sit-Com, and is busy penning another short film.

STAGE PLAYS

BEIGE

Genre: Comedy
Length: Approx. 20 minutes
Cast: 1 x Male 1 x Female

Synopsis: A contemporary comedy horror, exploring the mindset of a man who has just murdered his wife.

Beige is published by *Heartland Plays*, USA.

Author's note: *Beige* was the second play that I wrote, but was the first to be performed on stage. The piece received a rehearsed reading at a fringe event in London. It was then made into a short film, using the same actress who read Gayle at the reading. This script was the one which caught the eye of my agent.

Notice how I took advice with regards to small cast size/single setting/ simple props on board: it doesn't get much simpler to stage than a sofa/table and a telephone.

It has been described as a black, surreal comedy.

It is one of my favourite pieces.

Cast of Characters:
　Milton Woore
　Gayle Woore

ACT I

SCENE 1

At Rise: A sparse living room set comprised of a sofa, side table (with telephone) and other assorted furniture. MILTON is standing behind the sofa. He is holding a blood-soaked kitchen knife, and his shirt and face are splashed with blood. GAYLE is sitting on the sofa. As soon as the lights come up, she slumps onto her side. Milton points at Gayle.

MILTON
(Elated)

Ha!

Milton attempts to check for a pulse via Gayle's throat but pulls his hand away (due to the amount of blood coming from the wound in her neck) and opts for her wrist instead. Satisfied, he lets her arm fall.

MILTON
Ha! Didn't see that one coming, did you? Miss high and mighty . . . Miss always knows best!

Milton paces the stage.

MILTON
I can't believe I did it! I mean I just can't! It was so easy in the end . . . no need for all those sleepless nights! She was watching her soaps with her back to me; I found the knife in my hand and BAM! Dead wife! Ha!

DEAD STAGE

Milton stops by the telephone and taps the point of the knife repeatedly against his teeth. He reaches for the phone and begins to dial. He pauses and looks at the body of his dead wife.

MILTON

No Milton. This is not the way. You know what they will do to you in prison; you'll be passed around like currency.

Milton places the phone back onto the table.

MILTON

There's only one thing for it now.

Milton pulls his t-shirt up to expose his stomach and places the tip of the blade against his skin.

MILTON
(In between deep breaths)
Come on now, you can do this . . . just like the Samurai.

Milton prepares to plunge the blade into his stomach.
Gayle never moves her body during any of the exchange.

GAYLE

(Angry)
Do you mind telling me just what the hell that was all about?

DAN WEATHERER

Milton drops the knife and shrieks.

GAYLE
You've only gone and done it this time, haven't you?

MILTON
(Shocked)
Gayle?

GAYLE
Don't you Gayle me! Just what the hell do you think you are playing at? I'm sat here watching telly, not doing anything to anyone and—

MILTON
(Interrupting)
You are supposed to be dead!

GAYLE
Don't you go telling me what I'm supposed to be! I'll decide that; we've had words about this before!

MILTON
I stabbed you!

GAYLE
I know. Seven times—in the back might I add. Some man you are!

MILTON
I checked your pulse!

DEAD STAGE

GAYLE
You mean you actually touched me? That'll be a first!

MILTON
You were dead!

GAYLE
Do you really think I was gonna let you kill me and not have my say about it? You really don't know me at all do you, Milton Woore?

Milton approaches Gayle slowly and sinks to his knees so they are at eye level.

GAYLE
And don't you look at me with that tone!

Milton pokes her in the chest.

GAYLE
Oi! Keep your bloody hands to yourself! Don't you dare start getting any ideas about having your way with me now!

Milton stands up and backs away.

MILTON
(Disgusted)
God woman, what do you think I am?

GAYLE
Well, I thought I knew, but you really surprised me with your antics tonight!

Milton begins to pace the stage.

Pause.

> GAYLE
> Come on then . . . out with it!

> MILTON
> Out with what?

> GAYLE
> Why you did it? What have I done to warrant this then? I know at the end of all of this it will be your fault, but let's hear it anyway.

Pause.

> MILTON
> I thought you were having an affair.

> GAYLE
> *(Laughing)*
> How? I don't have the time for an affair. I'm far too busy cleaning up after you!

> MILTON
> I thought you were having one online. You are always in those chat rooms. I see you smirking to yourself when you read something you like. I figured you were going to meet up with one of your mystery men and leave me.

DEAD STAGE

GAYLE
Not bloody likely. The internet is full of weirdos!

MILTON
So what were you doing?

GAYLE
I was bored, OK? You never talk to me, and this was a bit of fun.

MILTON
How many men were there?

GAYLE
Just one.

Pause.

MILTON
Did you send him . . . Y'know . . . Intimate photos?

GAYLE
I did, yeah. Several actually.

MILTON
Oh god, I knew it, I bloody knew it!

GAYLE
They weren't of me though.

MILTON
(Horrified)
How do you mean . . . they weren't of me were they?

GAYLE
Get over yourself! They weren't of you. I'm not sure who they were of? I just looked them up online. I wasn't gonna go to all that effort tidying myself up for some weirdo I've never even met!

Milton calms a little.

MILTON
OK, then what about all the different colognes that I smelt on you?

GAYLE
I told you, male fragrances are much cheaper than female ones these days. I was trying to save you money, and I'm in the wrong yet again!

Pause.

MILTON
So you weren't having an affair?

GAYLE
No.

MILTON
Oh.

GAYLE
Oh indeed. See, I said it would be your fault . . . was I right? Was I ever!

DEAD STAGE

MILTON
I guess you were.

GAYLE
So you killed me over your misinterpretation of the facts?

MILTON
Yes . . . but . . .

GAYLE

(Interrupting)
Don't you think a conversation might have been more appropriate instead of some overly grand, and in my case, fatal gesture?

MILTON
Yes but . . .

GAYLE

(Interrupting)
Then why didn't you? You know I'm always—

MILTON

(Interrupting)
Because I can never bloody get a word in, woman!

GAYLE
Well . . . there's no need to interrupt is there?

MILTON

(Resigned)
No.

Pause.

GAYLE
Are you at least going to sit me up?

Milton sits Gayle up. Her head lolls to one side, and Milton uses a cushion to support it.

MILTON
There.

GAYLE
So, what's the plan now then, genius? How were you going to get out of this little pickle?

Milton stops and eyes the knife on the floor.

MILTON
Seppuku.

GAYLE
Seppoo-what?

MILTON
It means stomach cutting . . . it's the way a dishonoured samurai would commit suicide.

GAYLE
Oh, give me strength.

MILTON
Only I couldn't do it.

DEAD STAGE

GAYLE
Why not?

MILTON
I can't! You know I have a deep-rooted fear of Hell.

GAYLE
And where do you think butchering me is gonna get you? Buddy, you've already punched that ticket! Tell you what, give my dad a call—he'll be straight round to do it for you when you tell him what you've done!

MILTON
(Exasperated)
Oh, I wondered how long it would be until you brought daddy into this.

GAYLE
I was merely offering his help. You haven't the stones to off yourself, so let him do it for you.

MILTON
Because of course, he'd do a much better job of it than I would, right?

GAYLE
Without a doubt. Do you want his number? 0754—

Milton takes a seat next to the corpse of his wife.

MILTON
I'm not calling your father.

GAYLE
Of course you aren't. You are intimidated by him.

MILTON
No, I'm not!

GAYLE
Yes, you are. You are intimidated by him because he's a man's man. He knows things that men should know and you don't.

MILTON
So he fixed our boiler that one time . . . hardly qualifies him as an expert in all things now does it? Besides, he must have been lacking something for your mum to leave him.

GAYLE

(Infuriated)
What did you say?

MILTON

(Panicked)
Nothing . . . you must have misheard . . . it'll be all that blood in your ears.

GAYLE
And whose fault is that?

MILTON
So, we are back to blame again, are we?

DEAD STAGE

GAYLE
Yes, we are back to blame again! Let me ask you this . . . have I murdered you lately?

MILTON
(Timidly)
No.

GAYLE
Sorry, what was that?

MILTON
No.

GAYLE
Well then, as murder seems to be the hot topic tonight and I am the one lying dead, I'll apportion as much blame as I see fit, thank you very much!

MILTON
OK.

Pause.

GAYLE
So now what?

MILTON
I dunno.

GAYLE
Well, you can forget about dismembering me in the bathtub and leaving me out for the binmen . . . I look terrible in black.

MILTON
(Resigned)
I wasn't planning to. I remember Aunt Viv's funeral ... I've never seen PVC stretched so far as to become transparent.

GAYLE
What a bloody cheek! That cost you three hundred and fifty quid!

Pause.

Then what are you going to do?

Milton shrugs.

GAYLE
That's always been your problem. No foresight. You fail to plan—

MILTON AND GAYLE
—you plan to fail.

MILTON
Yes, yes I know.

GAYLE
It's a bloody good job you never gave me any kids, they'd be mortified to find out their daddy was capable of uxoricide!

MILTON
Huh?

DEAD STAGE

GAYLE
It means 'the act of stabbing your wife with a kitchen knife.'

MILTON
Oh. And why did you have to bring my weak swimmers into this? I told you . . . it's the stress of work that does it. It's not my fault, I always wanted children.

GAYLE
So did I, but you couldn't even manage that! And don't bring your job into it again. I suppose you never even gave work a thought in all of this?

MILTON
What do you mean?

GAYLE
Think of all the press attention your actions are going to bring! Working for the UK's largest supplier of kitchen utensils, you are hardly going to bring them the sort of attention that they would want! See, only thinking about yourself again. Typical Milton, it's all self, self, self.

Milton stands and begins to circle the sofa.

MILTON
(Sullen)
I don't really care. They never valued me. I'm middle management, strike one down and there are two more already waiting to take his place. I won't be missed.

DAN WEATHERER

GAYLE
Well, you should care! You'll want a good reference from them for when you get out. If you get out.

MILTON
Out?

GAYLE
Of jail.

MILTON
I'm not going to jail. This was a crime of passion.

GAYLE
Passion? Ha! That'd be a first!

MILTON
It was. Misinformed though I was, I killed you so that nobody else could have you.

GAYLE
How very thoughtful of you. Pity I didn't get a say in the matter.

MILTON
Besides, nobody knows you are dead yet. I could still hide your body . . . if you'd shut up long enough to let me think!

GAYLE
Let me get this straight. You want me to hold my tongue while you think of a way to dispose of my remains?

DEAD STAGE

MILTON
If you would.

Pause.

GAYLE
How about acid—or lime?

MILTON
Hmm, not sure where I'd get that from at this hour.

GAYLE
You could burn me?

MILTON
It's raining out, look can you just—

GAYLE
(Interrupting)
I was only trying to help.

Milton takes a seat next to Gayle.

MILTON
Did it hurt . . . When I . . . y'know, got all stabby?

GAYLE
Why do you think I was screaming? Of course it bloody well hurt!

MILTON
Oh. I figured you were just surprised, you made the same noise that time that the cat jumped out of the Christmas tree

Pause.

                MILTON
    What's it like, Death I mean?

                GAYLE
Bloody hell, what is this? Twenty questions?

                MILTON
    I just always wondered.

                GAYLE
(Thoughtful)
    OK . . . it's kinda like the colour beige.

Pause.

                MILTON
    Beige? Is that it?

                GAYLE
Yeah, I think that pretty much covers it.

Milton stands.

                GAYLE
    I'm starting to smell, aren't I?

                MILTON
    A little.

                GAYLE
Perhaps you should make that call?

DEAD STAGE

MILTON
And give myself up?

GAYLE
Yeah, why not? First offence . . . crime of passion and all of that . . . you'll probably get off with a fine and a stern word telling you not to do it again.

MILTON
You think so?

GAYLE
Oh God, yeah! The courts are so plugged up with real crimes these days, things like this are brushed under the carpet all the time!

MILTON
You might be right!

GAYLE
I am right. I'm always right. The way I've been prattling on tonight, I'll bet I had it coming anyway!

MILTON
Yes, you did! You so did!

GAYLE
So make the call, let's end this now. Get me all cleaned up and embalmed. The sooner this is dealt with the sooner you can crack on with your bachelor lifestyle. Besides which, I'm getting bored now. I can hear Aunt Hetty calling from beyond the veil . . . something about securing a badminton court but

only for the next half hour . . . God, I loathe Badminton. Perhaps I'm heading to Hell after all!

Milton sits on the edge of the sofa careful not to get too close to Gayle. He picks up the phone and dials.

MILTON
Hello, yes police please . . . and an ambulance—wait, do ambulances take dead bodies? Oh. OK. No, she's dead. Definitely dead. What happened? I stabbed her. Six times I think . . .

GAYLE
Seven. It was seven, the neck, remember?

MILTON
No, sorry my mistake, seven, it was seven—I forgot the one to the neck . . . Yes, it was my wife, how did you guess—wait, have you met her before?

FADE TO BLACK
END.

A QUESTION OF AUTHORSHIP

Genre: Comedy
Length: 10—15 minutes
Cast: 5 x male

Synopsis: Five of history's greatest playwrights meet to discuss the origins of the work penned in Shakespeare's name.

Cast of Characters:
    Arthur Miller
    William Shakespeare
    Sir Francis Bacon
    Christopher Marlowe
    William Stanley

ACT I

SCENE 1

At Rise: Heaven. ARTHUR MILLER, WILLIAM SHAKESPEARE, SIR FRANCIS BACON, CHRISTOPHER MARLOWE and WILLIAM STANLEY, are sitting at a table. Miller pours himself a glass of whiskey. Everyone else has a full glass. Miller sits centrally. Stage left is Shakespeare and Bacon. To Miller's right sit Stanley and Marlowe.

MILLER
Thanks for taking time out of your busy schedules to see me.

BACON
Not at all kind sir, the pleasure I can assureth thee is all mineth.

SHAKESPEARE
You can knock that off for a start, Bacon. Mr Miller isn't here for the tourist spiel.

MARLOWE
(Scoffs)
Idiot.
Marlowe takes a large sip of whiskey.

STANLEY
(To Shakespeare)
There's no need to be rude, William.

DEAD STAGE

SHAKESPEARE
(Mocking on the "WILL")
Oh, do shut up *Will*.

MILLER
Now gentlemen, please. Let us at least try to be civil. There is much to discuss and . . .

MARLOWE
(To Miller)
I'll take another dram.

Marlowe shoves his empty glass towards Miller.

MILLER
True enough to form, Christopher.

MARLOWE
Less talking, more pouring.

Miller pours Marlowe a measure of whiskey and passes it back via Stanley.

BACON
(To Miller)
Forgive me. May I ask as to why you requested our presence?

Marlowe downs his whiskey, slams his glass onto the table and gestures for the remainder of the bottle. Miller ignores him.

MARLOWE
Hear, hear!

Miller takes a sip from his whiskey and places it on the table.

Marlowe reaches for the bottle and pours himself another whiskey.

MILLER
Of course. Let's get right to it. It's a question that I have often pondered and I know it troubles a fair number of people down there . . .

Marlowe reaches for the bottle and pours himself another whiskey.

MARLOWE
Cheers!

SHAKESPEARE
(Groans)
Oh, not this again!

Miller produces a handful of books from beneath his chair. He places one on the table.

MILLER
It's simple, really. I wish to know who wrote this?

Shakespeare, Marlowe, Bacon and Stanley look at the book.

DEAD STAGE

ALL EXCEPT MILLER
I did!

MILLER
You all wrote Romeo and Juliet?

ALL EXCEPT MILLER
No. I did!

Miller places another book on the table.

MILLER
How about Hamlet?

ALL EXCEPT MILLER
I did!

Miller places the third book on the table.

MILLER
And Othello?

ALL EXCEPT MILLER
I did!

STANLEY
Actually sorry, I didn't write that one. My mistake. But I did write Twelfth Night so there's that . . .

Bacon stands in anger.

BACON
Liar!

(To Miller)
Stanley never penned a play worthy of note in his life!

(To Stanley)
Thou art a flesh-monger, a fool and a coward!

SHAKESPEARE
(To Bacon)
Nice. *Measure for Measure*. You really must have written it to quote it so eloquently?

MARLOWE
Sit down Bacon, before you hurt yourself.

Bacon sits.

STANLEY
(Hurt)
Not true. I thought Macbeth was worthy of note.

Bacon stands.

BACON
(Enraged)
Liar! Thou art as loathsome as a toad!

SHAKESPEARE
(To Bacon)
Oh, following up with a bit of *Troilus and Cressida* now. Well, that's me sold. How about you sit down and let the rest of us get a word in? As for you . . .

DEAD STAGE

(Turning to Stanley)
Signing yourself as W.S was never going to fool anyone. I mean honestly now, that has to be the weakest claim in the history of anything!

Bacon sits.

STANLEY
But I . . .

MILLER

(Interrupting)
Now gentlemen, please. We could quarrel and bicker until the end of days but that really isn't going to get us anywhere now is it?

MARLOWE
Get rid of him I say.
(Points to Stanley)
That one, I mean. Willie wannabe.

Bacon stands.

BACON

(Forceful)
Indeed.

Bacon sits.

SHAKESPEARE
Agreed.

DAN WEATHERER

MILLER
(To Stanley)
In the interest of moving the argument along, it seems that your claim as author to the works of Shakespeare is rejected. I must say it was always a flimsy argument at best. I'm surprised it survived as long as it did! Wouldn't you agree?

STANLEY
(Sulking)
Well . . . we do have the same initials. You cannot dispute that?

SHAKESPEARE
Yes, you and several hundred thousand others.

Stanley finishes his drink.

STANLEY
That many, huh?

Stanley stands.

I've got to go anyway. I have a first draft that needs my attention. It's a tragedy based on . . .

MARLOWE
(Interrupting/Dismissive)
Yes, yes. Good luck with that.

Stanley looks to the group.

DEAD STAGE

STANLEY
I'll see you . . .

SHAKESPEARE
(Interrupting)
So long, *Will*!

STANLEY
Yeah. Bye.

Exit Stanley.

Bacon stands.

BACON
(To Marlowe)
You may follow him, Marlowe. You are nothing but a drunk and a rakehell. I know not how you came to be the leading playwright of the day, such was the filth that you peddled!

MARLOWE
Rakehell? He's at it again! Have you spoken to anybody in the last hundred years?

BACON
Of course, I have! It's just that old habits die hard and you are a scheming rakehell. I can think of no other word that describes you better.

Marlowe stands.

MARLOWE
I'll not stand for this.
(looks down at feet)
Though remarkably, I am still able.
(To Shakespeare/Bacon)
I bested you in life, that'll do for me.

Marlowe snatches up the bottle of whiskey.

MARLOWE
(To Miller)
Nice meeting you, Art. Excellent work on *The Crucible*.
(To Shakespeare/Bacon)
Ladies.

Exit Marlowe.

Miller and Shakespeare look at Bacon.

Bacon sits.

MILLER
Well, that leaves the two most likely candidates?

BACON
As it ought.

Shakespeare snorts in derision.

BACON
What of it, man?

DEAD STAGE

SHAKESPEARE
Look, it's like this. You have ridden my coat tails for centuries now. Don't you think it's time to admit the truth?

BACON
Indeed.
(To Shakespeare)
So you concede that I penned the works in your name so that I might comment on the social policies of our day without fear of reprisal?

SHAKESPEARE
No, far from it. Though I will admit that you are a fraud and a coward.

Bacon stands.

BACON
(Enraged)
Outrageous! You are the son of an illiterate wool trader! You had little in the way of education! Ha! You were a failure of an actor at best! Nobody mourned your death. Nobody sang praise of your genius. You died penniless and unknown. I shall wager that you are not able to pen your own name!

SHAKESPEARE
You don't get it, do you? Though my legacy is assured, there was never any intention to leave one. Art exists for the sake of art. Not fame or glory. An artist doesn't care about how he is remembered, only that he prompted a reaction to his work. As for

genius, that is a title awarded by others better placed to judge the merit of my work than I. It isn't born of a good education and it isn't a reflection of one's upbringing. The gift is just that: a gift, given to the lucky few so that others might enjoy its fruit.

Shakespeare stands

SHAKESPEARE
(To Miller)
Enough now. I must be off. Lady Aline is waiting. Mr Miller. Sir Bacon.

Miller nods farewell.

Exit Shakespeare.

Bacon sits.

Miller finishes his drink and begins to gather up his books.

MILLER
I think I have my answer.

BACON
(Aghast)
Surely you cannot think he is the true author? The man is a fraud! His . . . his portraits look nothing like him!

Miller stands.

DEAD STAGE

MILLER
Irrelevant. I do not think . . . I know. Now if you will excuse me?

Exit Miller.

Bacon sits a moment. He is flustered and angry.

Bacon stands and follows after Miller.

BACON
Mr Miller! Sir! Do be a gent and wait a moment? Did I ever tell how I came to write King Lear? I based it on a dear friend of mine from the court!

Exit Bacon.

END.

CRIPPEN

Genre: Drama
Length: Approx. 100 minutes

Synopsis: Early Twentieth Century England—The true story behind the infamous Dr Crippen, his crimes, his capture and his execution. Was the body in the cellar really that of Cora Crippen?

Crippen brings to life the events that led to the hanging of Hawley Crippen and his place in history as one of England's most notorious murderers.

With his marriage hanging by a thread and the theatrical career of his wife Cora in tatters, Dr Crippen seeks counsel in the young and beautiful Ethel. A proud Protestant, he vows never to act upon his feelings, but after returning home and finding his wife in the arms of another, Hawley and Ethel spend the night together.

Cora learns of Hawley's affair and confronts Ethel, knocking her to the floor causing her to lose the unborn child that Ethel had previously kept from Hawley.

With his hopes of fatherhood dashed and Cora's threat of making his affairs public, thus ruining his reputation as a respected homoeopathic physician, Hawley decides to take matters into his own hands.

Whilst Dr Hawley Crippen was tried and found guilty for the murder of Cora Crippen, DNA tests carried out a century later reveal that the body found under the flagstones of his cellar was not that of Cora's. Nor was it female.

DEAD STAGE

Who then, fell victim to Dr Crippen's murder plot and what happened to Cora?

Cast of Characters:
  Hawley Crippen
  Belle Elmore/Cora Turner
  Ethel Le Neve
  Simon Harper
  Marcie Whittingham
  Florie Shaw
  Chief Inspector Walter Dew
  Maid
  Officer
  Officer
  Guard
  Guard
  Priest
  Judge
  Prosecution
  Confession Crippen

ACT I

ACT 1-1

At Rise: Stage—CORA TURNER (aka BELLE ELMORE, late thirties, dark-haired, pretty)/SIMON HARPER (early twenties, dark hair, handsome) are on stage.

Audio cue—Lacrimosa (Mozart's Requiem in D minor)

(2-3 minutes of performance set to musical score)

Belle/Simon are acting out the final scenes of an unnamed dance in which Belle's character is dying. She drops to the floor. It is an experimental performance.

Lights out.

Sound cue—polite applause

Lights up.

Simon has left the stage.

Belle rises to her feet and revels in the applause. Simon enters stage right to give Belle a bouquet of flowers. He disappears off stage to allow her to savour the moment.

DEAD STAGE

Exit Simon

Belle continues to milk the applause

Belle responds angrily to an unseen prompt to leave the stage.

LIGHTS OUT

ACT 1-2

Backstage: Belle enters a sparsely furnished dressing room. She throws the flowers to the ground and takes a seat at her dressing table. She begins to brush her hair. HAWLEY CRIPPEN (Early forties, slim, moustachioed) is standing in the corner of the room.

BELLE
(excited)
Did you see me? I was magnificent!

Hawley fidgets but does not answer.

BELLE
How many were there tonight? Two, three hundred?

HAWLEY
(uneasy)
I don't know.

Pause.

Perhaps thirty?

Belle slams her hairbrush onto the dressing table.

BELLE
Nonsense! Absolute nonsense! It was deafening in there! Did you not hear their applause?

DEAD STAGE

HAWLEY
I was stood amongst them for act 1, perhaps there were nearer forty but no more.

Belle stands and turns towards Hawley.

BELLE
Why do you insist on darkening my mood? Tonight was a triumph! I was majestic! They shall sing praise of this evening for months to come!

HAWLEY
I can check the registers if you insist . . . but the truth is that we lost money tonight.

Belle returns to her dressing table and resumes brushing her hair.

BELLE
Then you shall have to step up your efforts. How can I be expected to fill seats if people do not even know that I am performing? No—it is you who have failed tonight, not I and not the dance. You and your lack of vision are to blame. By rights, the theatre should be packed to the rafters night upon night!

HAWLEY
It is not simply a matter of throwing money at the situation. I have my research to fund—

Belle stops brushing her hair and glares at Hawley via her mirror.

BELLE
I am tired of hearing about your research! Forever do you promise me that your formula is nearing completion—that you shall revolutionize homoeopathic medicine and be paid a fortune for it! Am I ever going to see the fruits of your labour?

HAWLEY
Yes.

BELLE
(laughing)
Doubtful! How many years is it now?

HAWLEY
Four.

BELLE
The very reason we came to this country was so that you could set up a practice based upon your own cures, yet here we are—four years later and no closer to that goal. Need I remind you of what I gave up for you. I was a star in New York—yet I believed in your ideas . . . Now, look at us. I should be climbing the ladder—I should be performing at The Alhambra! Not performing to a handful of philistines!

HAWLEY
And you shall. It just appears that London is slow to warm to your charms. But we need to invest in my remedies before committing financially to your theatrical adventures. I have already invested a larger sum than we agreed—

DEAD STAGE

BELLE
(interrupting)
Piffle! Explain to me why it must be my career that stagnates? One cannot simply put the arts on hold! One has to live them whilst within the grip of her fervour!

Pause.

Belle resumes brushing her hair.

HAWLEY
(tentative)
I'm sorry to say that tonight was to be our last performance. The owner of the theatre insists that he has given you enough time to—

Belle slams her hairbrush down for the second time. She remains seated and turns towards Hawley.

BELLE
(angry)
How dare he! This is outrageous! Does he not know who he is about to cast out? Tell him that I am above this paltry theatre! Tell him that I shall forever tarnish his name amongst the artistic community . . . I shall say that he made advances towards me. He shall struggle to book all but the most desperate of acts!

HAWLEY
He has rent to meet and your act is not bringing in enough customers. Can we not accept that this

particular piece is not to London's taste and bow out with our dignity intact?

BELLE
I shall say that he propositioned me and because I spurned his advances he withdrew his services. Yes, that shall set this matter right!

HAWLEY
Cora, I hardly think that this is the correct way in which to carry oneself—

BELLE
(angry)
How many times have I told you not to call me that? I am Belle Elmore . . . and I hardly think that you are in a position to speak on this matter! Had you backed me as a husband ought I would not be in this predicament!

HAWLEY
There was a time when I admired your passion but this issue of money is overshadowing our happiness. We both have paths we are required to tread—

BELLE
It is not simply about the money Hawley! We came here together! We shared a dream! We were to take London by storm . . . with I a roaring hit on stage and you with your revolutionary treatments making waves throughout the medical community. Our success was never in doubt . . . yet look at us now. Somewhere along the way, we lost ourselves. The

DEAD STAGE

stage became all I have . . . and I trust that your vials and test tubes became just as meaningful to you. We can longer relate to one another. Could we ever?

HAWLEY
I have tried to understand your Cora but life has a habit of making demands which require my attention and—

There is a knock on the dressing room door.

BELLE
Enter!

Simon enters the dressing room.

SIMON
Forgive me, Belle, have you heard?

BELLE
Yes-yes, Hawley just informed me. Fear not, I shall find us another stage upon which to perform.

HAWLEY
But Belle it will not be quite so—

BELLE
I have not the time to entertain your negativity now. Simon and I are to discuss our next move.

Simon looks at Hawley.

> BELLE
> Oh don't worry about him, he was just leaving.

Hawley looks at his feet.

> HAWLEY
> Yes. Quite.

Hawley passes Simon and heads towards the exit.

> HAWLEY
> *(To Simon)*
> Good evening.

Exit Hawley.

Simon approaches Belle and wraps his arms around her.

> SIMON
> I cannot for the life of me understand what you see in that pitiful excuse of a man!

> BELLE
> His devotion is unquestionable and his pockets deep. You would struggle to believe it but there once beat the heart of a vibrant man, determined to change the world. Sadly, the fog of this cursed city seems to have swallowed his desire. You provide what he lacks. How I wish that you and he were one and the same.

Belle turns towards Simon and they kiss.

DEAD STAGE

BELLE
We shall perform again my love, London has yet to see the last of Belle Elmore!

FADE TO BLACK.

ACT 1-3

Office: Hawley is seated at his desk. The office is sparsely furnished. He is reviewing notes. There is a knock on his door.

                    HAWLEY
  (without looking up)
                    Enter.

Enter ETHEL LE NEVE (Late teens, pretty) with a stack of papers.

                    ETHEL
          Good morning Doctor.

Hawley places his work aside and rises to greet Ethel.

                    HAWLEY
Please, there is no need for such formalities when it is only you and I.

Ethel places the papers onto Hawley's desk.

                    ETHEL
Sorry. I get so used to keeping up appearances.

Hawley touches Ethel on the cheek

                    HAWLEY
I know that it is hard for you, I too feel the burden of our love, yet we must maintain a proper distance.

DEAD STAGE

Ethel nods and Hawley takes his seat.

ETHEL
These are the interview transcripts that you requested. All are new to the clinic so I'm afraid they are a little lengthy.

HAWLEY
Understood. Thank you, Ethel.

Hawley flicks through the pile of papers. He seems tired and agitated.

ETHEL
How does your research progress?

HAWLEY
(gruffly)
It does not.

ETHEL
Forgive my concern but are you well?

Hawley stops what he was doing.

HAWLEY
Cora is without a stage again.

ETHEL
Oh.

HAWLEY
She is not the draw that she has me proclaim her to

be and it is only a short matter of time before audiences realize her shortcomings. Alas, she is oblivious.

ETHEL
I understand why it is that you remain with her, I—I just . . .

HAWLEY
(frustrated)
If only it were so simple Ethel, I would leave it all behind and start afresh with you yet my faith . . . my morals forbid be. Unhappy though I am, I must remain true to my vows.

ETHEL
(resigned)
I know.

Hawley stands and crosses to his window.

HAWLEY
Without a platform to call her own, she will become unbearably tiresome. It falls upon me to finance her next venture yet I am at a loss as to how to proceed!

ETHEL
You work so hard Hawley, surely she must see that?

HAWLEY
I'm afraid she sees little beyond the spotlight.

Pause.

DEAD STAGE

ETHEL
I should let you be in peace.

Hawley returns to his desk.

HAWLEY
Thank you.
(*taps papers*)
I have much to occupy myself with.

Ethel nods and exits. Hawley returns to his work.

FADE TO BLACK.

ACT 1-4

Dining room: Hawley and Belle are seated at opposite ends of a large dining table. They are eating dinner in silence.

Long pause.

BELLE
Have you given thought as to how you shall fund my next performance?

HAWLEY
Do you have a theatre in mind?

BELLE
All of them. None of them. What does it matter? You did not answer my question.

Pause.

HAWLEY
As of yet, I have not.

BELLE
Your income will no longer suffice. I shall require more in the way of finance if I am to return to the stage.

HAWLEY
I suspected as much. I cannot devote any more money to finance your endeavours. My research must come—

DEAD STAGE

BELLE
(interrupting)
You shall need to work longer hours.

HAWLEY
There are no more hours in which to work.

Pause.

BELLE
Then we shall have to take in lodgers. We have room. I know of several actors in the city in desperate need of accommodation.

Hawley places his cutlery aside.

HAWLEY
Do you really wish to open our house to others? Are you not afraid that they will learn of our unfortunate situation?

BELLE
To what are you referring?

HAWLEY
This house is bitter. No love resides within these walls. Would that it be any lodger wished to remain here.

BELLE
And? Do you really think that I shall let that stand between me and my dreams? Hawley, you know of my desire.

HAWLEY
Yes, and that is the very crux of the matter!

Belle stands.

BELLE
(angry)
How dare you! You shall retract those words immediately!

HAWLEY
(bitter)
I retract nothing.

BELLE
If this is about us having children again—

HAWLEY
A wish of mine that you cruelly deny!

BELLE
There is no place for children in my plans. They demand attention and patience, neither of which I have an ounce of to spare!

HAWLEY
You wish only for your own success—your own happiness.

BELLE
(assertive)
No, but I must endeavour to work towards it. If you refuse to provide extra funding for my career,

DEAD STAGE

choosing to selfishly pursue the hopeless idea of your miracle cure then this must be done. We shall have lodgers and you will work towards making each of them welcome. Our relationship is of no concern in this. If I am to return to the stage, then lodgers are a must. Unless you are prepared to backtrack on your reluctance to finance my plans?

HAWLEY
I am not reluctant . . . I am unable. A line must be drawn. I remain dedicated to my work. As for longer hours; there are only so many patients in the city at any given time.

BELLE
Oh, piffle! I am on to you Hawley Crippen, you wish to see me back in the gutter . . . you wish to see me broken and hopeless!

HAWLEY
And why would that be? Do tell. After all, I have supported you thus far?

BELLE
Because you live in my shadow. I have everything that you ever desired. I have talent, I have admirers and devotees. I touch people with my performances—I am a star.

HAWLEY
(dismissive)
I never wished for anything such.

BELLE
Liar! I've seen the way you look at me when I am surrounded by my adoring public. You turn positively green! I shall never capitulate, I shall never run back to my father and admit that I failed. I was born for better.

Hawley stands up.

HAWLEY
Do as you must. Take in your lodgers. I shall not stop you, nor could I if I tried.

Hawley exits the room. Belle pours herself a glass of wine and takes a sip.

BELLE
Indeed. For mine is the only way.

FADE TO BLACK.

Act 1-5

Dining room: Night. Belle is entertaining MARCIE WHITTINGHAM and FLORIE SHAW (Both late thirties/early forties, well dressed)

(laughter)

MARCIE
You must enlighten Belle regarding the latest exploits of Cherie Mon' Lette!

BELLE
That little harlot? Where has she been flaunting it now?

FLORIE
Well, you know the owner of the Old Mo?

BELLE
A gentleman by the name of Leonard Fitzroy or so I am led to believe?

FLORIE
Indeed, well it seems that Cherie gave herself over to him several times under the pretence of a Saturday night performance this coming weekend.

BELLE
Harlot.

FLORIE
Only having never met Mr Fitzroy and desperate as she were, she ended up sleeping with the theatre pianist thinking it was Leonard!

(laughter)

MARCIE
Serves her right! She has little in the way of talent. I've heard she spends more time on her back than she does in front of an audience. Why ever do those devoid of talent choose to flaunt the few blessings that the Lord gifted to them?

FLORIE
It is beyond me! I have no time nor respect for any woman who chooses to open her legs rather than have the conviction of one's expertise in the arts!

BELLE
Unless of course, one's expertise is on one's back!
(laughter)

Pause.

FLORIE
We simply must have you back where you belong Belle, London is positively crying out for a talent such as yours!

MARCIE
I agree! Everything has gotten awfully stale without your presence, though the Music Hall Ladies Guild is

DEAD STAGE

delighted to name you amongst our number . . . it is the stage upon which you truly belong.

BELLE
Your kindness knows no end. It seems that my latest vision is not to taste—I am pondering a change of act.

FLORIE
Nonsense! The London audience prides itself on breaking new art! The Guild, Marcie and I are beside you all of the way!

MARCIE
Absolutely. Now when do you propose to return to the stage?

BELLE
(sullen)
I cannot say . . . I have the means in place, at least some of them, yet Hawley is reluctant to help.

FLORIE
Why would he not? Can he not see the greatness in your performance?

BELLE
Lately, I think not. His mind is occupied by his failing efforts. He understands my struggles less each day.

MARCIE
That is unfortunate—Florie and I shall speak to the guild, perhaps we can—

DAN WEATHERER

Simon enters the room.

SIMON
Oh! Pardon me, forgive my intrusion, I knew not that you were entertaining.

BELLE
(brightening)
Not at all! Please, join us.

Belle motions for Simon to join her. He is reluctant.

SIMON
(flirtatious)
Dare I trust myself amidst as fine a collection of ladies as I have ever set eyes upon? I think not!

BELLE
(flirtatious)
Oh, you had better if you wish to remain as lodger!

SIMON
(To Belle)
If I may, I had matters to discuss with you, but they can keep.

MARCIE
(playful to Florie)
I imagine that Belle is only too keen to bid us farewell so that she can direct her full attention to whatever the matter is.

DEAD STAGE

BELLE
(To Marcie and Florie)
And who could blame me!

FLORIE
(laughing)
Oh come now Marcie, let us away and leave these two in peace. I'm quite sure that the fine gentleman has better things to do than listen to our frivolous talk.

MARCIE
(To Belle)
My—isn't he a handsome fellow.

Belle smiles at Marcie

BELLE
He is the perfect lodger that one could wish and nothing more. Isn't that right Mr Harper?

Simon gives a wry smile.

FLORIE
Come now, let us be away. Good evening to you both.

Marcie and Florie exit.

Simon maintains his position by the door.

BELLE
It is safe to approach. They shall not return. Nor shall they speak of you. We three have a bond that I trust implicitly.

SIMON
I had hoped to catch you alone my darling. Have we time to be together this night?

Belle stands and approaches Simon. She places her arms around his neck and looks into his eyes.

BELLE
He shall be away for another hour.

Simon smiles and the pair kiss. Passions begin to overflow.

Enter Hawley.

Hawley sees Belle and Simon. He remains by the door.

Simon sees Hawley and pushes Belle away.

SIMON
(shocked)
Hawley! I—we—forgive me.

Hawley does not answer.

Belle composes herself.

BELLE
I understood that you were to be back later this evening.

DEAD STAGE

HAWLEY
(dejected)
My—My plans have changed.

Pause.

SIMON
Forgive me, sir, I—

BELLE
Ask forgiveness for nothing! He suspected long ago . . . He was merely too weak to confront the matter. Were you not?

Hawley looks at the couple for a moment before turning towards the door.

Exit Hawley.

SIMON
He didn't say an awful lot.

BELLE
He never does. Likely that he will find a tavern in which to brood before returning here, drunk and apologetic.

SIMON
But why should he be the one to be sorry?

BELLE
Men such as Hawley always are. No matter the situation they are always the source of the misfortune that surrounds them.

SIMON
But—

Belle places her finger over Simon's lips.

BELLE
We still have the evening to ourselves. Would that we waste it?

Simon pauses for a moment before giving in to temptation. They resume their embrace.

FADE TO BLACK.

ACT 1-6

Small living room complete with table and two chairs.

Enter Ethel and Hawley.

HAWLEY
(agitated)
Forgive my calling upon you at such an hour. I had no other place to visit. I shall be damned if I am to return home just yet!

ETHEL
Hawley dear, whatever has happened? You are a dreadful shade!

Hawley takes a seat. Ethel sits opposite.

HAWLEY
My damnedest fears were presented to me this night. I returned home to find Cora with another.

Pause.

ETHEL
If I may, you always suspected as much. We have spoken of this many times.

Hawley rises from his chair and begins to pace.

HAWLEY
Indeed, that much is true. Yet far from my sight it bothered me not. Setting eyes upon her as she cavorted with another, it was too much for me to stomach. A suspicion or an idea can be pushed to the farthest reaches of the mind. Once one is witness to something first-hand it becomes all the more tangible and much harder to ignore.

ETHEL
Do you still love her?

Hawley takes a seat.

HAWLEY
This is not a question of love; you know that my heart belongs to you.

ETHEL
As mine does to you but—

HAWLEY
(angry)
It is the sheer audacity of the woman! In my home, under my nose . . . whilst I toil for her so that she may return to the stage! Her lack of respect for me is beyond compare!

Pause.

ETHEL
All the while we long for one another whilst she cavorts behind your back. Tis most unjust. You

DEAD STAGE

deserve a woman who believes in you. A woman who would take care of you. Belle—she takes from you Hawley... your money and your spirit. Can you not see?

Hawley looks into Ethel's eyes.

HAWLEY
I am a conflicted man. I burn for you but my faith permits me from acting upon my desires.

ETHEL
(reluctantly)
I understand.

HAWLEY
Yet...

ETHEL
Yes?

HAWLEY
Yet seeing how little I am respected by her, despite how hard I labor... why do I continue to attempt to please her when it is you that I wish to be with?

ETHEL
Why did you come here?

HAWLEY
I had to. Whether I admit it to myself or not, tonight I have awoken from a terrible nightmare.

Hawley stands and takes Ethel by the hand. She stands.

HAWLEY
Ethel, I adore you. We have shared many hours in the company of one another yet all I ever wanted to do was this.

Hawley kisses Ethel.

Ethel pulls away. She is shy and unsure.

ETHEL
Could I be who you really want?

HAWLEY
Yes, my dear. Of that I am certain.

Ethel moves to kiss Hawley.

FADE TO BLACK.

ACT 1-7

Hawley's Dining room—Belle, Florie and Marcie are enjoying a glass of wine.

Laughter

BELLE
We really should arrange to meet more often. It has been several weeks since you last blessed this house with your company. I might almost venture that I missed you both!

MARCIE
You know how it is, the Guild needs to keep up appearances.

FLORIE
Our diary is positively brimming with engagements!

BELLE
One can imagine.

Pause.

FLORIE
Tell me, where is that delightful young fellow that interrupted us the last time that we met here?

MARCIE
Oh yes! Will he be joining us again?

BELLE
(dismissive)
Simon? Oh, I sincerely doubt it. I'll wager that he is enjoying the evening somewhere tasteful and expensive with another of his co-stars. He has a taste for those that walk the stage . . . a taste that soon sours once one is no longer a draw.

FLORIE
Oh, a shame for sure.

Awkward silence. Florie and Marcie exchange glances.

BELLE
Is there something that you wish to say?

Florie and Marcie exchange awkward glances.

BELLE
Oh for heaven's sake, out with it?

MARCIE
I don't really know how to—

FLORIE
This is about your husband.

BELLE
Hawley? Must we speak of him?

FLORIE
I'm afraid we must. One of the ladies of—

DEAD STAGE

BELLE
Who?

MARCIE
She wishes to remain anonymous.

BELLE
Whatever for?

Pause.

BELLE
My patience wears thin, out with it at once!

FLORIE
Your husband has been seen dining with another.

MARCIE
On several occasions.

BELLE
Oh.

FLORIE
Whilst we are sure that you were unaware of his actions—

MARCIE
—and it upsets us a great deal that we are to be the ones bearing such bad tidings—

FLORIE
You understand that as Guild Treasurer there are certain standards which need to be met in order to protect our reputation.

BELLE
(distant)
... of course.

MARCIE
It would be wise to resolve this issue in as polite and dignified a manner as possible.

FLORIE
In the interests of all concerned of course.

BELLE
(distant)
Of course.

MARCIE
Please endeavour to keep us informed of any developments. It goes without saying that your position is as secure as ever ...

FLORIE
Oh of course it is ... but the Guild needs to be seen in only the purest of light.

Belle rises from her seat.

DEAD STAGE

BELLE
(assertive)
I understand. If you will forgive me, ladies, I need to clear my head in order to decide how best to tackle this most unfortunate of matters.

Gestures towards the door.

BELLE
If you please.

Marcie and Florie rise. They are visibly put out.

MARCIE
Of course.

FLORIE
We shall be in touch soon. My deepest apologies.

MARCIE
Yes—our deepest apologies.

BELLE
Thank you, I am touched. Now if you will excuse me.

Belle motions Marcie and Florie out of the door.

Exit Marcie and Florie.

Belle returns to her seat and pours herself a glass of wine.

BELLE
Who would have thought that the miserable weasel could catch the eye of another?

Belle takes a gulp of wine.

BELLE
I'll wager she is the desperate sort . . . large and plain. Either way, this will not do.

FADE TO BLACK.

ACT 1-8

Outer office: Ethel is typing whilst sitting at a small table.

Enter Belle.

Ethel looks up from her work.

ETHEL
Good afternoon, how may I help you?

Belle looks at Ethel for a moment. Ethel begins to wilt and looks away.

BELLE
I'm here to see Hawley.

ETHEL
Dr Crippen is currently out of the office. May I take a message?

BELLE

(assertive)
Do you know where he is?

ETHEL
He is taking note of an order; he should be back later this afternoon. I will ensure any message left is passed to him upon his return.

Belle turns towards the exit.

BELLE
No, I shall speak to him when he returns home.

ETHEL
(taken aback)
Oh. Yes. I shall tell him that his wife called in.

Belle pauses.

BELLE
Are you not going to ask for my name? It is extremely rude to pass on a message without a name attached.

ETHEL
Oh yes . . . of course. Do you prefer Belle or Cora?

Belle turns towards Ethel.

BELLE
You are the one, aren't you?

ETHEL
(scared)
I-I don't know what you mean!

BELLE
You are the little whore that my Hawley has been seen out with! Who else could it be? He never was much of a socialite . . . and you are oh so his fancy!

ETHEL
(flustered)
Mrs Crippen, I—

DEAD STAGE

BELLE
Don't refer to me using that name, I'm Belle Elmore and you are having relations with my husband, are you not?

ETHEL
Mrs Elmore I—

BELLE

(angry)

Are you not?

Pause.

Ethel stands.

ETHEL

(assertive)
Hawley is a lovely man and he deserves to be treated in a proper manner. He works hard, his ideas could change the world yet you insist on breaking his spirit and holding him back!

BELLE
I will not take counsel regarding my marriage from the likes of you and I'll tell you to—

ETHEL

(interrupting)
I am the woman that Hawley should be with! I would care for him, support him, encourage him to be all that he could be! You do not deserve him! He has stood by you, sacrificed so much for you, yet you are blinded by selfish desire! You have lost his heart—

BELLE
(fuming)
Don't you ever tell me—

Belle pushes Ethel to the ground.

BELLE
. . . what my husband needs from me. Do you hear?

Ethel is sitting on the ground. She is shaken and afraid.

ETHEL
I-I'm sorry but Hawley and I—

BELLE
I don't want to hear of it. If you ever go near my husband again I shall have you beaten to within an inch of your life. Do you hear?

ETHEL
(sobbing)
Yes . . . Yes, I understand.

Belle takes a long look at Ethel who is seated upon the floor.

BELLE
Pathetic. You cannot hope to hold a candle to me.

Exit Belle.

DEAD STAGE

Ethel continues to cry and begins to suffer stomach pains. She climbs to her feet in an obvious amount of pain. With her back to the audience, she checks her abdomen. Her hand comes back bloody. Ethel collapses to the floor and begins to wail.

FADE TO BLACK.

ACT 1-9

Outer office: Hawley enters the office. Ethel is sitting on the floor. She has a distant look in her eyes and her abdomen is covered in blood.

HAWLEY
I'm sorry that I am later than expected—Did you close the surgery early—My God! What has happened here? Are you alright?

Hawley rushes to Ethel's side.

HAWLEY
Whose blood is this?

Ethel does not respond.

HAWLEY
Ethel, are you hurt? Talk to me!

ETHEL
(distant)
It did hurt at first but now I just feel . . . numb.

HAWLEY
(panicked)
    Whatever has happened here?

ETHEL
(breaking down)
    I'm sorry my dear, I'm so sorry!

DEAD STAGE

HAWLEY
Are you hurt? Come, we must get you to a physician at once!

ETHEL
It's our baby . . . it's gone. I'm so sorry . . . I know how much you wished to be a father . . . I couldn't even give you that. Our baby . . . my baby.

HAWLEY
(shocked)
Our baby?

ETHEL
(anguished)
I was going to tell . . . I was! When I knew for sure . . . I mean a mother knows but I needed to be sure for you . . . but with the stress you were under . . . it could keep, I could manage.

HAWLEY
My God! You were pregnant? I . . . Was I to be a father?

ETHEL
Cora came to see you . . . she lost her temper . . . she threw me to the ground . . .
(Breaks down)
I'm sorry Hawley, I could no longer hold my tongue! She is a vile creature! She has taken everything from me . . . from us!

HAWLEY
(shocked)
She did this to you?

Ethel nods.

ETHEL
Yes . . . but I said such awful things to her . . . this is my fault. I'm so sorry Hawley. I wanted to give you a child . . . I'm so sorry.

HAWLEY
(tearful)
Come, you need medical attention. Do not dwell on the events of the day. Perhaps all can be saved.

Hawley helps Ethel to her feet.

ETHEL
Our baby is gone Hawley . . . she took it from us. I'm so sorry, I should have held my tongue.

Hawley helps Ethel towards the door

HAWLEY
Nonsense. Do not apologize. Let us see you well, you are my concern now. Do not worry about anything else.

Exit Hawley and Ethel.

FADE TO BLACK.

ACT 1-10

Night: Hawley's Office. Hawley is drinking at his desk.

HAWLEY
(upset)
I was to be a father. A blessing I had sought for so long.

Hawley takes a gulp from his glass.

HAWLEY
(angry)
Yet that woman denied me. Again and again . . . she delights in my torment! I shall never be truly happy until I am rid of her. She has to go. I can no longer stand to live this way. She has to go.

Hawley takes a small envelope from his pocket and places it on his desk.

HAWLEY
This shall be the answer to my woes.

He opens the envelope and studies the contents for a moment.

HAWLEY
My hand is forced; anger holds me within its toxic grasp. No longer can I live this way. My child . . . my child is dead.

DAN WEATHERER

Hawley finishes his drink, picks up the envelope and returns it to his pocket. He takes a pistol from his desk, stands, removes his coat from the coat stand and exits the office.

FADE TO BLACK.

ACT 1-11

Morning: Hawley is standing by the dining room window. His attention is fixed on the outside.

Enter Belle

BELLE
Oh . . . Good morning.

Hawley remains still.

BELLE
I did not hear you return.

HAWLEY
Time ran away with me. I wished not to disturb you.

BELLE
Strangely courteous of you, though I must say it is rare for you to work so late.

HAWLEY
I wished not to return to a similar scene as witnessed before.

BELLE
I was trying to be courteous, there is no need for such uncouth a tongue as yours at this early hour.

HAWLEY
Of course. How rude of me.

BELLE
Besides, Simon is gone. He shall likely not return. No doubt he is with another much younger and prettier than I.

HAWLEY
Forgive me if I feel little in the way of compassion.

Pause.

HAWLEY
You visited my surgery yesterday, correct?

BELLE
I did, you were not there.

HAWLEY
No, I was not. You spoke to my secretary.

BELLE
(laughing)
Pah! Your secretary—is that what she is?

HAWLEY
You struck her.

BELLE
I did no such thing! The woman is a liar, as are you!

HAWLEY
Meaning?

DEAD STAGE

BELLE
She is no more your secretary than I am your darling wife.

HAWLEY
Yet you are my wife, at least according to the court.

BELLE
You shall do well to remember that. I will not stand for you gallivanting around the city with that whore of a woman. Should you continue to see her I shall make it public knowledge of your extramarital affair! Your reputation as a respected Homeopathic Physician shall be ruined and I shall take all that remains of your estate.

HAWLEY
You have already taken enough.

BELLE
Oh, I haven't even started yet!

Pause.

BELLE
Hadn't you to work?

HAWLEY
Yes.

BELLE
Be sure to end matters with that girl. I want her out of a job by midday. Do you hear?

DAN WEATHERER

Hawley does not respond.

Exit Belle.

After a moment's further contemplation Hawley turns towards the dining table. He takes the pistol from his pocket before returning it and removes the small envelope. He empties the contents into a bottle of red wine which is resting on the dining table.

Exit Hawley.

FADE TO BLACK.

ACT 1-12

Night: Bathroom. Stage lights rise and fall in synchronicity to a loud, audible heartbeat which quickens as the scene continues.

Hawley is seen standing next to a bathtub filled with blood. He is dishevelled and his clothes are bloodstained. He is sobbing and upset. There is a reluctance and a tiredness in his movement. There is a metal bucket by the bath and a solitary sink in the corner of the room. Hawley is holding a saw and is looking into the bathtub.

In between lights up/out Hawley is heard cutting with his saw. He is seen carrying an arm and placing it into the sink, first one, then another.

Two legs are then stacked neatly by the bathtub.

The fifth and final cut is accompanied by the clanging of the metal bucket as something unseen is dropped into it.

Hawley is seen holding the bucket at eye level before him. A wisp of dark hair is visible above the lip of the bucket.

LIGHTS OUT.
CURTAIN FALLS.
END OF ACT ONE.

ACT 2

ACT 2-1

Lights up: Office. Morning.

Enter Hawley carrying a bag. He is dishevelled and edgy. He hangs his coat upon the coat hook, takes a seat and places the bag on his desk. He begins to rummage through the contents of the bag.

Enter Ethel.

Hawley closes the bag.

ETHEL
Good morning.

Hawley mumbles a greeting.

ETHEL
Darling, you look terrible! Is anything the matter?

HAWLEY
(agitated)
Close the door. Please. Are you well?

Ethel closes the door.

ETHEL
I am. I missed you. Though I rested, it was you that I needed more. I'm sorry.

DEAD STAGE

Pause.

HAWLEY
She left me.

Pause.

ETHEL
Did she? I didn't ever think that she would but—

HAWLEY
She went last night. It's for the best. You and I know that it is.

ETHEL
Of course. Are you alright?

Hawley stands and faces the office window.

HAWLEY
I shall be . . . in time. It is what I wanted after all . . . it just came as somewhat of a shock.

ETHEL
Yes. I suppose it must.

Hawley turns his attention to Ethel.

HAWLEY
How are you feeling? I know that I have been of little help of late. The loss hit me hard and I should have been there for you . . . it's just with Cora and everything I—

ETHEL
I am well, at least I try to be. It is a difficult time for me—for us, and the loss will always remain . . . but at least now we can face it together?

Pause.

ETHEL
Forgive me.

Hawley approaches Ethel and places his hands upon her shoulders.

HAWLEY
My sweet girl, of course we can. Belle is no longer a part of my life, she shall not return, of that I am certain. You and I, we shall overcome all of our hardships together.

ETHEL
And those plans that we made? Your elixir? Your clinics?

HAWLEY
We are free to pursue them. All of them.

They embrace

HAWLEY
As for the moment, I have a favour to ask of you.

ETHEL
Anything.

DEAD STAGE

Hawley returns to his desk and opens the bag.

HAWLEY
Come . . . see what I have for you.

Ethel approaches the desk. Hawley takes out a handful of jewellery.

HAWLEY
These are for you. A gift.

Ethel takes the jewellery.

ETHEL
These were Cora's . . . I cannot possibly—

HAWLEY
Paid for by me. She no longer wants them; I shall only pawn them should you decline to accept them . . . however, these pieces would look positively exquisite upon you.

Ethel smiles first at the jewellery and then at Hawley.

ETHEL
If you insist.

Hawley smiles and nods.

HAWLEY
It would make me very happy if you were to accept them.

DAN WEATHERER

ETHEL
Thank you.

Ethel places the jewellery into her pocket.

Hawley returns his attention to the bag.

HAWLEY
As for the rest of the pieces, would you please sell them? I am not so interested in price; I just wish to be rid of them.

ETHEL
Of course. I know of a few places.

Ethel picks up the bag and turns to leave.

HAWLEY
One more thing.

Hawley removes a letter from the desk drawer.

HAWLEY
Deliver this to the Ladies Guild. They shall be wary of Cora's absence. This letter explains that she has left the country in order to aid a sick relative.

ETHEL
Oh. But—

DEAD STAGE

HAWLEY
I know that is not the truth of the matter but I cannot bear to have my personal affairs discussed among their number.

ETHEL
I understand. I shall deliver this right away.

HAWLEY
Thank you.

Ethel smiles.

ETHEL
There is no need to thank me.

Exit Ethel.

Hawley takes a moment to compose himself before beginning his work.

LIGHTS OUT.

ACT 2-2

Street: Night. Hawley and Ethel are walking arm in arm.

ETHEL
I have thoroughly enjoyed this evening. I do not believe I have ever dined in such splendour! You really are good to me.

HAWLEY
Now that we are free to enjoy the company of one another I want you to experience the best that the city has to offer.

ETHEL
Do you think it wise that we attended the Guild ball?

HAWLEY
I think our presence was expected.

ETHEL
Perhaps yours but not so much mine.

HAWLEY
Cora is gone. It is time that the guild realized that. Perhaps tonight we put a stop to a large amount of tongue wagging.

They pause.

DEAD STAGE

ETHEL
It is so good to see you smile.

HAWLEY
It feels good to do so. You must take credit for my current happiness.

Ethel and Hawley kiss. They resume their slow walk.

Hawley observes something unseen and begins to feel uneasy.

HAWLEY
Come, let us cross . . . quickly!

ETHEL
(surprised)
Why? Whatever is the matter?

HAWLEY
(agitated)
Come now, do as I say!

Enter Florie and Marcie.

MARCIE
Why, good evening Dr Crippen.

FLORIE
I see you have wasted little time in acquiring yourself a partner?

DAN WEATHERER

Hawley and Ethel pause.

HAWLEY
Good evening ladies. I trust that all is well?

MARCIE
We have had no word from Belle despite repeated attempts to contact her.

FLORIE
We wondered if she had established contact with you?

HAWLEY
Why on earth would she? She left me with not a moment's notice. As far as I am concerned she is gone for good. I would advise you to recruit for her post, she shall not return—not if I know Cora.

Marcie notices the brooch that Ethel is wearing. She approaches her and reaches out to touch it.

MARCIE
Is that not Belle's brooch?

Hawley pulls Ethel from the reach of Marcie and Ethel turns away from her.

ETHEL
The brooch is mine. It was a gift.

DEAD STAGE

FLORIE
I would have imagined Belle would have taken her jewellery with her—

MARCIE
A lady never travels without her jewellery!

HAWLEY
Belle left in a hurry. She took all the pieces of value and left those she favoured least. Anything left behind falls under my ownership.

MARCIE
(To Florie)
She often wore that piece. It was one of her favourites.

FLORIE
Indeed. It became so often a talking point due to its extravagant design.

HAWLEY
(flustered)
What can I say? A woman changes her mind as often as the wind changes direction. Now . . . if you will excuse us. The hour grows late.

MARCIE
She never did speak of an ailing relative—

FLORIE
And she trusted us with her most personal affairs.

MARCIE
The truth Hawley—out with it.

HAWLEY
(flustered)
This is hardly the time—

FLORIE
We shall not rest until we know that she is well.

HAWLEY
Then I regret to inform you of her recent passing.

Ethel, Marcie and Florie are shocked

MARCIE
What?

FLORIE
You mean to say that Belle is deceased?

ETHEL
Hawley I—

HAWLEY
Alas, she passed away last month.

MARCIE
This is—this is terrible!

HAWLEY
Indeed, now if you shall excuse us.

DEAD STAGE

FLORIE
What of her body?

HAWLEY
She was cremated. It was her final wish.

FLORIE
I see. How awful.

HAWLEY
Quite, now we must be off, I dislike speaking of such tragedy in such a hasty manner.

Marcie and Florie regard the couple.

MARCIE
Of course. Good evening.

ETHEL
(timid)
Good evening.

Exit Ethel and Hawley.

FLORIE
Well . . . what do you make of that?

MARCIE
Dead? It cannot be!

FLORIE
More so, as a Catholic, she would be fiercely against cremation.

MARCIE
And that was Belle's brooch of that I am certain.

FLORIE
Why admit now that she had passed, why not at the dinner or before now . . . why only when pushed?

MARCIE
I do not know but this whole affair sits uneasily with me. I suggest that we take our fears to the constabulary.

FLORIE
For peace of mind—I agree. Come, the night grows cold and there is still wine to be drunk. Let us toast the passing of a great actress.

MARCIE
The potential passing.

FLORIE
Yes, of course . . . let us not be so hasty to accept his story.

Marcie grabs her friend by the arm.

MARCIE
Then lead on dear friend! A drink shall calm my nerves!

Exit Florie/Marcie.

LIGHTS OUT.

ACT 2-3

Inspector Dew's office: Enter INSPECTOR DEW, (early thirties) Marcie and Florie.

INSPECTOR DEW
If you would care to take a seat?

Florie and Marcie take their seat. Dew takes his seat behind his desk.

FLORIE
Thank you for agreeing to see us, Officer.

Inspector Dew takes a notepad from his desk and begins to write.

INSPECTOR DEW
Inspector actually—and not at all. So—let me get to it, my colleague informs me that you have concerns regarding a friend of yours?

MARCIE
She is more of an associate really. Belle Elmore—sorry, Cora Crippen.

INSPECTOR DEW
(impatient)
Well—which is it?

FLORIE
Belle is her stage name, she hated any other.

DAN WEATHERER

INSPECTOR DEW
Cora Crippen. Age?

MARCIE
Well . . . I wouldn't like to say . . .

INSPECTOR DEW
I shall need this information in order to compile an accurate profile. Age?

Marcie and Florie look at one another.

MARCIE
Possible late forties, early fifties?

Florie nods.

Dew sighs and makes a note.

INSPECTOR DEW
And what are your concerns?

FLORIE
Her husband told us that she had left the country in order to aid a sick relative, yet she left in an awful hurry—

MARCIE
She never even said her farewells or took any of her jewellery!

FLORIE
That's right! We saw his latest lady friend wearing one of her brooches at the Guild ball!

DEAD STAGE

Inspector Dew stops taking notes.

INSPECTOR DEW
In grave times people often up and leave without the thought of others.

FLORIE
There's more . . . we received her resignation from her husband—

MARCIE
It was not penned in her handwriting.

INSPECTOR DEW
I see. What position did she hold within your organization?

MARCIE
She was the head of the fundraising committee for the Ladies Music Hall Guild.

FLORIE
A position that she took most seriously.

MARCIE
She was a remarkable aid to our cause—an actress such as she is a—

INSPECTOR DEW
An actress you say? Could she have taken leave in order to find work?

Marcie and Florie look at one another.

FLORIE
I suppose so—she was adamant that she needed to return to the stage.

MARCIE
It seemed that theatres in London were no longer in need of her services but—

Inspector Dew places his pen on the desk.

INSPECTOR DEW
Ladies, I understand your concern but you must agree that it is entirely plausible that your acquaintance has left London for either of those reasons. I see no cause to investigate further.

MARCIE
Please, inspector, there is still more to tell. Her husband was having an affair.

FLORIE
We saw him entertaining a young lady on several occasions.

MARCIE
And when last we asked after Belle he informed us of her death!

Inspector Dew resumes his note-taking.

INSPECTOR DEW
You suspect foul play?

DEAD STAGE

MARCIE
To be honest we are not sure what to think! He changed his story in a matter of seconds. Hearing him say that she had passed away . . . it didn't sound convincing.

FLORIE
His lover was there when he made this admission. She seemed as shocked as Marcie and me!

INSPECTOR DEW
Hmmmmmm. Was Mrs Crippen aware of this affair?

FLORIE
Yes—we informed her.

INSPECTOR DEW
I see. And how did she take this news?

Florie and Marcie regard one another again.

MARCIE
I would say . . . not well.

INSPECTOR DEW
Her husband's name, please.

FLORIE
Hawley Crippen. He is a Doctor of some sort.

INSPECTOR DEW
And his address?

DAN WEATHERER

MARCIE
39 Hilldrop Crescent, Holloway.

INSPECTOR DEW
Thank you. That should be enough for now.

Dew places his pen down and stands. Marcie and Florie stand.

FLORIE
Shall you speak to Hawley?

INSPECTOR DEW
Though I suspect that there is nothing untoward regarding the disappearance of Mrs Crippen, I shall at least pay him a short visit. The fact that he has changed his story seemingly on a whim suggests that there may be more to this tale.

MARCIE
Thank you. That is all we ask. Something feels amiss in all of this. For instance, Belle would not stand for cremation. She was a devout Catholic.

FLORIE
That would not be her wish at all.

Dew shows Marcie and Florie to the door.

INSPECTOR DEW
I am sure that we shall resolve the matter quickly. Leave your details with my colleague and I shall be in touch.

DEAD STAGE

FLORIE
Thank you, inspector.

Exit Florie/Marcie.

Dew returns to his desk and examines his notes.

FADE TO BLACK.

ACT 2-4

Dining room: Enter Ethel and Inspector Dew. Hawley is seated at the dining table reading over a collection of notes.

                    ETHEL
(nervous)
            Inspector Dew to see you.

Hawley stands. Dew approaches to shake hands.

            INSPECTOR DEW
              Dr Crippen?

                  HAWLEY
Indeed. Ethel, that will be all. Thank you.

Exit Ethel. Dew and Hawley shake hands.

                  HAWLEY
          Pleasure. Please sit.

Dew takes a seat.

                  HAWLEY
     How may I be of assistance?

Dew takes out his notebook.

            INSPECTOR DEW
Forgive my line of questioning, the matter is

DEAD STAGE

somewhat delicate yet I have received a visit from friends of your wife . . .

Dew checks his notebook.

HAWLEY
Cora.

INSPECTOR DEW
Yes! That's it. They were concerned about her sudden disappearance and came to me with all sorts of theories.

HAWLEY
They told you that I said she was dead. Correct?

INSPECTOR DEW
In a manner of speaking yes. Though they insisted that at first you had told them that Cora had returned home to tend to a sick relative. Home is in this instance?

HAWLEY
The United States. New York. It is true. I told them both of those things.

Pause.

INSPECTOR DEW
So which is correct? Did your wife pass away?

HAWLEY
No. She is alive . . . at least as far as I am aware.

INSPECTOR DEW
I see. Did she return home?

HAWLEY
Yes.

INSPECTOR DEW
To tend to a sick relative? Though I must advise that the ladies in question are adamant that they would have heard of such a relative. They were quite open in their business by all accounts.

Pause.

HAWLEY
No. Though she did likely flee there . . . with him.

INSPECTOR DEW
I see. Would you care to explain what really happened?

HAWLEY
I concocted the stories about her tending to a sick relative and later died in order to save face. My wife left me for another. He lodged here . . . I caught them together.

INSPECTOR DEW
Was she having an affair?

HAWLEY
Yes.

DEAD STAGE

INSPECTOR DEW
As were you?

HAWLEY
Yes-no, not at that time. I had never acted upon my feelings. Cora was a difficult woman to love but we had made a promise to God. However, she realized her future lay elsewhere and the pair of them left last month.

INSPECTOR DEW
Why did you not just tell the truth?

HAWLEY
I was ashamed. I could not admit that she had chosen another after all that I had done for her. My practice is all that I have left—the fear of my patients hearing of my failed marriage . . . it was too much to comprehend. I knew that Cora would not return so in order to safeguard my reputation I invented those stories. I apologize, it was foolish of me.

INSPECTOR DEW
And the lady who let me in? Is she your lover?

HAWLEY
Her name is Ethel. It is true that she and I are in love yet our relationship blossomed after Cora had left me. Without her, I sincerely doubt I would have continued to live . . . as was my grief.

Inspector Dew returns his notebook to his pocket.

DAN WEATHERER

INSPECTOR DEW
I understand. My apologies for wasting your time.

HAWLEY
Not at all. It is your duty and nothing more.

Hawley and the inspector stand.

HAWLEY
I shall show you out.

Hawley and the inspector move towards the door.

INSPECTOR DEW
Thank you. Oh! One last thing. Why did your wife elect to leave her jewellery behind?

HAWLEY
I'm sorry?

INSPECTOR DEW
One of the ladies that came to see me insisted that ... Ethel, was it?

HAWLEY
Yes.

INSPECTOR DEW
That Ethel was wearing one of your wife's brooches.

HAWLEY
(abrupt)
Then they are mistaken.

DEAD STAGE

INSPECTOR DEW
They seemed quite adamant.

HAWLEY
My wife took everything of worth—hence my determination to keep my reputation intact and my practice profitable.

INSPECTOR DEW
I understand. Could it be possible that she forgot a piece?

HAWLEY
No. Those that came to see you are mistaken. Now, if we are done here?

Pause.

Dew regards Hawley for a moment.

INSPECTOR DEW
Yes, that concludes my business for now. I shall return if I have any further questions. Good day Dr.

HAWLEY
And to you.

Exit Inspector Dew.

HAWLEY
(flustered)
Ethel! Come here this instance!

DAN WEATHERER

Enter Ethel. She is pale and flustered.

ETHEL
Is everything alright?

Hawley looks through the window before turning to answer.

HAWLEY
(panicked)
Pack your things, we need to go!

ETHEL
Go? Go where?

HAWLEY
I-I don't know . . . Canada . . . Quebec, how does Quebec sound?

ETHEL
It sounds far away—whatever has brought about this sudden change?

HAWLEY
There shall be time for answers later, please trust in me.

ETHEL
What of your practice? This makes no sense at all?

HAWLEY
We shall only be away for a while—a year perhaps . . . just until the attention has passed. Besides—I can start a Practice there. They have sickness in Canada

DEAD STAGE

too.

ETHEL
I don't understand? What about our plans?

Hawley crossed the room and places his hands upon Ethel's shoulders.

HAWLEY
My dear, people are talking . . . and talking leads to scandal. I have seen it happen many times, tongues can be vicious. They can break careers and shatter relationships such as ours. It is better that we are far removed from their sight.

ETHEL
But I . . . are you sure?

HAWLEY
I am sure. Were we to remain our lives would fall under constant scrutiny and you and I would find little time to enjoy one another's company. Though I curse her name to Hell and back, we must accept that her elopement shall forever haunt us unless we act upon it now.

ETHEL
I would follow you to the ends of the earth, you know that, but I have family here. What shall I tell them?

HAWLEY
Tell them . . . tell them that you are to see the world whilst you are still young. Tell them that you are with the one that you love and you shall want for nothing.

DAN WEATHERER

              ETHEL
Do you have the means to make this so?

             HAWLEY
The means and the desire.

Ethel smiles.

             HAWLEY
So will you come away with me to Canada?

             ETHEL
I shall.

Hawley and Ethel embrace.

             HAWLEY
Quickly now, we must make haste. The sooner that we are able to leave the better!

Ethel nods.

Exit Hawley and Ethel.

          FADE TO BLACK.

ACT 2-5

Office: Inspector Dew is sitting at his desk.

Enter Florie and Marcie.

Dew rises to meet them.

INSPECTOR DEW
Good morning, thank you for attending at such short notice.

FLORIE
Not at all. We trust that you have news?

Marcie and Florie sit.

INSPECTOR DEW
I do. I visited Doctor Crippen yesterday evening—

MARCIE
What did he tell you? Is Belle really dead?

INSPECTOR DEW
He says not and I believe him.

FLORIE
What makes you so sure?

INSPECTOR DEW
He admitted that he had invented the story of her death to prevent loss of face. You see Cora was having an affair—

DAN WEATHERER

FLORIE
Nonsense!

MARCIE
We'd have known about it were it true!

INSPECTOR DEW
Ladies—if you will permit me to finish. He returned home early one evening only to stumble upon his wife with another—a lodger of theirs by all accounts.

Florie and Marcie look at one another.

INSPECTOR DEW
The marriage deteriorated and Cora left for the United States with her lover. Hurt he turned to confide in another and as you have seen for yourselves, their relationship has blossomed. As a respected practitioner of homoeopathic medicine, he wished to keep word of his failed marriage to himself. Alas, under interrogation by your good selves her felt forced to concoct a story—foolish as it were, in order to end the interest in Cora's disappearance.

Pause.

MARCIE
Well . . . I never.

FLORIE
(To Marcie)
It must have been with that young fellow who

DEAD STAGE

interrupted us that night. I was not aware of any other lodger.

Marcie nods.

INSPECTOR DEW
I'm afraid that there is little in the way of evidence that should lead me to doubt his claims so—

MARCIE
This doesn't make sense.

FLORIE
(To Dew)
Before being informed of Belle's death—which we now know to be untrue, we had a contact of ours check the shipping records regarding any departures for the United States surrounding the date of Cora's leaving that Hawley had supplied to the guild in the resignation letter.

MARCIE
We had to be sure that he was telling the truth. There was no ship bound for that destination on the date proposed and of the ships that set sail near to that date . . . Mrs Crippen was not listed as a passenger.

INSPECTOR DEW
I see. Why did you not mention this before now?

FLORIE
We decided to look into this ourselves after our meeting with you.

DAN WEATHERER

Inspector Dew takes out his notebook and begins to write.

INSPECTOR DEW
It is possible that your contact overlooked something—however I shall check this myself. I still have no reason to believe that Mrs Crippen did not leave her husband, however . . . in the interests of being thorough and for your peace of mind, I shall attain confirmation of her journey.

Inspector Dew stands.

INSPECTOR DEW
Thank you for your information. I shall be in touch. Now, if you please?

Inspector Dew motions towards the door.

Marcie and Florie stand.

MARCIE
Of course. We are just happy to help.

FLORIE
We care dearly about Belle and wish to know that she is safe and well.

INSPECTOR DEW
Of course. She is blessed to have friends such as yourselves. I shall be in touch.

Marcie and Florie exit the office.

DEAD STAGE

Inspector Dew returns to his desk and picks up the phone.

                    INSPECTOR DEW
Operator . . . White Star lines, please.

                    FADE TO BLACK.

ACT 2-6

Dining room: MAID and Inspector Dew enter the dining room.

MAID
Please come in . . . I'm not sure I can help you though.

INSPECTOR DEW
I'm here to see Dr Crippen, I tried his practice but it was closed. Is he here?

MAID
I'm afraid not. The Doctor and Miss Le Neve left this morning.

INSPECTOR DEW
Left? For where?

MAID
I'm not sure.

INSPECTOR DEW
It is important that you try and think. Did you hear them discussing potential destinations?

MAID
I did hear Canada mentioned . . . along with a place named Antwerp . . . I was tasked with preparing the house for an extended absence.

DEAD STAGE

INSPECTOR DEW
(assertive)
Touch nothing else. I shall be back shortly with a warrant and several officers. This house is a potential crime scene. Remain here but again I must add—do not touch or move anything.

The Maid nods.

Exit Inspector Dew

FADE TO BLACK.

ACT 2-7

Dining room: Dew is searching the room.

Lights on/off to symbolize passing of time. Each time the lights come up Dew is in another position. Sometimes alone, sometimes joined with another officer.

Final lights up—Evidence lies on the table.

Inspector Dew and OFFICER 1 examine it.

OFFICER 1
This envelope was found beneath a loose floorboard in one of the back bedrooms.

Inspector Dew opens it carefully.

INSPECTOR DEW
Seems to be some kind of powdered medicine. It's not labelled . . . better get it looked at.

OFFICER 2 hurries into the dining room. He is pale and in a state of shock.

OFFICER 2
Sir . . .

INSPECTOR DEW
(without turning around)
What is it, officer?

DEAD STAGE

OFFICER 2
We've found a body buried beneath the cellar floor.

Inspector Dew turns to face officer 2

INSPECTOR DEW
Cora Crippen?

Officer 2 takes a moment to compose himself. He looks as though he is about to vomit.

OFFICER 2
I can't say for sure . . . there's no head.

INSPECTOR DEW
My God!

Inspector Dew pushes past Officer 2 and heads to the cellar. Officer 1 follows after him.

Exit Inspector Dew/Officer 1.

Officer 2 sits on the floor and puts his head in his hands.

FADE TO BLACK.

ACT 2-8

Office. Inspector Dew is at his desk. He busies himself with a pile of papers.

VOICEOVER: The murder of Cora Crippen made headline news and was carried by newspapers across the continent. Not since the days of Jack the Ripper, had London played host to such savage a crime—A manhunt was launched and the nation observed with interest.

Enter Officer 1

OFFICER 1
Telegram for you sir. Marked as urgent.

Inspector Dew takes the telegram and opens it.

INSPECTOR DEW
For the attention of Chief Inspector Dew STOP, Captain Kendall of the SS Montrose sighted Dr Crippen and Ethel Le Neve travelling under false alias STOP, Mr and Master Robinson STOP, Bound for Quebec STOP, Request assistance on this matter END.

Inspector Dew places the telegram on the desk.

INSPECTOR DEW
The destinations check out, at least according to what the maid said. Has the ship sailed?

DEAD STAGE

OFFICER 1
White Star informs us that it has.

INSPECTOR DEW
Damn it!

OFFICER 1
However, the SS Laurentic leaves Liverpool on the morrow. It shall arrive in Quebec before the Montrose.

Inspector Dew stands

INSPECTOR DEW
Then get me on that ship!

OFFICER 1
Right away sir!

Exit Officer 1.

FADE TO BLACK.

ACT 2-9

Voice over: The transatlantic chase gripped the country. Newspapers carried daily updates on the progress of the two ships and the love triangle between Cora, Hawley and Ethel became familiar breakfast reading. The nation held its breath.

Deck of the SS Montrose: Hawley and Ethel (disguised as a male) are standing on the deck of the Montrose.

HAWLEY
We made it dear. Canada welcomes us.

ETHEL
The crossing seemed to take forever.

HAWLEY
We can finally breathe again. This could be a new beginning for us!

ETHEL
Are you contemplating never returning to London?

HAWLEY
I must entertain the idea! The air is crisper here— there is no choking smog to dull the senses. Yes . . . We could be happy here. Perhaps we could start a family?

ETHEL
I'd like that very much.

DEAD STAGE

Hawley kisses Ethel.

ETHEL
But what of your house, your practice?

HAWLEY
Ours is an age of wonder. With the arrival of the telegraph, one no longer needs to rely on the letter. I can easily settle my affairs from here. I see a market for my products here, and time to devote to their perfection.

ETHEL
So long as I am with you it matters not where we call home.

Ethel and Hawley hold one another and embrace.

Enter inspector Dew disguised as a pilot.

Hawley sees Dew and releases Ethel. He tries to avoid making eye contact with Dew.

INSPECTOR DEW
Good morning, Dr Crippen. Do you know me? I'm Chief Inspector Dew from Scotland Yard.

Hawley and Ethel pause, neither daring to look at Inspector Dew.

Dew removes his hat.

DAN WEATHERER

INSPECTOR DEW
I came a long way to see you, the least you could do is acknowledge me.

HAWLEY
(To Ethel)
Forgive me, my dear.

Hawley lets Ethel go and slowly turns towards Inspector Dew.

INSPECTOR DEW
And you must be Miss Le Neve?

Pause.

HAWLEY
(To Inspector Dew)
Thank God it's over. The suspense has been too great. I couldn't stand it any longer!

Hawley holds out his hands in order to be cuffed.

Ethel begins to cry.

ETHEL
(anguished)
Hawley dear . . . whatever are you doing?

Inspector Dew handcuffs Dr Crippen

INSPECTOR DEW
Hawley Harvey Crippen, I am arresting you for the

DEAD STAGE

murder of Cora Crippen, you are not obliged to say anything unless you wish to do so but what you say may be given in evidence.

HAWLEY
I understand.
(To Ethel)
I'm sorry Ethel. Truly I am.

ETHEL
(breaking down)
No! No surely not! This has to be a mistake?

HAWLEY
Know that I love you Ethel and that the man you fell in love with is not the villain that you are about to hear of.

INSPECTOR DEW
Ethel Le Neve, I am arresting you on suspicion of accessory to murder and of being a fugitive from justice. You are not obliged to say anything unless you wish to do so but what you say may be given in evidence. Alas, only one pair of handcuffs is issued per officer so—

ETHEL
(ignoring Inspector Dew)
She left you Hawley . . . you insisted that she left you!

HAWLEY
Please, Ethel, let us comply with the inspector's wishes.

INSPECTOR DEW
You will both accompany me back to England immediately. We have a ship waiting. I must warn you that your exploits have become quite well known in your absence.

HAWLEY
I see.

ETHEL
(upset)
What exploits? Hawley, what have you done?

HAWLEY
(To Ethel)
It is better for us both if I say little.

Inspector Dew motions for them to disembark.

INSPECTOR DEW
This way . . . we leave at once.

Ethel is crying yet obeys the inspector's command. Hawley and Inspector Dew follow her off stage.

Exit Hawley, Ethel and Inspector Dew.

FADE TO BLACK.
CURTAINS CLOSE.
END OF ACT TWO.

ACT 3

ACT 3-1

At Rise: Courtroom. Hawley stands in the dock on the left side of the stage, Ethel on the right. The Spotlights illuminate each character in succession (when addressed by the judge.) The judge/prosecution appears in voice only. Both Hawley and Ethel address the audience for the duration of this scene.

Illuminate Hawley

JUDGE
Hawley Harvey Crippen, you are charged with the murder of Cora Crippen and of being a fugitive from justice. How do you plead?

HAWLEY
(reluctant)
Not guilty.

Illuminate Ethel

JUDGE
Ethel Le Neve, you are charged with being an accessory to murder and of being a fugitive from justice. How do you plead?

ETHEL
(sobbing)
Not guilty, your honour.

DAN WEATHERER

Illuminate Hawley

PROSECUTION
Human remains were unearthed from beneath your cellar. Though the body had been dismembered in order to prevent identification, an identifying mark confirmed that the body was indeed that of Cora Crippen.

HAWLEY
Cora is alive and well.

PROSECUTION
Then how do you explain the body beneath your cellar?

HAWLEY
We had not long moved into the property—barely a year or so ago. The body was left by a previous tenant.

PROSECUTION
Yet I have documents that claim to the contrary—you have in fact lived at 39 Hilldrop crescent for a number of years . . . five in fact.

HAWLEY
I know not how the body ended up there, nor as to whom it once belonged.

Illuminate Ethel

DEAD STAGE

PROSECUTION
What is your relationship with Dr Crippen?

ETHEL
I suppose you might call us lovers.

PROSECUTION
And when did your relationship begin?

ETHEL
We became friends when I began to work for Hawley, that would be in 1903.

PROSECUTION
Friends or lovers?

ETHEL
Just friends. Yes, I felt for him a great deal and I suspected that he might also, yet his religion and his marriage vows, they prevented him from acting upon any desire he might have harboured towards me. He is a good man.

PROSECUTION
Yes-quite. But you did admit to being lovers, correct?

ETHEL
Yes, but not until recently. Hawley discovered that his wife was having an affair. Our relationship blossomed not long afterwards.

PROSECUTION
Whilst Cora Crippen was still living with Hawley Crippen?

ETHEL
(reluctantly)
Yes.

Illuminate Hawley

PROSECUTION
Would you say that you had a tempestuous relationship with your wife?

HAWLEY
Cora was a difficult woman to live with. She was often taken to wild flights of fancy, flights which I was expected to finance. Yet I loved her all the same.

PROSECUTION
It is said that she courted numerous lovers. Were you aware of this fact?

HAWLEY
No.

PROSECUTION
So you were unaware of her affair with a lodger by the name of Simon Harper?

HAWLEY
(flustered)
I was unaware, yes.

PROSECUTION
Yet you told Chief Inspector Walter Dew that Cora had in fact left you for one of your lodgers? Correct?

DEAD STAGE

HAWLEY
No—well yes but I panicked. I made that up.

PROSECUTION
You told the Music Hall Ladies Guild that Cora had left to attend to the needs of a sick relative? Correct?

HAWLEY
Yes.

PROSECUTION
You also told said members of the Ladies Guild, that Cora had fallen ill and passed away . . . and her body cremated, correct?

HAWLEY
Yes.

PROSECUTION
Neither of these stories is true. Records indicate that Cora Crippen did not travel to the United States during any of the periods of her reported missing. Nor was anyone by that name cremated.

HAWLEY
She likely travelled under another alias—perhaps her real name—Kunigunde Mackamotzki.

PROSECUTION
Lies upon lies Dr Crippen. What a wicked web you weave!

Illuminate Ethel

PROSECUTION
When Hawley informed you of his wife's departure, how did you feel?

ETHEL
Relieved. It meant that we could finally be together.

PROSECUTION
Did her leaving not strike you as somewhat sudden?

ETHEL
A little, but I knew that tensions had been building for a while. She was prone to unpredictable outbursts . . . she . . .

PROSECUTION
Go on.

ETHEL
Once she knew about Hawley's affair she came to the office. I don't know how but she realized that it was I Hawley was involved with. She got angry . . . she pushed me to the ground . . . I was pregnant and I . . .

Ethel begins to cry.

PROSECUTION
I know this is difficult, but please go on.

ETHEL
I was pregnant and I lost the baby that night.

DEAD STAGE

PROSECUTION
As a result of Cora's assault.

ETHEL
Yes.

Illuminate Hawley

PROSECUTION
Your young lover Ethel Le Neve, she was pregnant, wasn't she?

HAWLEY
Yes.

PROSECUTION
I say was because there was an altercation between Cora and Ethel which resulted in the loss of her child.

HAWLEY
Yes. Cora pushed her to the ground.

PROSECUTION
This made you angry?

HAWLEY
(angry)
Of course it did! I had only ever wanted to be a father! Belle had no time for children. She saw them as a drain . . . a distraction . . . a hindrance to her career.

DAN WEATHERER

> PROSECUTION
> Angry enough to kill?

> HAWLEY
> No! Nor could I do the unspeakable things that I am accused of! I am a practitioner of homoeopathic medicine . . . only a monster could have committed the atrocities that you bring before me!

> PROSECUTION
> A monster indeed. Let it be known to the court that a sizable amount of hydro-bromide of hyoscine was found concealed beneath the floor of 39 Hilldrop Crescent. For those of you unfamiliar with medicine hydrobromide of hyoscine is used to slow a rapid heart rate. A high dose can result in death.

> HAWLEY
> I have no idea how that substance came to be in my house.

Illuminate Ethel

> PROSECUTION
> How did Hawley take the loss of your child?

> ETHEL
> He was upset. He was angry—angry that she had taken the chance of fatherhood from him.

> PROSECUTION
> And it was shortly after this that Mrs Crippen disappeared?

DEAD STAGE

ETHEL
Yes.

Illuminate Hawley

PROSECUTION
We have a multitude of stories regarding Cora's disappearance, none of which have an ounce of evidence to support them. We have a mutilated corpse buried beneath your cellar floor—no more than a few months old. We have a sample of a highly toxic chemical which was hidden within your property—

HAWLEY
Which I told you I know nothing about.

PROSECUTION
I'll wager we even have a motive! Not only was your wife conducting numerous affairs beneath your nose—all of which you were aware of—

HAWLEY
That was not the case!

PROSECUTION
You were also angry at her for the loss of your child—brought about by her actions. I put it to the jury that you drugged her, dismembered her corpse in order to prevent identification and buried her remains beneath your cellar floor. Ironic that the healer has become the murderer.

DAN WEATHERER

>HAWLEY
>I did no such thing!

>PROSECUTION
>Tell the court, where is her head? Where are her limbs?

>HAWLEY
>I know not! She left me, she went back home to the United States using another name!

>PROSECUTION
>And why would she use a false identity?

>HAWLEY
>I don't know . . . so that I couldn't trace her perhaps?

>PROSECUTION
>But if she were in the United States and you did wish to contact her . . . you would know where to look, correct?

Hawley does not answer.

>PROSECUTION
>What did you do to her Dr Crippen?

>HAWLEY
>I told you she left.

>PROSECUTION
>With another?

DEAD STAGE

HAWLEY
No. She was not having an affair. We merely fell out of love.

PROSECUTION
Why will you not admit that you knew she was having an affair?

HAWLEY
Cora was many things but I shall not have her name tarnished in this court, not while she still lives and breathes.

PROSECUTION
Quite. Why did you elect to leave the country after speaking with Inspector Dew?

HAWLEY
I suggested that it was time for a break. The stresses that we had both endured had taken a large toll on us.

PROSECUTION
An extended break by all accounts. Your maid was instructed to prepare the house for a long absence.

HAWLEY
She was mistaken.

PROSECUTION
You can understand how it looks to the rest of us—an innocent man leaving for another continent after the sudden disappearance of his wife.

> HAWLEY
> Yes.

Illuminate Ethel

> PROSECUTION
> Did you suspect foul play?

> ETHEL
> No, not at all! Nor can I believe it now!

> PROSECUTION
> Though the evidence remains.

> ETHEL
> Yes.

> PROSECUTION
> Did he ever mention anything that may have led you to believe that Cora was in fact dead?

> ETHEL
> No, only that he was convinced she would never return to cause us grief.

> PROSECUTION
> Miss Le Neve, let me put it to you thus—did you help in the murder of Cora Crippen?

> ETHEL
> *(desperate)*
> No!

DEAD STAGE

PROSECUTION
Did you help in the concealment of Cora Crippen's body?

ETHEL
(sobbing)
No . . . no. I just did what Hawley wanted. He wanted to get away from the stares and the accusations . . . I believed that Canada could offer us a fresh start!

PROSECUTION
No further questions.

JUDGE
Thank you, Miss Le Neve. I turn to the members of the jury, it is up to you to decide whether Miss Le Neve played an active part in the murder and concealment of Cora Crippen, or whether she was merely following the will of a man whom she loved and would do anything to be with.

Illuminate Hawley

PROSECUTION
You believe that Cora is alive and well?

HAWLEY
Yes.

PROSECUTION
And you insist that you do not know the identity of the body found beneath your cellar, nor how it ended up there?

DAN WEATHERER

HAWLEY
I maintain that I have no idea.

PROSECUTION
No further questions.

JUDGE
Members of the jury may I remind you of the facts . . . The body in the cellar, fresh and dismembered to prevent identification. The poison was hidden beneath the floorboards and the loss of Ethel Le Neve's baby. Let us not forget the Atlantic chase. I ask you to consider only the facts and that you arrive at a majority verdict.

Lights illuminate Hawley and Ethel in turn. Synchronized to a loud and quickening (audible) heartbeat.

Illuminate Ethel.

JUDGE
Ethel le Neve, the jury have found you not guilty of all charges. The court believes that you had no prior knowledge of Hawley Crippen's heinous crimes.

ETHEL
(sobbing)
Thank you . . . Thank you.

JUDGE
You are free to go.

DEAD STAGE

Illuminate Hawley.

JUDGE
Hawley Harvey Crippen, you have been found guilty of the murder of Cora Crippen.

HAWLEY
(*shocked*)
No-no this is a mistake I tell you—a mistake!

The judge places a black cap on his head

JUDGE
I sentence you to be hung by the neck until you are dead. Take him down.

Lights dim as Hawley delivers this next line

HAWLEY
No . . . you've gotten this all wrong! She returned home to her parents—I swear! I didn't kill her—I didn't!

FADE TO BLACK.

ACT 3-2

Lights up: Small space representing a cell (stage left) complete with a bare mattress on the floor, bucket and a large bookcase. A solitary book lies upon its shelf. A plate of bread and cheese lies on the bed.

GUARD 1 and GUARD 2 escort Hawley to the cell. Hawley is bound by the wrists. Guard 1 opens the cell door whilst Guard 2 undoes the wrist restraints.

GUARD 1
This'll do for you now.

Hawley rubs his free wrists and peers into the cell.

HAWLEY
How long will I be here?

GUARD 2
Till we fetch you.

Guard 2 pushes Hawley into the cell.

GUARD 1
Better make the most of your time. How about a book?

GUARD 2
Don't be saft! As like he can't read!

Guard 1 shuts the cell door and locks it.

DEAD STAGE

GUARD 1
(laughing)
Right you are! It's wasted on the lot of 'em. You know that I found one of the bastards used it to wipe his arse!

GUARD 2
Vermin aren't they. Hope you told them to use the short drop on that one.

Guards make way off stage

GUARD 1
Nah, I was too late wasn't I? Fella had already been done.

GUARD 2
Hey—Have ye heard this?
Dr Crippen killed Belle Elmore
Ran away with Miss Le Neve
Right across the ocean blue
Followed by Inspector Dew
Ship's ahoy, naughty boy!

HAWLEY
(angry)
I despise that infernal song!

The guards laugh. Hawley sits on his mattress and looks at his surroundings. After a while, he picks up a slice of bread from the plate and quickly drops it.

HAWLEY
I request the presence of a priest! Do you hear me?

Pause.

Do you hear me?

Hawley returns his attention to the plate of food.

HAWLEY
Blasted roaches crawling over the last meal of a dead man! Wheresoever there is suffering it is the roach that inevitably feasts!

He pushes the plate aside, stands and takes the book from the shelf.

HAWLEY
(laughing)
The Bible . . . What use is this to a man in my predicament?

He places the book back upon the shelf.

Enter Guard 1 and Priest.

Guard one unlocks the door and lets the priest into the cell.

GUARD 1
Hurry it up.

Guard one locks the cell door.

DEAD STAGE

Exit Guard one.

Hawley and the priest regard one another.

PRIEST
Did you request my company?

HAWLEY
That I did.

PRIEST
Do you seek confession?

Hawley sits on the bed. The priest remains standing opposite Hawley.

Hawley looks to the floor.

HAWLEY
They won't inform me of Ethel's fate. Tell me, did they find her guilty?

PRIEST
They did not. The jury decided that she was innocent of all charges.

HAWLEY
I have not heard from her. I had hoped that she might write.

PRIEST
Perhaps it is best that she does not. She grieves you. The man she loved was not the man she knew . . .

surely you can appreciate her feelings on the matter.

Hawley stands.

HAWLEY
Can I be saved? Can God's mercy apply to me?

PRIEST
Only if you are to confess.

Hawley turns to face the audience.

HAWLEY
Cora lives. I am not guilty of her death yet forever shall I be known as the doctor who butchered his wife.

PRIEST
The Lord sees all, though his mercy is only for those who seek to repent their sins.

The following confession is acted out stage right by Belle, Simon and a replacement Hawley. The Hawley character could be masked with a plain face for extra dramatic impact.

Lights up on the dining room. Simon is laid on the floor and Belle is trying to rouse him.

Real Hawley begins to pace.

DEAD STAGE

HAWLEY
It is true that I am innocent of Cora's murder, though it was my intention to kill her. I had added a large amount of hydro-bromide of hyoscine to a bottle of red wine which I knew Belle would ingest. Yet upon my return later that night I was confronted by the sight of Simon collapsed upon the floor and Cora weeping over his prone body. As it transpired, Simon had returned to Belle in order to reignite their relationship. He drank the majority of the wine whilst trying to explain his recent actions, thus succumbing to the poison. I panicked. Belle was hysterical—she spoke of calling the police. I drew my pistol and threatened her. As a means of punctuating my threat, I shot Simon in the chest. Shocked, she pleaded her life and me, weak that I was, spared her on the condition that she leave right away and never speak of the matter again. I did not expect her to believe my threat yet she did as I asked. I gave her money with which to travel. I know not where she went but she is still alive.

Lights out on re-enactment

HAWLEY
This left me with a body that I needed to conceal quickly for my maid was due to start her chores at first light. I took his body into the bathroom and set upon the bloody task. First I removed the limbs—the head followed after. These were added to a weighted sack which I disposed of in a nearby canal. I then removed the internal organs, followed by the ribs and long bones—leaving me with a fleshy shell that

would be impossible to identify. The bones were incinerated in the kitchen hearth . . . never have I encountered a sicklier stench than the smoke that poured into my kitchen that night. The organs I left in the bathtub, a small amount of lime reduced them to a slush that was easily washed into the sewer. As you know . . . the carcass I buried beneath the cellar.

Hawley falls to his knees before the priest.

HAWLEY
Forgive me, father, I beg of you. That is the truth of it, horrific though it may be.

PRIEST
Though you did not kill your wife as most believe, you still committed the sin of murder. May God forgive you and have mercy on your soul.

HAWLEY
(weeping)
Thank you, father. Please ensure that Ethel receives the benefits of my estate.

Priest nods.

Audio cue—Lacrimosa (Mozart's Requiem in D minor) plays throughout this part of the scene.

Enter Guard one and Guard two.

Guard one unlocks the cell.

DEAD STAGE

Both Guards enter.

Hawley stands.

GUARD 1
It's time.

Hawley nods.

HAWLEY
I'm ready.

The Priest begins his address. The guards begin to bind Hawley's wrists (front).

PRIEST
Let us pray. Most gracious God, Father of mercies and God of all consolation, Thou wish none to perish that believes and hopes in Thee, according to Thy many mercies look down favourably upon Thy servant Hawley whom true faith and Christian hope commend to Thee.

The guards begin to bind Hawley's legs at the knees.

HAWLEY
Wait! How will I walk?

GUARD 1
It's not far. Pay it no heed.

Guard two opens the bookcase revealing a room

set behind the cell. The silhouette of a noose can be seen.

>GUARD 2
>This way, please.

Hawley obliges.

>PRIEST
>Visit him in Thy saving mercy, and by the passion and death of Thy only-begotten Son, graciously grant to him forgiveness and pardon of all his sins that his soul in the hour of its leaving the earth may find Thee as a Judge appeased and being washed from all stain in the Blood of Thy Same Son may deserve to pass to everlasting life. Through the same Christ our Lord.

A hood is placed over Hawley's head.

The bookcase slams shut followed immediately by—

Audio cue—Lacrimosa should finish on "Amen."

>LIGHTS OUT.
>CURTAIN CLOSE.
>THE END.

ELOISE

Written by Dan Weatherer (Based on a concept by Mark Mooney)

Genre: Drama
Length: Approx. 6 minutes
Cast: 1 x Male

Synopsis: An elderly man comes to terms with the death of his wife.

Cast of Characters:
    Jim

ACT I

SCENE 1

At Rise: JIM (Mid-seventies, dressed in a black suit/tie) sits in a large armchair. To his left is a small table. On it is a black hat, a large glass of whiskey, an empty whiskey bottle, a lamp and a black and white photograph of a young woman.

Jim takes the photograph from the table and looks at it. He shows it to the audience.

JIM
Eloise. Taken in nineteen sixty-four, I think. Brighton Pier. We'd ride down on me old Triumph Bonneville. It stayed nice all weekend, but then the sun always seemed to shine back then.

Jim pauses to look at the photograph.

JIM
I buried 'er this morning.

Jim places the photograph back onto the table and turns his attention back to the audience.

JIM
Reverend gave a lovely service. Church was packed. There were faces there I hadn't seen fer years! Charlie Pipp were there with his missus Angie, as was Bertie Fife, me old drinkin' buddy from the Tanner's Arms. 'e were looking knackered, but then

DEAD STAGE

'e always did look like he were about to keel over, even back when we drank together. Aye, they did 'er proud they did. She'd 'ave been 'appy with the turnout would Eloise.

Jim takes a tub of tablets from his pocket and pours some into his palm.

JIM
Excuse me a moment. For the pain.

He swallows the tablets with a sip of whiskey.

JIM
She were always around was Eloise. We grew up near one another. She lived on the next street . . . Pembroke Road it were called. We went to the same schools. I saw 'er almost every day. We started courting after I'd left school. The plan was I was to follow me old man into the pits, but they closed a few years earlier. Me dad, ever the resourceful type, opened up 'is own garage, and I followed 'im into the business instead. Taught me everything I know about cars 'e did. There were nowt we couldna fix between us. It were bloody cold in that workshop mind . . . and we'd keep all hours, y'know, to make ends meet. I still don't know what she saw in a lanky streak of piss like me. I'd come out of the shop late on, covered in muck an' oil, black as the Ace o' spades. She'd be waiting for me, sitting on the wall outside by Brock's Butchers. She went to college and studied dressmaking or home economics, I forget which. She were brilliant with a needle and thread though. Back

then, when we first moved in together money was scarce. She'd make all 'er own clothes. She were a proper stunner. All the lads were jealous. She went on to run 'er own dressmaking business, even had a shop at one time. She did all the designs, alterations, everything herself . . . till 'er eyes gave out, then she had to get help in. It were never the same after that. Still, she loved 'er work. I couldna believe me luck landing a catch like that . . . Me working in muck and grime, stinking of sweat and oil, an 'er making clothes the likes of which you have never seen! She 'ad a gift that one. We shouldna 'ave worked, we were like chalk n cheese . . . but we did.

Jim quickly takes a couple of tablets and follows them with a gulp of whiskey

JIM

I don't know about true love an' all that. You young un's, listen up. It ain't like the movies say. It's not all flowers an' chocolates, or poems and all that romance malarkey. Sure, it can be like that at the beginning . . . when everything is new and exciting. You feel butterflies when they walk into a room . . . she were the only one to make me feel like that. Savour those times because they don't last. But that doesn't mean the love don't last. It changes, and some can't hack that change. There's nobody to blame for that you understand, some folk just grow apart. You see marriage takes work . . . it does, no two ways about it. But with me an' Eloise, the effort came easy. Why? I dunno. Perhaps we were lucky? Perhaps we just fit. I always thought we did. We just

DEAD STAGE

slotted together. Nothing was awkward between us, nothing was ever an issue. Everything was spoken about an' there was never any friction, not really . . . not like some folk have. Sure, we had our fair share of rows, but that's all part of it. Frustrations come out but you work through them together. At least that's what Eloise and I did.

Jim quickly takes a couple of tablets and follows them with a gulp of whiskey.

JIM

So, back to what I wanted to talk to you about, before I forget what I were saying. Is there such a thing as true love? I think so . . . I think that when two people stand together, accept one another, faults an' all, and face what the world throws at them, supporting one another through the bad times, savouring the good times together and creating memories together . . . then yes, I'd say that would be love. If it ain't, then it's pretty damn close. Like I said, it ain't about buying presents or singing her praises . . . that gets old and fast. Love for someone can be shown in the smallest of gestures. The squeeze of a hand, the gentle brush of an arm, a smile or even a look. It's about being a rock for someone, unselfishly though . . . without thought or reason. It's about sharing a life together.

JIM

And that we did. In a way, our lives were one, and now that she's gone . . . well . . .

Jim quickly takes a couple of tablets and follows them with a gulp of whiskey.

Pause.

We never 'ad children. I always said that the good lord blessed us in other ways. It would 'ave been nice to raise young 'uns, but we still had enough good times. I never felt like we missed out. I'm not sure Eloise might say the same but she was happy, that I know.

Jim places the last of his tablets into his hand and places the empty container onto the table.

JIM
(Getting upset)
I . . . I just never told her how proud I was of 'er. For doing what she loved, for standing by me, for allowing me to share 'er life. I hope that she knew . . . but it isn't the same as saying it out loud. I'm sorry . . . I'm babbling now.

Points to the glass

JIM
It's the drink talking. Forgive me.

Pause.

It's been twelve days since she went. Since I was a boy, there was never more than a couple of days that I didn't see her.

DEAD STAGE

Pause.

JIM
These twelve days have been the longest of my life.

Jim looks up. There are tears in his eyes.

JIM
Please forgive me, Eloise. You always did say I'd be hopeless without you.

Jim takes the last of the tablets and finishes his drink.

LIGHTS OUT.
END.

KILLING GARY

Genre: Comedy
Length: Approx. 15 minutes
Cast: 1 x Male 1 x Female 1 x optional

Synopsis: An apprehended serial killer with an unusual modus operandi, is interviewed in custody.

Author's note: *Killing Gary* was performed in the finals of The Congleton Players International One-Act Festival, 2016. It was adapted from a short story of the same title, contained in *Neverlight*. As the set up consisted of three characters talking in an interrogation room, I concluded that it would be a simple transition from short story to stage play.

Cast of Characters:
Kirsten Shaw
Detective Honeysett
PC Nelson

ACT I

SCENE 1

At Rise: Interrogation Room

Lights up on a sparsely furnished interrogation room. There is a table with two chairs. One is occupied by KIRSTEN. There is a tape recorder on the table. PC NELSON stands guard at the only door to the room.

Enter DETECTIVE HONEYSETT with an armful of files. He dumps them on the table before Kirsten and begins to address her.

> DETECTIVE HONEYSETT
> Seven years work.

Kirsten stares at the Detective.

> DETECTIVE HONEYSETT
> Seven years, countless sleepless nights, untold resources and man-hours, all spent trying to apprehend you.

Detective Honeysett taps on the pile of folders.

> DETECTIVE HONEYSETT
> This . . . all of this . . . it's down to you!

DAN WEATHERER

KIRSTEN
Allegedly.

DETECTIVE HONEYSETT
There's no allegedly about it! Not this time! I've got you good!

PC Nelson Coughs

PC NELSON
Are we ready to begin the interview now, sir?

Detective Honeysett nods and takes a seat. He sets the tape recorder in motion.

DETECTIVE HONEYSETT
This is the interview of Kirsten Shaw, in regards to the murder of one Gary Howe. The date is the fifteenth of March and the time is nine forty-two a.m. Present are myself DCI Honeysett, and PC Nelson.

Detective Honeysett begins to organise the files. He opens one and begins to look through it.

DETECTIVE HONEYSETT
(absently)
Do you wish to request the services of a lawyer?

KIRSTEN
Killed my last lawyer.

DETECTIVE HONEYSETT
Ah yes . . . so you did—Mr Gary Harlow, correct? Met

DEAD STAGE

him a few times. He represented only the finest class of scum. You fed his face into a paper shredder if I remember right? Nice. Chalk that one up as a confession Nelson.

PC NELSON
(nodding)
Aye, Sir.

KIRSTEN
I wouldn't call it a confession as such. That would imply that I felt remorse or sought forgiveness . . . neither of which is true.

DETECTIVE HONEYSETT
Perhaps, perhaps not. In that case, shall we start with your latest Miss Shaw?

Kirsten raises her hands in mock surrender.

KIRSTEN
Seems as good a place as any, after all, you caught me dead bang!

DETECTIVE HONEYSETT
Let's see . . . Gary Howe, thirty-three, divorced, Gas safety engineer. According to forensics . . . you beat him to death with his own wrench whilst he serviced your boiler . . . that sound about right?

KIRSTEN
(chuckles)
Yep, first thing that came to hand. I hate to shatter

your illusion Detective but there was no master plan at work here, no weeks of planning or anything like that. This was spontaneous, a crime of passion if you will!

DETECTIVE HONEYSETT
Passion? You mean you were involved with Gary?

KIRSTEN
Hell no! I killed the greasy son of a bitch because I was passionate about his disgusting body odour not polluting my kitchen! And there was his massive ass crack . . . staring me in the face . . . I couldn't stand it . . . he had to go!

DETECTIVE HONEYSETT
So you killed him?

KIRSTEN
Yep.

DETECTIVE HONEYSETT
Dragged his body outside and left it on the kerb?

KIRSTEN
Yep, his tools too. Figured the gipsies might want a look.

DETECTIVE HONEYSETT
You left a dead body at the side of the road, a man you killed because of his poor posture and dubious personal hygiene, in the hope that the gipsies might get rid of him for you?

DEAD STAGE

KIRSTEN
Oh no, not the body . . . just the tools. What would gipsies want with a dead gas man?

DETECTIVE HONEYSETT
You knew you'd be caught right?

KIRSTEN
Right.

DETECTIVE HONEYSETT
Leaving a corpse out for the binman, it's a tad reckless, isn't it?

KIRSTEN
Suppose so, yeah.

DETECTIVE HONEYSETT
So, why then? Why now? Why like this?

KIRSTEN
(shrugging)
I dunno. Maybe I'd gotten tired of killing Gary.

DETECTIVE HONEYSETT
Perhaps.

Detective Honeysett closes one file and opens another.

DETECTIVE HONEYSETT
How about Gary Govik, forty-one, civil servant . . . killed by a dustbin lorry . . . you know anything about that?

DAN WEATHERER

> KIRSTEN
> Oh, that one.

> DETECTIVE HONEYSETT
> So, you do? Care to elaborate?

> KIRSTEN
> He was the bloke I spoke to about bi-monthly bin collections. Patronising jobsworth, he was! I found out his address online . . . it's easy enough if you know where to look. Then on the morning of the grey bin collection, I waited until the crew had gone in for lunch and took their lorry . . . I-I didn't mean—

Kirsten begins to cry.

> DETECTIVE HONEYSETT
> You didn't mean to kill him? So you do feel remorse for this one!

> KIRSTEN
> No, it's not that . . . I tried to get him under the wheels but I misjudged it and caught him between the wheelie bins instead. Not what I had hoped for at all.

Kirsten cries harder.

Detective shakes his head.

> DETECTIVE HONEYSETT
> Jesus Christ, you are a piece of work, aren't you?

DEAD STAGE

Detective Honeysett closes the file, opens another and shows it to Kirsten.

DETECTIVE HONEYSETT
How about this one then? Gary Farthwright, twenty-one, student . . . killed falling off a bridge.

Kirsten sits up straight.

KIRSTEN
OK, that wasn't me. I saw that one in the papers, they said he jumped . . . wasn't he the depressive sort anyway? Nope, not me. Next one.

Detective Honeysett closes the file.

KIRSTEN
(mumbling)
Still, did me a favour, one less for me to do.

Detective Honeysett slams his hands onto the table and stands up, startling Kirsten and PC Nelson.

DETECTIVE HONEYSETT
(angry)
Alright, enough of the crap! How many was it? Give me a number, no more bullshit theatrics! I wanna know just how busy you have been!

Kirsten thinks for a moment.

KIRSTEN
I'd say fourteen. Well, fourteen and a half . . .

DAN WEATHERER

DETECTIVE HONEYSETT
(interrupting)
Fourteen and a half! How the hell does that work?

KIRSTEN
There was the rude waiter from Nom, he went into the storage refrigerator with a cleaver in his head, he was called Gary. There was Gary the driving instructor who failed me . . . stabbed him in the eye with his pen but pushed a little too far . . . then there was . . .

DETECTIVE HONEYSETT
(interrupting)
The half! Get to the half!

KIRSTEN
Oh yeah—Gary the half! Sorry . . . once I start reminiscing it's hard to get me back on track! He was a mechanic doing my MOT. Wanted to fail me on emissions so I slammed the bonnet on his head a few times. Thing is they make them so bloody light these days it only knocked him out. I drove past a few days later to see him working on a new Kia! I count him as my half.

DETECTIVE HONEYSETT
(exasperated)
Ah, now I see how that could be interpreted as half a murder, how short-sighted of me!

Detective Honeysett crosses over to PC Nelson and mutters something inaudible. PC Nelson nods and leaves the room.

DEAD STAGE

KIRSTEN
Don't stress it, we all make mistakes right?

Detective Honeysett moves back to the table.

DETECTIVE HONEYSETT
Interview suspended at nine fifty-five am.

He leans in close to Kirsten.

KIRSTEN
Woah there tiger, you wanna back up?

DETECTIVE HONEYSETT
Who was the first? Tell me.

KIRSTEN
Well . . . Gary obviously.

DETECTIVE HONEYSETT
(getting angry)
Which Gary?

KIRSTEN
Gary Baker, my first love. He had a moped and a middle parting. He was gonna work at the pot bank and we were gonna have kids and a nice terraced house, the lot . . . till he went and messed it all up.

DETECTIVE HONEYSETT
What did he do?

KIRSTEN
He sold the moped and went to college to study media. After that, things were never the same between us. He'd talk about Blue-skying and PowerPoint presentations; it was like he was from another planet! He broke my heart so I broke his . . . with a lump hammer.

DETECTIVE HONEYSETT
You are telling me that you killed all of those men just because someone broke your heart?

KIRSTEN
Well, not just because. I mean there's something about Garys isn't there? Something weasel like? Let's be honest, it's the kind of name you give to the kid that you dropped on the head right? You'd be all like *Oh sorry darling I just dropped baby on his noggin but at least we don't need to struggle thinking of a name now . . . it's gotta be Gary, right?*

Detective Honeysett tightens his jaw.

KIRSTEN
And they are all so stupid with their eyes so close together and awful personal hygiene! Can you even name one Gary who has contributed anything to the good of the human race? Any at all? I challenge you . . . you can't, because all Garys are losers.

Detective Honeysett rises from his chair.

DEAD STAGE

KIRSTEN
Honestly, I'm doing the world a favour . . . if I'd started younger maybe I'd have culled their numbers more . . . I guess we'll never know now.

DETECTIVE HONEYSETT
I have a middle name.

KIRSTEN
You do?

DETECTIVE HONEYSETT
I do. I rarely refer to it but in this instance, it seems rather appropriate.

KIRSTEN
You don't want to say what I think you are going to say.

DETECTIVE HONEYSETT
Do you want to know what it is?

KIRSTEN
I'm warning you!

DETECTIVE HONEYSETT
Gary. Detective Inspector Scott Gary Honeysett. That's why I took such a special interest in this particular case. Call it a sense of pride, I was doing my bit for Garys everywhere.

KIRSTEN
You—You're one of them!

DAN WEATHERER

DETECTIVE HONEYSETT
A card-carrying Gary, yes I am.

For a moment neither moves as each regards the other intently, then with a shriek, Kirsten launches herself at the Detective, desperately trying to wrap her hands around his throat. After a brief, largely silent struggle Honeysett manages to pry Kirsten's hands free and call for help. PC Nelson enters the room to see the two of them struggling on the floor and uses his Taser on Kirsten.

Honeysett stands up and catches his breath. Nelson handcuffs Kirsten and rolls her into the recovery position.

PC NELSON
You told her your name was Gary, didn't you Sir?

DETECTIVE HONEYSETT
I did yes.

PC NELSON
Why? Your middle name is Hugo.

DETECTIVE HONEYSETT
Gary is my dog's name; I'd be damned if I was going to let her continue to dirty his good name!

PC NELSON
Really? What breed?

DEAD STAGE

DETECTIVE HONEYSETT
Chihuahua. The wife chose the breed, I chose the name, that was the compromise. A good marriage is all about compromise, Nelson.

PC NELSON
Ah. Right you are.

DETECTIVE HONEYSETT
Anyway, lock this one back up; let's hope Judge Gary Willis is in session for her hearing.

Detective Honeysett straightens his tie and exits the room.

END.

ONE FOR THE ROAD

Genre: Drama
Length: Approx. 12 minutes
Cast: 2 x Male

Synopsis: An elderly man reflects on his life and comes to terms with mortality.

Cast of Characters:
　Alf
　Man

ACT I

SCENE 1

At Rise: ALF (late sixties) is sitting with a pint of bitter in his hand. There are tattered beer mats and an empty packet of pork scratchings on the table.

After a moment of drinking alone, a MAN (mid-forties, well dressed) approaches Alf.

MAN
Mind if I join you, Alf?

Alf checks his watch and looks up at The Man

ALF
What time d'ya call this?

MAN
I'll take that as a yes.

The Man takes a seat next to Alf

ALF
You want a drink before—

MAN
I don't partake. Thank you, though.

ALF
No . . . I suppose not.

Alf takes a sip of his pint

> ALF
> You took your time.

> MAN
> You know how it can be.

> ALF
> Aye, I can imagine.

Pause.

> MAN
> Is now a good time for you?

> ALF
> Isn't that for you to determine?

> MAN
> In a manner of speaking, however, there are exceptions. I have been known to grant a temporary reprieve on occasion.

> ALF
> Nah, it's OK. I've nothing to sort. Now works for me, so long as you let me finish ma' pint?

The Man nods

> MAN
> Of course.

DEAD STAGE

Pause.

MAN
Tell me, how is your son?

ALF
That waste of space? He's doing OK. Why do you ask? You thinking of paying him a visit?

MAN
No. Not for a while at least.

Pause.

ALF
Suppose that's something, gives him time to sort himself. I don't really think bad of the boy.

MAN
I know.

ALF
It's just that he misses so much, y'know? He's got his whole life before him, two little kiddies, and he's pissing it all away in back street boozers.

MAN
Like you did?

ALF
Aye, like I did. But you don't want that for yours, do you?

MAN
I wouldn't know.

ALF
You don't, trust me. An' you try and tell 'em but they don't wanna hear it. You just have to sit back and watch them make the same mistakes you did.

MAN
Such is life.

ALF
Aye, such is life.

Alf takes a long drink

ALF
But he's a good sort. He'll come around.

MAN
I don't doubt it.

ALF
Have you seen much o' Margy?

MAN
Last I heard she was settling well. You needn't worry.

ALF
No . . . I know. I miss her, though.

MAN
I know.

DEAD STAGE

ALF
Will she want to see me?

MAN
I couldn't say. That's beyond me.

Alf takes sip of his drink

ALF
I suppose it is. Sorry.

MAN
No need to apologise.

ALF
She made me happy y'know. Made me complete.

MAN
I know.

ALF
When you took her, well . . . I didn't see a reason to carry on.

MAN
But you did.

ALF
Aye, I did. I did.

MAN
You've had a good go at it.

DAN WEATHERER

ALF
Life? Yeah, I suppose I have. There's my boy of course, then all those years at the pot bank. Y'know many people saw it as just a job but not me. I saw every piece I worked on as a lasting reminder of me . . . sort of my legacy. OK, I know I was just painting designs and the like, but those will be on mantelpieces long after I've gone. They will be appreciated by countless folk. I take a certain degree of pride in that.

MAN
So you should. I see so many leave nothing behind but misery and ruin.

ALF
There's enough of that too . . . but still.

MAN
Terry will come around.

ALF
Too late, I fear.

MAN
It's never too late, that you shall see.

ALF
I miss him.

MAN
I know. And he misses you.

DEAD STAGE

ALF
If you say so.

Pause.

MAN
Shall we?

ALF
Is this getting awkward, only I've not finished my drink?

MAN
I'm just not accustomed to conversation.

ALF
Why's that then?

MAN
I am a visitor that most are unhappy to see. There are exceptions . . . such as yourself.

ALF
I wouldn't say I'm elated to see you, I just know how it is.

MAN
Few are as open to the realities of life as you. It often reminds me of a child with a favoured toy. I have observed this numerous times. When it is time to put it away, one tries to talk them into letting go but so often one has to pry it from their hands by force.

Alf takes a drink from his pint.

ALF
Sounds like it can get messy?

MAN
It can.

ALF
You ever see it from our point of view?

MAN
Aside from the analogy I just gave you?

ALF
Yeah.

MAN
No. I am unable.

ALF
Suppose, but you gotta try to see it from our side. Life is all we have . . . it's all we know. It gives us so much, why should we want to let it go?

MAN
You are afraid.

ALF
Most, but not me.

MAN
It is the fear that prevents acceptance of one's own mortality.

DEAD STAGE

ALF
Do we need to be afraid?

MAN
No.

Alf takes a sip of his drink

ALF
Why'd you take her when you did?

MAN
It was her time.

ALF
Aye, no doubt—but who decides that? You?

MAN
I am the means to the passing. That is all. The plan comes from a higher power.

ALF
You mean God?

MAN
Some may call it that.

ALF
A lot'o folk do.
MAN
It is the order of things. A balance must be maintained. I ensure this is so.

ALF
Aye, I suppose. Does it bother you, what you do?

MAN
You ask a lot of questions.

ALF
Aye, I do. Best way to get to know someone I reckon. I've still a few sips to go so please . . . go on.

MAN
To be bothered implies that I have the emotional capacity to do so.

ALF
Don't you?

MAN
Emotions are a part of the gift of life, and it truly is a gift. I often wonder why so many take their blessing for granted.

ALF
Aye, me too. I suppose we get so caught up in routine that we fail to see what we really have. Really had.

MAN
It is never all in vain.

ALF
I know. I left my mark. I learned a little too late to appreciate my time but I know that the price of life is death.

DEAD STAGE

MAN
And do you accept that?

ALF
Yes.

Alf finishes his drink and places the empty glass on the table

ALF
I'm ready.

MAN
Good. Close your eyes.

ALF
Thank you, I mean for what you have done, you could have just taken me without all of this and—

MAN
No need to thank me. Close your eyes now.

Alf closes his eyes.

The man touches Alf on the forehead and Alf slumps in his seat. He has a smile on his face.

The Man leaves the stage.

CURTAIN FALLS.
END.

PARENTS

Genre: Comedy/Drama
Length: Approx. 20 minutes
Cast: 2 x Male 2 x female 1 x female voice over

Synopsis: Parents of reception pupils waiting to see their child's teacher, discuss the finer points of parenting in the modern age.

Parents was a finalist in the **Blackshaw Showcase Writing Award, 2017**.

Cast of Characters:
  Gilly Marston
  Steff Lightwood
  Tom Hanton
  Marianna Hanton
  Voice of Woman

ACT I

SCENE 1

Parents Evening: Reception class, Western Primary.

At Rise: School corridor complete with children's paintings and school notices etc. on the wall. There are four seats next to the classroom door. STEFF is sitting in the seat nearest to the classroom.

Enter GILLY.

GILLY
(To Steff)
Alright?

STEFF
(shy)
Hiya.

There is a moment of awkward silence as Gilly chooses which seat to take.

GILLY
Mind if I take this one?

Steff shakes her head. He sits next to Steff, who shuffles away from him.

Another awkward pause follows.

> GILLY
> You been waiting long?

> STEFF
> About twenty minutes. She's got a couple in there now. Frea's parents I think.

> GILLY
> Ah right. Not a name I recall. Bethany talks about her friends all the time, but it's in one ear, out the other, you know how it is? Some names stick, others don't.

Steff nods.

> GILLY
> Don't get me wrong, I wanna keep track of who is who, I think it's important to know the names of your kid's friends, but after twelve hours at the warehouse, it's kinda difficult to keep up with her. She can chatter for England that one.

Steff laughs politely.

> GILLY
> Which one's yours?

> STEFF
> I've two actually. Adam and Joe.

> GILLY
> Oh, the twins! Bethany is always talking about those two! She knocks about a fair bit with 'em.

DEAD STAGE

STEFF
Hope they aren't leading her into mischief? I keep telling them to behave but do they listen?

GILLY
Nah, it's OK. Boys will be boys. I think it's good that she mixes with the lads too. She never has a bad word to say about 'em . . . Not like that Rebecca.

STEFF
Yeah, she sounds a right one! Adam has told me about her a few times.

Gilly leans into Steff and lowers his voice.

GILLY
Did you hear about Mitsy, the class hamster?

STEFF
No?

GILLY
The way Bethany tells it, and bear in mind that she has a highly active imagination so I can't say for sure just how much of this is true, but apparently Rebecca force fed the hamster plasticine balls!

STEFF
Oh! That's awful! Was the Hamster OK?

GILLY
Bethany said so, though it wasn't moving for a while! She said the teacher mended it though.

STEFF
Thank God for that! What a terror she sounds, I'd hate to have to hear about one of mine doing something like that!

GILLY
Yeah, same here. Still, Ms Dooley sounds like she has it under control. If you can give CPR to a Hamster I'll bet there isn't much she can't handle!

Steff laughs.

Awkward pause.

GILLY
So, twin boys then. Bet they keep you on your toes eh?

STEFF
They do! There's always something. I never get five minutes these days. They are good kids but they just never stop! I don't know where they get the energy from! Still, I'd not have it any other way.

GILLY
Aye, nor me. Well. I would but—

Enter TOM and MARIANNA.

TOM
Ah, here we are! The Reception class . . . finally! Maisie's directions were hopeless. It's like a bloody maze in here!

DEAD STAGE

MARIANNA
I shall have words when she arrives tomorrow. I'll not look the fool on my first parent's evening!

GILLY
Evening.

TOM
Good evening.

Marianna looks at Gilly disapprovingly before taking the seat furthest from him.

STEFF
Hiya

Tom nods and takes the seat next to Gilly.

MARIANNA
Good evening.

Awkward Pause.

TOM
Tell me, is there much of a wait? I have a meeting at eight and I really need to be back at my desk. Multi-million-pound deal on the—

GILLY
'fraid so mate. I've been here five minutes, but this one—

STEFF
Steff.

GILLY
(To Steff)
　　Sorry, where are my manners? Steff.
(To Tom)
　　Steff here has been waiting a while now.

TOM
Oh.

Awkward Pause.

Marianna leans forwards so that she can address Steff at the far end of the row of chairs.

MARIANNA
Would you be a dear and let us go before you? Thomas has an awfully important Skype call at eight and he really ought to be on time. His associates would look upon his tardiness most unfavourably.

STEFF
Erm . . .

GILLY
(To Marianna)
Sorry love, it doesn't work like that. You should have gotten an earlier appointment. We all have to wait our turn.

MARIANNA
Oh, but we did.

DEAD STAGE

TOM
Our nanny gave us terrible directions. Couldn't find the bloody place. Missed our slot.

Gilly and Steff look at one another. Gilly mouths the word "nanny" and they both smirk.

MARIANNA
Yes, She'll be getting quite the telling off when she arrives tomorrow morning.

GILLY
That still makes you late.

MARIANNA
We arrived here in good time, we just couldn't locate where we were meant to be, could we darling?

TOM
No. A minor hitch.

Gilly and Steff look at one another.

Pause.

STEFF
(To Tom and Marianna)
Is this your first time at the school?

TOM
Yes, it is. Seems rather . . . rudimentary.

MARIANNA
Indeed. This wasn't our first choice, not at all. We wanted to send Rebecca to Saint David's in Chelmsford, however, we couldn't bear to send her away could we darling?

Gilly and Steff look at one another again and smirk upon hearing that they are Rebecca's parents.

GILLY
(To Tom and Marianna)
You er . . . you got any pets at your place?

MARIANNA
Certainly not!

TOM
Oh God lord, no.

MARIANNA
Filthy things. What with all the faeces and such! Plus, Archie has allergies.

TOM
Archie is our eldest. Twelve, strapping lad. Good head for business already. He started a lunchtime sticker shop last week, made an absolute fortune. Buy low, sell high, that's what I always tell him! Terrible allergies though. If he gets even a whiff of peanut butter we have to take him into A and E. Head swells like a balloon—

DEAD STAGE

MARIANNA
Yes, alright Thomas, that's enough. I'm sure they don't want Archie's complete medical history.

Pause.

GILLY
(To Tom)
What did you mean earlier when you said it all seems rudimentary?

TOM
Well . . . look at it. The paintings on the wall . . . ill-defined . . . sloppy use of form and colour. And those posters, at five I could already count to one hundred . . . backwards too.

MARIANNA
It just seems a little . . . simple for our tastes. At Saint David's they have the reception class reading music by the end of the year. You know, nursery rhymes and such. Not symphonies . . . That's for year one.

GILLY
Impressive. Still, sounds a bit much. I mean they are only five.

MARIANNA
It's never too early to plant the seeds of culture. That's what award-winning author and child development expert Dr Lucille Roathings says, and I for one agree with her. Rebecca is enrolled in Tap,

Ballet, Contemporary dance and is a keen player of the piano.

TOM
When we can get her to practice that is.

MARIANNA
Yes, well . . . I've said to Judith before, she needs to be stern with her.
(To Steff)
Judith is our daughter's Piano tutor. She charges fifty pounds an hour but came highly recommended by the Dean of Saint David's.

TOM
Yes, she's his wife.

Gilly and Steff stifle a laugh.

Pause.

Gilly nudges Tom in the ribs.

GILLY
Hey, I bet this takes you back eh? Sitting outside the classroom, waiting for the headmaster to come and give you a rollicking? Eh?

MARIANNA
I think not! Thomas was a perfect student. Weren't you Thomas?

DEAD STAGE

TOM
I was but I had my moments.
(To Gilly)
There was this one time I said I'd eaten all of my vegetables so that I could move onto my treacle sponge . . . but I hadn't! I'd left the cauliflower! I just scooped it onto the floor when the dinner lady was breaking up a fight behind me! Oh, I was a sod in those days! It's a miracle I'm as successful as I am now.

GILLY
Did you hear that Steff? We've a real bad 'un here.

Steff smiles

MARIANNA
You never told me that story before! Why now, in front of total strangers? Whatever will they think of us?

TOM
Hey, you knew I had a wild streak when you married me.

Pause.

TOM
(To Gilly)
What do you do then?

GILLY
I'm a Storage Expediter.

DAN WEATHERER

TOM
I see, sounds impressive. And what does that entail?

GILLY
I load stock onto the back of a lorry. It's a posh way of saying warehouse worker. Still, it keeps the wolves from the door. You?

TOM
I'm in property acquisitions. I buy and sell large estates . . . surprisingly demanding work. Keeps me at the office until all hours. It's like I say to Marianna, commerce never sleeps!

MARIANNA
He rarely sees the children; such is his dedication to his work. Nor do I really, we are a very productive family when it comes to our work.

STEFF
(To Marianna)
What is it that you do?

MARIANNA
Me? I represent one of the leading retailers of beauty products. I've a team of fifty sales reps beneath me. My team is current county leader in terms of sales.

STEFF
Oh, are you with that Forever lot then? I've had some of their stuff. Brought me out in a rash.

DEAD STAGE

                    MARIANNA
(flippant)
Forever is a brand for the more discerning skin type.
       Our products don't suit just anybody.

                     STEFF
(taken aback)
                      Oh.

Pause.

                      TOM
(To Steff)
            So what does your partner do?

                     STEFF
          Last I heard an eight to ten stretch.

                TOM AND MARIANNA
                      Oh!

                     GILLY
                What did he do?

                     STEFF
Armed Robbery. Well, attempted, but he had priors.
He knocked off a Gregg's with a water pistol and a
sock. The police arrested him in the bookies next
door. Couple of witnesses in the shop at the time saw
him go in. He robbed them first thing in the morning
so the tills were almost empty. Figured he could
double his money betting on the 12:20 at Kempton.
              Never was that bright.

GILLY
No, doesn't seem the smartest move. Do you see much of him?

STEFF
You mean do I visit him inside? Nah. I won't have the kids in a place like that. Besides, he was a waste of space. We were done with a long time before he pulled that stunt.

TOM
I'm sorry to hear that. Dreadful luck.

STEFF
Luck had nothing to do with it. He made his bed.

Pause.

MARIANNA
So, do you work?

STEFF
No. My boys keep me busy enough.

MARIANNA
So what do you do for money, if I may ask?

STEFF
I claim. It's all I can do.

MARIANNA
(aghast)
You live on benefits?

DEAD STAGE

STEFF
It's not a dirty word. Yes, my boys and I make do.

TOM
Can't you get a job?

GILLY
Hang on a mo, let's not pry. Her business is her business.

STEFF

(To Gilly)
No, it's OK.

(To Tom)
Easier said than done. Try getting a job that pays a living wage and fits in with my childcare needs. There aren't many about. It's either take a job paying less than I claim now, or work all of the hours God sends and never see my kids. I've no-one to help with the boys, no-one to take them before or after work, so I'm kinda stuck. I don't like to claim but I do what I can for my boys.

GILLY
As do we all.

There is an awkward pause.

Sound of Door opening and departing footsteps.

WOMAN'S VOICE
Miss Lightwood, please?

Marianne nudges Tom.

TOM
I know we touched on this earlier but I do have a terribly important call to take . . .

STEFF
(annoyed)
No, go ahead. Don't mind me.

TOM
Thank you. Darling?

Marianna and Tom stand.

MARIANNA
(softly)
Thank you.

Sound of footsteps.

TOM
Mr and Mrs Hanton, delighted to finally meet you, Ms. Dooley.

Sound of door closing.

GILLY
I'm sure they didn't . . .

STEFF
(interrupting)
No, those type never do, do they? Winds me right up!

DEAD STAGE

Makes me feel like I have to justify myself. I mean they have a nanny for God's sake. They practically pay someone to bring their kid up for them!

GILLY
I'm sure it's not as clear-cut as that. I know what you are getting at though. I'd kill to spend more time with Bethany. My shifts mean it's either first thing in the morning, or last thing at night when I see her.

STEFF
How do you manage? I'd hate that. You miss so much.

GILLY
Can't be helped. My parents help. They are a Godsend, and Bethany loves spending time with them. I need to work, I'm fortunate to have a job with decent money. Lets me take her away on holiday and do things she enjoys on my days off.

STEFF
That's nice.

GILLY
You been away yet this year?

STEFF
No. Not yet. We get away when we can, y'know, on those newspaper deals. The boys love it.

GILLY
I'm taking Bethany to Greece later this year.

STEFF
Oh, I went there before we had the boys. It's nice. Hot though. I'm not sure where we stayed exactly but it was a bit dodgy.

GILLY
Dodgy how?

STEFF
Well, we kept getting approached by men trying to buy our passports. Put me right off going back!

GILLY
(laughing)
I'll be sure to keep an eye out for them, thanks for the tip-off!

Sound of door opening followed by hurried footsteps.

Sound of door closing.

MARIANNA
(flustered)
Of all the cheek!

TOM
(assertive)
Now dear . . .

MARIANNA
I'll not have a bad word said about our daughter! She has to be mistaken! Rebecca would never kick the

DEAD STAGE

hamster ball across the classroom with the hamster still in it . . . she adores animals!

Tom and Marianna move to leave the stage.

TOM
I'm positive that she is mistaken. It will be another little girl, don't you worry.

MARIANNA
I'm going to call the head teacher in the morning. I'll not stand for this!

Exit Tom and Marianna.

GILLY
Wow. She really has got it in for that hamster!

Steff laughs.

STEFF
I guess nobody wants to hear bad about their child. Still, if it's the truth, it needs addressing. I'd want to know, and believe me, I've heard plenty of what my boys have been up to before now!

GILLY
Me too. Tough as it may be, teaching your child what is acceptable and what isn't, is part of the job of being a parent.

STEFF
I couldn't pass that job over to a nanny, even if I had

the money to. I like sharing the day with my boys, good and bad. Sure, they wind me up something chronic but that's what families do. That's what makes us close. I'd do anything for my boys.

GILLY
I know, but I guess they are doing what they think is best for Rebecca. You do what you can don't you, whether you think people agree with your methods or not. So long as the children are happy and provided for.

Pause.

STEFF
Do you try to see the best in everyone then?

GILLY
(laughing)
I try to yes . . . but it's bloody difficult sometimes!

Sound of door opening.

WOMAN'S VOICE
Miss Lightwood?

Steff stands.

STEFF
Well, that's me. Nice chatting to you.

GILLY
Same. And as for those two just now, don't let their

DEAD STAGE

opinions get to you. From what I hear of the twins, you are doing a cracking job. Same time next parent's evening?

STEFF
Sure. I'd like that. Thanks. See you around Gilly.

Sound of footsteps.

Sound of door closing.

END.

PENKHULL PARANORMAL

Genre: Comedy
Length: Approx. 30 minutes
Acts: Two
Cast: 4 x male 5 x female

Synopsis: A group of amateur ghost hunters embark on an investigation only to find that paranormal activity is not the only topic on the night's agenda.

Cast of Characters:
   Angel
   Colin
   Ben
   Cindy
   Rick
   Selena
   Hannah
   Steve
   Aggie

ACT I

SCENE 1

At Rise: COLIN (Mid-forties) and ANGEL (Early forties) are standing by a table in a darkened room. On the table lie an assortment of gadgets and camera equipment.

COLIN
Should be a good one tonight. Small group, so—

ANGEL
(interrupting)
How many?

COLIN
Six I think. You got the history of the place memorized?

ANGEL
How many times do I have to tell you? I don't need notes . . . the spirits give me all the information I need.

COLIN
Right you are.

Colin begins to fidget with the equipment on the table.

DAN WEATHERER

ANGEL
Must you? Everything is where you left it? The dead have no need to steal your stuff y'know?

COLIN
Just checking and rechecking . . . you can never be too prepared.

Enter BEN (mid-thirties) and CINDY (Early Thirties.) Cindy is smoking a cigarette and Ben is holding a hip flask.

CINDY
(To Ben)
Told you we'd be the bloody first ones here.

BEN
Better early than late, that's what my mam always used to say.

CINDY
I dunno . . . I'd prefer you late in the bedroom if you know what I mean!

BEN
Cheeky!

ANGEL
(To Ben and Cindy—overly theatrical)
Good evening! Welcome to Penkhull Paranormal. Penkhull's only paranormal investigation team. I'm your spirit guide Angel. Pleased to meet you.

DEAD STAGE

Angel shakes hands with Ben and Cindy.

CINDY
Bit cold in here ain't it? They gonna put the heating on?

ANGEL
I don't know.
(To Colin)
Are they gonna put the heating on dear?

COLIN
I doubt it. Place has been abandoned for years. Doubt the boiler even fires up. Besides, it all adds to the atmos eh? I'm Colin by the way.
(To Cindy)
There's no smoking in here, so if you could just . . .

CINDY
There's no one here? Who is it gonna bother?

BEN
Just put it out, love.

COLIN
Aside from the effects of second-hand smoke on others, it can affect my equipment.

BEN
You wanna see a doctor about that pal.

Cindy hits Ben on the arm.

CINDY
Less of your cheek!

BEN
I'm just joking about, he knows I am, right mate?

Colin smiles weakly. Ben takes a sip from his hip flask

COLIN
(tentative)
Erm . . . there's no drinking either.

BEN
Oh, bloody hell . . . some Saturday night this is turning out to be.
(To Cindy)
I thought you said it was gonna be a night spent in the company of spirits?

Cindy hits Ben on the arm again.

CINDY
You know what I mean.
(To Colin and Angel)
He knows what I mean.

Ben puts his hip flask into his pocket.

Moment of awkward silence.

BEN
So, is Angel your real name then?

DEAD STAGE

COLIN
Funny story actually, no—

ANGEL
(interrupting)
Yes. Yes, it is.

BEN
Oh. Seems rightly fitting that. You dealing with the dead and all . . .

Angel glares at Colin. More awkward silence.

Enter RICK (late forties) and SELENA (early twenties.) Rick has a large camera hanging from his neck and is carrying a large, metallic case.

ANGEL
(To Rick and Selena)
Oh hello again, Rick, great to see you!

COLIN
(To himself)
Oh great.

Rick places the case onto the floor and kisses Angel on her cheek.

RICK
Good to see you. Looking forward to tonight, I've a new camera to try out, 20.2-megapixel 1-inch Exmor CMOS sensor, 10 frames per second burst mode, the works!

DAN WEATHERER

Rick begins to fidget with his camera.

RICK
You got one of these yet Colin?

COLIN
No.

RICK
Guaranteed to snap a ghost or two with this bad boy. Will be clear as day too, not like your blurred efforts of late.

ANGEL
(To Selena)
And who is this delightful young lady?

Rick answers without looking up, stopping Selena from speaking.

RICK
Selena. My daughter. She's a bit shy so probably won't say a lot. Isn't that right, dear?

Selena attempts to answer

RICK
Like her mother this one. Never says a word. Always up to me to do the talking. Honestly . . . I despair sometimes.
(To Colin)
Here, check out the flash on this.

DEAD STAGE

Rick uses the flash in Colin's face.

COLIN
Argh!

Colin tries to shield his eyes but to no avail.

COLIN
Yes . . . very impressive.

Colin returns to his gadgets on the table.

ANGEL
(To Selena)
Is this your first ghost hunt dear?

RICK
It's her first time out on a Saturday night! Never mind her first ghost hunt. No confidence at all have you, dear?

Selena attempts to answer but opts to shake her head.

ANGEL
Aw, bless. Well, you are in good hands with me.

Enter HANNAH (mid-thirties) and STEVE (late thirties)

STEVE
Oh, how original . . . a nut house. Straight out of the ghost hunter's handbook that!

DAN WEATHERER

HANNAH
Will you be quiet! We've not even started yet and already you are spoiling the evening!

ANGEL
Ah, more for the hunt! Pleasure to meet you. I'm Angel, your medium for the evening—

BEN
(interrupting)
More like our large for the evening!

CINDY
Ben!

Hannah shakes Angel's hand.

HANNAH
The pleasure's all mine. I read your last interview with Psychics Weekly. Fascinating. I never knew that the reincarnation of Elvis Presley married the reincarnation of Cleopatra! And to think they live right here in Stoke! Amazing!

STEVE
Oh, good Lord.

ANGEL
Well, celebrity attracts celebrity, even after death . . . I'm writing a book on that very subject. "History's Icons—married with kids." Can I put you down for a copy?

DEAD STAGE

HANNAH
Yes, please! Oh, where are my manners, I'm Hannah by the way and this is my husband Steve. He's a bit of a sceptic Frederick by the way.

ANGEL shakes STEVE by the hand.

ANGEL
(To Steve)
Oh, I've met your sort. I'm pretty confident that I'll make a believer out of you before the night is done, mark my words.

STEVE
Doubtful. I've yet to see any credible proof of the afterlife, what with all of the heavily doctored videos and photographs doing the rounds . . . you are all doing more harm than good!

ANGEL
Yes. Quite.

Enter AGGIE (Early Sixties.)

Angel's cheerful disposition falters.

ANGEL
Aggie.

AGGIE
Angel.

COLIN
Aggie.

AGGIE
Colin.

COLIN
You keeping well?

AGGIE
When the spirits let me rest, yes. However, it's all go at present. There is a disturbance in the veil—

BEN
(interrupting)
I'm sure there is, Darth.

Cindy hits Ben hard on his upper arm.

CINDY
Ben! For the love of!

BEN
Ouch, woman!

ANGEL
(To Aggie)
Yes, I feel it also.

AGGIE
Well, I felt it first.

DEAD STAGE

COLIN
Right! Now that we are all here, shall we make a start?

STEVE
Is this it then?

ANGEL
Perhaps people were too afraid to join us, given our exclusive location tonight. Did you know that—

STEVE
Doubtful! Scared of paying thirty quid for a sham of an investigation more likely!

COLIN
Actually, we prefer smaller group sizes as it helps to eliminate outside interference should we encounter something deemed paranormal.

HANNAH
(To Steve)
Yeah Steve, smaller group sizes as it helps to eliminate outside interference should we . . . erm, yeah. It's just better with a small group.

ANGEL
OK, show of hands . . . who here has seen a ghost?

AGGIE
Spirit, dear. They prefer to be known as Spirits.

DAN WEATHERER

ANGEL
Who here has seen a spirit then?

STEVE
Ghost—the disembodied spirit of a dead person, supposed to haunt the living as a pale or shadowy vision, Collins Dictionary. Doubtful any of us have seeing as they don't exist.

Ben and Hannah raise their hands.

ANGEL
Hannah?

HANNAH
I have yeah, loads. On Youtube . . . you just search—

COLIN
Social Media doesn't count. We want to hear about actual physical sightings.

Ben strains his hand higher.

ANGEL
Go on.

BEN
I saw one when I was serving in the army.

COLIN
Oh really, an apparition on the battlefield, how exciting!

DEAD STAGE

BEN
No, shore leave. Portsmouth it were. Me an' the lads had had a skinful and I'd passed out in the bogs of the Hand and Hounds. Quality boozer that. Anyway, I woke up and all me mates had gone back to base. The pub was locked up tight and I couldn't find a way out. I found myself at the bottom of a staircase and I saw this old fella, dressed in white, standing at the top. He started to yelling at me to "leave this place immediately." I bolted and squeezed my way through an open bog window. Shit myself I can tell you.

There is a moment of silence.

STEVE
Could it have been the landlord that you saw you reckon?

Ben shuffles on the spot as all eyes turn to him.

BEN
Oh. Aye, I guess it coulda been. Sorry.

Cindy hits Ben on the arm again.

CINDY
You bloody daft sod! Stop showing me up, will you!

BEN
Sorry, duck. I never really thought about it until just now.

STEVE
So we can safely say that none of us here have seen a ghost then?

AGGIE
I have. I've seen loads.

ANGEL
(quickly)
I've seen more.

Selena attempts to speak but is cut off by Rick.

RICK
Show us your gear then, Col!

Ben sniggers. Cindy shoots him a warning look.

COLIN
OK, well tonight we shall be using a variety of equipment such as . . .

Colin picks up a small, cheap looking K2 meter.

COLIN
This K2 meter. It's used for—

Rick produces a larger K2 meter from his case.

RICK
Check. This piece of kit will detect any anomalies in the surrounding electromagnetic field up to a range of 100 metres. What's the distance on yours?

DEAD STAGE

                    COLIN
(sheepish)
                    Five.

Colin picks up a small, plastic device.

                    COLIN
            Then there's the ghost box.

Hannah gasps in awe.

                    STEVE
        Is there an actual ghost in that then?

                    COLIN
                 No, it's for—

                    STEVE
(interrupting)
                 Thought not.

Rick produces a larger version of the same device.

                    RICK
This sucker rapidly scans am/fm frequencies, the theory being that spirits use radio waves to communicate. I can scan over 5000 frequencies in under six seconds with this piece of kit . . . how about yours Col?

                    COLIN
            Three hundred. AM only.

Rick stifles a laugh and places the device back into his case.

RICK
I've also got light grids, UV torches—one each, EVP recorders three of and a set of cutting-edge motion detectors which emit a beep if anything crosses their scan range. Most Haunted ain't got nothing on me!

COLIN
I've got some chalk. Oh, and some tennis balls . . . for trigger objects.

RICK
(unimpressed)
Right.

ANGEL
Well, between the two of you we've got it covered, yes?

Colin nods and despondently begins to pack his gear away.

COLIN
(To himself)
Knew I should have brought the wide angle IR.

Rick produces one from his case and waves it at Colin.

ANGEL
Right then, that's the tech talk done. Now it's

DEAD STAGE

important that we keep together. This place is dark and not all areas are safe for public use. Plus, we never know who might be lurking in the shadows, this is an old mental asylum after all!

AGGIE
You got your stooges here tonight then?

CINDY
Stooges? This better not be a setup, eh Ben?

BEN
No, it better bloody 'adna!

ANGEL
Of course not guys—Aggie is confusing me with another of the local clairvoyants. I've never stooped to using tricks on my ghost hunts. Everything you experience is one hundred percent genuine! Now, if you will just allow me a moment to tune in.

AGGIE
Pah! You couldn't tune your TV!

Ben and Steve snigger.

COLIN
I'll just take a moment to say that we don't make enough from these ghost hunts to pay anyone else, so you can be sure there's no one lurking in the shadows, waiting to jump out and scare you. Least not on our payroll.

ANGEL
(annoyed)
Well thanks for that, dear. Very reassuring. Now If we could all join hands and I'll evoke a quick protection spell before we proceed.

The group join hands. Ben is uncomfortable holding Steve's hand and vice versa.

AGGIE
I'll say one too. Just in case yours has holes in it. Better to be safe than sorry when dealing with the spirits, that's what I always say.

ANGEL
(forced polite)
Thank you, Aggie.

BEN
S'alright folks. We dunna need no protection. Any funny business from the dead or alive and I'll nut 'em!

Ben makes a headbutt motion towards the centre of the circle

Angel begins a blessing.

FADE TO BLACK.

SCENE 2

At Rise: The group enter (Angel leads, followed by Aggie and the rest) a rundown office, complete with desk, chair and empty bookcase. Colin and Rick are overloaded with gadgets and equipment.

ANGEL
Come, come, the gates are still open, we have yet more to experience!

BEN
What do you mean more? We haven't experienced anything other than a few creaky doors and someone's bad gas!

Cindy hits Ben in the arm

CINDY
Ben! Don't be so vulgar!

BEN
It inna me, love!
(speaking to group)
But whoever it is dropping air biscuits, I suggest you see a doctor sharpish!

COLIN
Ah, the director of the facilities office. This is a ghost hot spot.

DAN WEATHERER

AGGIE
Spirit hot spot.

CINDY
(To Angel)
Can you call out and see if my mother is here?

ANGEL
Of course. Did she work here or?

CINDY
She was committed here. Long story.

BEN
She lived on Hanley Park for five weeks back in the late nineties. Ending up going feral.

STEVE
(To Cindy)
You let your mother live rough in the park?

CINDY
We tried to coax her back with scratch cards and Bovril, but she were 'aving none of it.

STEVE
I can't believe what I am hearing! You should have brought her home!

BEN
Hey, it wasn't that easy, mate! Sprightly old bird when she wanted to be, 'er mother. Showed us a clean pair of heels several times, I can tell you!

DEAD STAGE

ANGEL
Oh. Oh my. Well, I shall ask. What is her name?

CINDY
Mavis. Though you might have more luck with Earth Maiden Fleo . . . it's what she went by towards the end.

ANGEL
I see. Well, give me a moment.

Angel adopts a stance of concentration.

HANNAH
Oh, I can't wait! Are you picking up anything Angel?

ANGEL
Not yet—I . . .

AGGIE
(interrupting)
I am. Tall fellow. Old.

HANNAH
How old?

AGGIE
Not too old.

HANNAH
About forty?

DAN WEATHERER

AGGIE
He's about forty. He's directing. He's the director of this facility.

STEVE
(sarcastic)
And here we are in his office . . . what a coincidence!

HANNAH
Shush, Steve! I mean where else would he haunt?

Rick and Colin begin taking photographs of the office

COLIN
If he's here, I'll get a shot of him.

RICK
Not if I do first!

ANGEL
(dramatic)
Oh, I see him too, he's there by the window.

Angel points to where Selena is standing. Colin and Rick begin to photograph her. She moves away. Angel continues to point at Selena.

AGGIE
Is he 'eck! He's sat in the chair!

Colin and Rick start to photograph the chair.

DEAD STAGE

ANGEL
Must be a different director I'm seeing. A previous one from an older time.

STEVE
Of course! How convenient!
(To Hannah)
Are you really buying this gubbins?

HANNAH
(excited)
Shush! There are two ghosts! Two!

AGGIE
Spirits, dear.

HANNAH
Sorry.

BEN
They are having a ghost off!

STEVE
They are having a laugh is what they are having!

ANGEL
Mine is younger. Says his name is Otis.

AGGIE
Mine says nobody by that name worked here. He also called you a charlatan.

The group gasp. Colin and Rick stop taking photographs.

ANGEL
Well, mine called you a dried up old has-been, who only comes to events like this to make herself look important, when in reality you are no more psychic than a can of instant gravy granules.

The group gasp again.

BEN
Now this is more like it!

AGGIE
You take that back! I was reading palms while you were still messing your nappy!

ANGEL
True, but you were just as much of a fake then as you are now! Why not leave the ghost hunting to the real experts?

AGGIE
(angry)
Spirits! They prefer to be called Spirits!

ANGEL
And we all know what spirits you spend your time with!

Angel makes a drink motion

DEAD STAGE

ANGEL
Glug, Glug, piss yourself, pass out!

AGGIE
Why you dirty mouthed!

Aggie instigates a struggle with Angel. The group watch as the two pull at one another's hair and generally scuffle.

AGGIE
Bitch!

ANGEL
Phony!

AGGIE
Drag queen!

ANGEL
Pisshead!

Colin and Rick intervene but are thrown aside.

SELENA
(shouting in a gruff voice)
STOP THIS AT ONCE!

Aggie and Angel stop fighting. All attention turns to Selena.

RICK
Are you OK sweetie? That sounds kinda sore?

SELENA
Enough of this nonsense! How dare you call yourselves professional ghost hunters.

AGGIE
They prefer Spir—

SELENA
(interrupting)
We don't give a shit either way! We are dead!

CINDY
We?

BEN
Is she ok?

HANNAH
She's possessed!

STEVE
She's what?

AGGIE
I agree. Has to be. Look at her sickly skin tone . . . look at the coldness in her eyes. We need to get this girl exorcised at once!

RICK
I did think she was a looking a little peaky.

STEVE
You mean you think your own daughter is possessed?

DEAD STAGE

RICK
Well . . . yeah. First time I've heard her speak this week . . . and I mean look at the state of her.

STEVE
Oh, dear Lord.

ANGEL
(To Steve)
Yes! That's what we need . . . prayer. Everybody follow Steve's lead!

HANNAH
Oh, I'm so proud of you, honey!

STEVE
What? I'm not leading any exorcism!

SELENA
(uncertain)
Yes . . . OK, I am possessed. My name is Otis and I've something to say. We've lived our lives and we seek peace. We are mighty sick of people like you disturbing our rest. Always ordering us to knock on walls or move objects, all for your amusement. We are dead, we deserve a break dammit! We aren't performing seals for God's sake! It's the living that you need to concern yourselves with.

ANGEL
How do you mean?

SELENA
Take this girl, has anyone ever given her the chance to speak? Has anyone ever taken time to get to know her? Sure, she may be quiet and a little reserved, but she doesn't need anyone to answer for her. Especially not her father.

The group turn to look at Rick. He lowers his head and accidentally takes a picture of himself with his camera. The flash startles him.

SELENA
I suggest we stop antagonizing those who have passed on and start taking note of what is going on around us. There will be time for answers later. Death comes for us all. Spend your time living life. A little mystery goes a long way towards making life interesting. I mean who wants to watch the film if you already know the ending—

BEN
(interrupting)
Alright, alright, you don't have to keep on about it. We get the idea.
(To Cindy)
Jeez, are all the dead this bloody boring?

CINDY
Don't be so disrespectful!
(To Selena)
Erm, dead fella . . . please go on.

DEAD STAGE

SELENA
As for this infighting, it has to stop! I mean how can you earn the respect of the scientific community and the world at large if you all continue to belittle one another. It's pointless and it makes you look unprofessional and petty. You should all support one another should you wish to be taken seriously, after all, you are all working towards the same goal . . . correct?

ANGEL
Correct.

AGGIE
Aye . . . aye we do.

SELENA
Right, well I've said my piece, now if you will excuse me.

Selena shudders gently for a moment.

The group edge closer

RICK
Are . . . are you OK sweetie?

SELENA
(coughing)
I'm fine daddy. What's the matter?

ANGEL
There's no one else in there with you?

SELENA
No, of course not why?

AGGIE
We were visited by another.

HANNAH
And he had a message.

SELENA
He did? Wow, I'm sorry I missed that. I must have dozed off or something. I'm sure whatever he had to say was very important though . . . right, dad?

RICK
Erm . . . yes, I suppose so.

ANGEL
I guess that's it then, for the tour I mean . . . now we've been told to pack it in.

AGGIE
Yes. I think it ought to be, after what was said an' all.

BEN
Thanks for the floor show ladies. Same time next week?

CINDY
(To Ben)
Will you give it a rest!
(To group)
Thank you for a wonderful evening.

DEAD STAGE

Exit Ben and Cindy.

STEVE
(To Hannah)
C'mon Hannah, I've seen enough of this. Next time you think about dragging me to one of these things you think again!

HANNAH
But I thought you believed it all!

STEVE
I believe these people need serious therapy!

Exit Steve/Hannah

Colin packs up his gear.

RICK
(To Colin)
You know your gear's pretty good mate. I mean it's not the latest stuff but it's still pretty solid.

COLIN
Thanks. It serves a purpose. I can't be doing with buying new gear just to keep up.

RICK
I understand, takes a lot of money and dedication. You are best off leaving it to the big boys.

COLIN
Yeah. Sure.

RICK
C'mon. Let's go home. You can tell your mam all about it.

SELENA
If I can get a word in edgeways.

Exit Rick/Selena

ANGEL
I didn't mean what I said earlier, about calling you a fake.

AGGIE
I know dear.

ANGEL
Did you?

AGGIE
Did I what?

COLIN
Oh no. Now ladies, remember what the ghost—erm spirit said just now . . .

ANGEL
(interrupting)
Did you mean what you said?

AGGIE
Yes. Every word. I've seen more convincing acts of clairvoyance coming from my pet goldfish!

DEAD STAGE

ANGEL
Why you spiteful old witch!

Angel moves to attack Aggie.

LIGHTS OUT.
END.

POINTS

Genre: Comedy
Length: Approx. 10 minutes
Cast: 2 x male 1 x female

Synopsis: An official from the Department of Work and Pensions, has troubling news for the wife of the recently deceased Mr Willis.

Cast of Characters:
    Mr Willis
    Mrs Willis
    DWP Official

ACT I

SCENE 1

At Rise: MR WILLIS is lying on a table. He is covered with a sheet. MRS WILLIS stands by his side.

MRS. WILLIS
(sobbing)
Oh, Frank, why did this have to happen now? You were always so careful about what you ate as well! It was the stress that did it . . . I know it was! How many times did I have to say it?

Beat.

Now what will I do without you?

Enter DWP OFFICIAL.

Character is dressed in a cheap suit and carries a pen/clipboard.

DWP OFFICIAL
Excuse me, Mrs Willis, is it?

Mrs Willis nods takes a tissue from her sleeve and dabs her eyes.

DWP official points at the body of Mr Willis with the tip of his/her pen.

> DWP OFFICIAL
> Mr Willis?

> MRS. WILLIS
> Yes.

DWP official approaches the body of Mr Willis and throws back the top half of the sheet, exposing the head/bare chest of Mr Willis.

DWP official scribbles notes on a clipboard while circling body.

> MRS. WILLIS
> (confused)
> I'm sorry. Who are you?

DWP quickly flashes lanyard towards Mrs Willis while keeping attention on the body of Mr Willis.

> DWP OFFICIAL
> I'm with the Department of Work and Pensions.

DWP official continues with his/her notes.

> MRS. WILLIS
> (more confused)
> The DWP? I don't understand. Why are you here?

DWP official answers without stopping his/her note taking.

DEAD STAGE

> DWP OFFICIAL
> Routine, madam. It's just routine.

> MRS. WILLIS
> Do you have a name?

Choose required name depending on whether actor playing DWP official is Male/Female.

> DWP OFFICIAL
> Of course. I'm Simon/Elaine.

> MRS. WILLIS
> Simon/Elaine what?

DWP official looks up from the body of Mr Willis and turns his/her attention to Mrs Willis.

> DWP OFFICIAL
> (quickly)
> I'm not at liberty to say.

Beat.

Mrs Willis, the cause of death was cardiac arrest yes?

> MRS. WILLIS
> The doctors said he had a heart attack.

DWP official ticks a box on his paperwork.

> MRS. WILLIS
> How did you know?

DWP OFFICIAL
I spoke to the presiding doctor before I came in, no need to worry. So I see from the marks on his chest that they tried resuscitation, correct?

MRS. WILLIS
Yes.

DWP OFFICIAL
And I'm informed by the presiding Doctor that they employed the use of a defibrillator?

MRS. WILLIS
They shocked him yes. It didn't work though.

DWP OFFICIAL
Mrs Willis, could you tell me how many times they used the defibrillator on your husband?

MRS. WILLIS
(confused)
I'm . . . I'm not really sure. There was so much to take in I—

DWP OFFICIAL
It is very important that you remember.

Mrs Willis takes a moment to think.

MRS. WILLIS
I really couldn't—

DEAD STAGE

> DWP OFFICIAL

(interrupting)

> Was it two?

> MRS. WILLIS
> I-I think so.

DWP ticks another box.

> DWP OFFICIAL
> Excellent.

> MRS. WILLIS
> I don't see how that is relevant. Are you here to judge if there is a case of malpractice—should they have done more?

> DWP OFFICIAL
> Oh good lord no! Two uses of the defibrillator is the maximum allowed under new government measures.

> MRS. WILLIS
> I-I don't understand?

> DWP OFFICIAL
> It's simple Mrs Willis. In this challenging economic climate, one cannot simply waste resources. The NHS operates on a strict budget. Gone are the days of careless spending, where doctors were free to use the defibrillator willy-nilly. Why I heard of cases where a patient was shocked sometimes, thirteen . . . maybe even fourteen times, with no improvement. And that was just one example, in one trust, on any

given day. Can you imagine the cost of wasted electricity across the entire NHS for the last calendar year if this was the case elsewhere? Staggering . . . truly staggering. So, under new austerity measures, every patient is entitled to two jolts of the defibrillator in any given calendar year, running April 1st to April 1st. Two should be more than enough.

MRS. WILLIS
(shocked/upset)
I—I don't understand? This is a lifesaving treatment you are talking about here! One more shock could have brought my Frank back!

DWP official turns his/her attention back to Frank.

DWP OFFICIAL
Indeed, it could have, it certainly would have helped matters today . . . which brings me to the reason that I am here. You see, while claiming incapacity Benefit for your husband's back injury sustained . . .

DWP official checks notes.

DWP OFFICIAL
. . . July 2014, it seems that you were in receipt of several overpayments . . . amounting to a total cost of . . .

DWP official checks notes again.

DEAD STAGE

DWP OFFICIAL
... Two thousand, seven hundred and eighty pounds and thirty-two pence.

DWP official looks at Mrs Willis.

DWP OFFICIAL
An amount still owed and required to be paid in full.

MRS. WILLIS
I-I don't have that kind of money? My husband just died, there's his funeral to pay for and—

DWP OFFICIAL
(Interrupting)
Well, hold on a moment. Let's not get too hasty. You see I've carried out my examination and I regret to inform you that your husband hasn't scored enough points to be declared unfit for work.

MRS. WILLIS
(stunned)
What? How can ... Don't be so—

DWP official sidles up to Mrs Willis and shows her the clipboard.

DWP OFFICIAL
I'm afraid so. It's all here in black and white. See here where it says number of limbs, and I've put four ... you'd agree he has four, correct?

MRS. WILLIS
Yes, but?

DWP OFFICIAL
And you'd also agree that he is completely intact?

MRS. WILLIS
Well, yes but his heart . . .

DWP OFFICIAL
He's not broken any bones either?

MRS. WILLIS
No, but his—

DWP official withdraws clipboard.

DWP OFFICIAL
Further, the nature of his original claim focused on, and I quote, his inability to straighten his back.

MRS. WILLIS
That's right. He could barely lie down.

DWP official looks at Mr Willis.

DWP OFFICIAL
Looks to me like he's doing a pretty good job of it now.

MRS. WILLIS
Yes, but—

DEAD STAGE

DWP OFFICIAL
Then it's like I said. He hasn't scored enough points to be declared unfit to work. And as of The latest government legislation, because he has received a substantial overpayment of incapacity benefit, not only is he still liable for the debt, but he must return to work immediately so that he can begin repayment.

MRS. WILLIS
That is . . . that is absolutely ludicrous, how on earth do you expect him to do that when he is dead?

DWP OFFICIAL
Mrs Willis, please. I don't make the rules. I'm just doing my job. I suggest that you two sit down and discuss your options. Failure to comply will see sanctions applied to you both, meaning that any benefit you receive will be frozen until an agreement is reached between the DWP and your husband. There's plenty of low-paid, menial labour out there for those willing to get up off their backsides!

MRS. WILLIS
I-I have no idea what you expect me to do. I—

DWP OFFICIAL
I realise that news of the overpayment has come as something as a shock, and I am sorry to have to deliver . . .

DWP covers Mr Willis with a sheet.

DAN WEATHERER

>   DWP OFFICIAL
> ... it today of all days. But the matter stands. Expect us to be in touch shortly. Oh, and my condolences.

Exit DWP official.

Mrs Willis remains, mouth ajar, stunned and confused.

END.

THE MARCH OF THE PAGAN KING

Genre: Drama
Length: Approx. 5 minutes
Cast: 1 x male

Synopsis: Penda, King of England, delivers a rallying call to his people after a series of important victories on the battlefield.

Authors Note: This was the first piece that I wrote for the stage, and appears exactly as written.

Curtain up—The stage is empty apart from the solo actor who stands cloaked in darkness in the centre of the stage. The spotlight illuminates him and we see a middle-aged man wearing a gold crown above resplendent Armour. This is PENDA OF MERCIA. He looks out towards the audience and begins his address.

PENDA

Tonight I stand before you not as a King—but as a man. Alongside my noble brother Cadwallon, we have marched across this isle of ours, rightfully crushing all who dare oppose us. I see before me an army that is justly feared. An army that stood firm against the might of the Hwicce. An army that stormed the gates of the heretic Oswald and Edwin before him. An army that bled for me at Heavenfield, that died for me at Maserfield—all so that I may unite these lands under one rule—my rule! Verily, Tis not an army that I see before me tonight, but the sons of Mercia!

With God on his side, all things are possible. These . . .

Penda points to his left to indicate the presence of an unseen collection of objects

. . . trinkets of gold and silver that we took from the hands of our fallen foes are testament both to our strength and the righteousness of our claim. Tis a fine collection that we have carried out to this desolate place this night.

DEAD STAGE

The battles that we have fought and won have all but secured our place in history. Though they call me king slayer, oh yes—I know this to be true, the reign of King Penda will be spoken of through ages yet to come!

Though some may call me cruel, my rule is absolute and my ability to conquer undoubted. As for my thirst for death, what would they have me do? One must cut out the heart of the enemy to end the fight. Our Gods demand appeasement and we as willing subjects must pay heed to their call. Every drop of blood shed upon our conquered lands ensures that our fields will flourish for generations to come. It does not hurt that I am able to rid myself of an enemy monarch also.

In the beginning, our threat was not recognised amongst those that bickered and quarrelled over this divided isle of ours. Our warnings went unheeded and our movements went unnoticed. Our allegiance to the King of Gwynedd helped to strengthen both our claim upon Mercia and our growing repute as warriors. Our victory at Hatfield Chase finally captured the attention of our enemy, for not only did we slay King Edwin of Northumbria and ravage his lands, we took his son Eadfrith prisoner—his later execution was a further statement of our intent.

Egric and Sigevert, once both mighty kings, both heralded amongst the masses, were the next to fall by our blade. Our dominance over the East Angles enabled us to rise against the Northumbrians once more and force King Oswald from his throne. His dismemberment sent a clear message to those that would dare oppose the might of the Mercian army— do so at your peril. That those heathens made him a martyr is absurd! I for one shall never yield my faith in favour of this Eastern religion and nor shall the people of Mercia!

Tomorrow our armies march for Bernicia, our hold over Northumbria must remain total, yet those of you that stand before me now will serve your kingdom an even greater service! The spoils of a long and arduous war lie before us, a haul of gold and silver the likes of which no man has ever seen are ours to offer. Hilts and pommels lie alongside the relics of our enemies' doomed religion. We took everything from them, left them with nothing. The dead have no need for gold.

Yet it is true that the favour of the Gods does not come easily and it is now time for us to repay our debt.

Dig I say! Dig deep into the earth for the yule frost approaches and soon the ground will be as hard as the iron of our blades! Bury this hoard so that no man may claim it as his own, for this is Mighty Woden's treasure. This is our offering to him and him alone.

Penda reacts to an unseen voice addressing him from his right side.

DEAD STAGE

PENDA
I am told that one such piece carries the following inscription—Rise up, Lord; may Your enemies be scattered and those who hate You be driven from your face. Bury this piece deepest of all.

Penda turns his attention to the unseen companion.

PENDA
Captain, a word.

Penda lowers his voice

PENDA
Select five of your most trusted men . . .

Penda glances towards the audience

PENDA
Make sure that nobody leaves this place alive. This offering must remain hidden. Burn the bodies. Leave no trace.

Without looking back, Penda disappears into the blackness.

END.

A BROTHER BORN

Genre: Drama
Length: Approx. 45 Minutes
Cast: 4 x Male

Synopsis: A father's secret is exposed, and where once there were two, now there are three.

Cast of Characters:
  Cedric
  Francis
  Saul
  Anthony

ACT I

SCENE 1

At Rise: Public House. SAUL (tracksuit/beanie hat) is seated at a small table. There are several empty pint glasses littering the table.
He finishes his drink, burps, and places his empty glass with the others.
ENTER CEDRIC (Denim Jacket, T-shirt and dirty Jeans). He is carrying two pints of lager.

CEDRIC
There you go, lad.

Cedric passes one of the pints to Saul and takes a seat next to him.

CEDRIC
Get that down yer Gregory Peck.

Saul lifts his glass to meet Cedric's.

SAUL
Cheers, dad. I'll get the next round in.

CEDRIC
Don't worry about that lad, I know how hard up you are. It's only money.

Cedric takes a sip of his pint.

Saul nods.

CEDRIC
Besides which, I hate drinking on my own.

Saul takes a sip of his lager.

Cedric checks his watch.

CEDRIC
Late as bloody usual. Never any time for his family that one. It's always work, work, work with him.

SAUL
Yeah. He's always had it made has Francis. Coasting from one job to the next just because he went to university. He's got no idea how hard it is out there.

CEDRIC
You had much luck on the job front?

SAUL
No. Not really. I went for my review at the dole office this week though.

CEDRIC
Oh ar? How did it go?

SAUL
Shit. Same as ever. They wanted me to apply for a forklift job in Nuneaton. Said I could bus it there no problem. I'd have to bloody leave the house at five thirty every morning to get there for the half eight start!

DEAD STAGE

CEDRIC
Bloody scandalous that! A man needs his kip!

SAUL
I said I ain't even got my forklift license, and I've no experience doing factory work. They made me apply anyway. I'd get sanctioned otherwise.

CEDRIC
I tell you, I don't know what's happened to this country of ours?

SAUL
I do. It's all them immigrants . . .

CEDRIC
(interrupting)
Oh, don't get me started on them again! I came out for a quiet drink. You know how talking about that gets my heckles up.

SAUL
Sorry, dad. Just a bloody waste of time is all.

Beat.

(reluctant)
I should never have come out.

Cedric places his arm on his son's shoulder.

CEDRIC
Now, son, you weren't cut out for war, most men

aren't, there's no shame in admitting that. Just because I served, and my father before, and his father before him . . . you've not discredited the family name or owt. Them lads sounded like a right bunch of tossers. I don't want no son of mine taking a bullet for shits like that. You're better off out lad.

Cedric pats his son on the back and gives the back of his neck a playful squeeze.

CEDRIC
I don't want you overseas fighting a bunch of rag-heads anyway. Ain't no fight of ours! Better off out of it lad.

Enter FRANCIS carrying a solitary glass of wine. Francis is well dressed/groomed.

SAUL
Oh aye, here he is! The Probable son.

Francis takes a seat next to Cedric.

FRANCIS
You mean prodigal.

Cedric points to his watch.

CEDRIC
And what bloody time do you call this? We've been sat here ages!

Francis looks at the empty glasses on the table.

DEAD STAGE

FRANCIS
I can see that.

CEDRIC
You keep your punters waiting like this? I'd bloody hope not!

FRANCIS
(sighing)
No, dad.

SAUL
So, what's your excuse today?

FRANCIS
I couldn't find the place; I've not been here before—

SAUL
That fancy car of yours not got sat-nav?

CEDRIC
(To Saul)
Wouldn't surprise me if he had a bloke sat next to him directing from a bloody atlas, the amount he paid for that thing!

Saul and Cedric laugh.

FRANCIS
I'm here now.

Francis sits and takes a sip of his wine.

SAUL
So how's life in the justice system?

FRANCIS
I've told you before, I'm not that kind of solicitor.

SAUL
You got to court, don't you?

FRANCIS
Sometimes.

SAUL
So what's the difference?

FRANCIS
(sighing)
Well, there's the Crown court—

CEDRIC
(interrupting)
Enough shop talk. How are those grandkids of mine?

FRANCIS
They're good. Freddie is doing well at nursery and Eva is excelling at school.

CEDRIC
Good. Good.

FRANCIS
Of course you could always make the effort to stop by and see them yourself?

DEAD STAGE

CEDRIC
I will, I will. Y'know how it is and all? Time gets away from you.

FRANCIS
Bookies keeping you busy then?

Cedric mock punches Francis on the arm.

CEDRIC
Cheeky!
(To Saul)
Always had a tongue on him, this one!

SAUL
Yeah.
(To Francis)
Anyway, dad's had a couple of big wins.
(To Cedric)
Haven't you?

CEDRIC
(reluctantly)
I've done OK . . . nothing major.

FRANCIS
(To Cedric)
Don't worry yourself. I'm not about to ask for that money back. I said at the time, just as and when.

CEDRIC
I know, I know—and I will pay you back. It's just I've been off work a while and money has been tight.

FRANCIS
Why? What's the matter?

SAUL
Chest pains.

CEDRIC
(To Saul)
Now lad, I told you not to burden him!

FRANCIS
(To Cedric)
Have you been to the doctors?

CEDRIC
Aye.

Beat.

FRANCIS
(impatient)
And what did they say?

CEDRIC
(sighing)
Same as always, son. Slow it down, eat better and stay away from the gee-gees . . . and I will.

FRANCIS
When?

CEDRIC
Oh, come on now. You are starting to sound like your mother!

DEAD STAGE

FRANCIS
Yeah, well you never took any notice then and look where that's gotten you.

SAUL
It wasn't his fault mam left him—

FRANCIS
He was having an affair! Of course it was his bloody fault!

CEDRIC
Well, if she didn't nag all the time then—

SAUL
(interrupting)
See! She drove him away!

FRANCIS
You don't know what you are on about, you were just a kid. You didn't see what he put her through.

CEDRIC
Past is past boys, better to leave it be.

FRANCIS
I've heard that before.

SAUL
He said leave it be.

Beat.

FRANCIS
So when are you going to take the doctor's advice?

CEDRIC
Soon.

FRANCIS
When?

SAUL
Dammit, Francis, he said soon!

FRANCIS
(To Saul)
I wasn't asking you.

CEDRIC
(angry)
Soon! Alright? Soon. A man has needs. You think it's fun living on my own at my age? I need a release now and then. Keep me sane. Keep me away from the grave.

Beat.

SAUL
(softly)
Don't talk like that, dad.

CEDRIC
It's true! Wait and see. When you get to my age, you gotta take the wins wherever you find them. Mark my words.

DEAD STAGE

A brief moment of silence while all three take sips from their drinks and search for something to say.

FRANCIS
So . . . I take it I'm here because you finally told Saul? Can't think why else you'd request my company at such short notice?

SAUL
Told me what?

FRANCIS
(To Cedric)
Or you are going to?

SAUL
(impatient)
Going to tell me what?

CEDRIC
(annoyed—to Saul)
Nothing lad. I just fancied a catch up with my boys, that's all.

FRANCIS
You said you'd speak to him about all of this.

CEDRIC
I did, yes, but now's not the time.

FRANCIS
There isn't ever going to be a time dad. You dropped this on me and frankly, I'm tired of keeping it to

myself. I've got questions, Saul will have questions. It's only fair you answer them yourself. You can forget leaving this mess for me to clear up after you pop your clogs!

CEDRIC
I wasn't gonna keep it that long—

SAUL
(angry)
Tell me what? I'm sat right here! You always treat me like this, like I don't matter or I'm too stupid to be involved! I hate it . . . I always have!

Beat.

CEDRIC
(calm)
Of course you matter Saul, but we don't need to go into this now.

FRANCIS
I think we do. I need too.

SAUL
Just spit it out dad, are you ill?

CEDRIC
(To Francis)
You pushed this, Francis, remember that. I wanted to leave it until—

DEAD STAGE

FRANCIS
You wanted to leave it like you left him you mean?

SAUL
Him?

Cedric turns towards Saul. He appears weary and reluctant to speak.

CEDRIC
(sighing)
I didn't want it to come out like this . . . but . . . You've got a brother son, another one. Younger. I'm not sure how old—

FRANCIS
(interrupting)
He's seventeen.

Cedric turns towards Francis.

CEDRIC
And how do you know how old he is?

FRANCIS
His name is Anthony, dad. It wouldn't kill you to use it.

CEDRIC
You've spoken to him haven't you? I told you—

FRANCIS
(angry)

DAN WEATHERER

You told me I have a brother out there and you expect me to just carry on as though nothing has changed?

CEDRIC
I told you not to look him up! I told you that some things were better left be.

FRANCIS
And why was that? Scared of what truths I'd uncover about you? I hate to shatter any illusions you may hold with regards to yourself, but I saw through you a long time ago. You've your faults as much as any of us have. Perhaps it's time you face up to them.

Beat.

SAUL
Why are you telling me this now? Today? Why not before?

Cedric turns to Saul. Francis continues with his drink.

CEDRIC
Because it was my business son—

FRANCIS
(interrupting)
Bullshit! It's all of our business if it's blood.

CEDRIC
And you were too young to understand.

DEAD STAGE

SAUL
(motioning towards Francis)
How long has he known?

CEDRIC
Not long—

FRANCIS
A while. A year, perhaps.

SAUL
(To Francis)
And you kept this from me all that time?

FRANCIS
He told me to, plus I needed time to get my head around it. I wanted to tell you, but not knowing how I felt about it all . . . I wasn't sure I could be there to support you. I was angry. I still am.

Beat.

SAUL
Have you met him?

FRANCIS
No. Not yet.

SAUL
(To Cedric)
Have you? I mean like . . . did you ever take him out when he was little? Did you ever do the things you told us you were too busy to do . . . is that why you couldn't, because you were with him?

> CEDRIC
> No, son.

> FRANCIS
> He's never met him. At least Anthony can't remember doing so.

Beat.

Saul stands.

> SAUL
> I need a drink.

Francis motions towards Saul's pint glass.

> FRANCIS
> You've already got one.

> SAUL
> I need a real drink.

> FRANCIS
> Then I'll come with you.

Francis motions to stand.

> SAUL
> I'll be OK, I'll bring you one back if you want?

> FRANCIS
> No, I'm OK. I'm driving.

DEAD STAGE

SAUL
Suit yourself.

EXIT SAUL

CEDRIC
See what you've done now?

FRANCIS
What I've done? This was your secret. He had a right to know.

CEDRIC
I asked you for time, and you couldn't even give me that!

FRANCIS
I've given you plenty. You think this has been easy for me? I couldn't bury it like you did. I needed to know how he was doing. If he had a decent childhood. I needed to know he was OK without us.

CEDRIC
I didn't bury him.

FRANCIS
Looks to me like you did.

Cedric taps his head.

CEDRIC
Well you can't see in here can you lad? I thought about him every damn day. Sometimes only briefly,

wondering what he was doing, if he was safe. Hoping he had someone in his life to give him what I couldn't. It eats you up if you let it. So I didn't.

Beat.

> CEDRIC
> Did he ask after me?

> FRANCIS
> A little. He wanted to know where you were living. He's been trying to find you.

> CEDRIC
> *(Panicked)*
> You didn't tell him?

> FRANCIS
> *(annoyed)*
> No. Just that you were local. He wanted to know what you'd done with your life. So I told him.

> CEDRIC
> A short conversation then?

> FRANCIS
> Yeah.

Beat.

> CEDRIC
> How is Suzanna? She doing OK?

DEAD STAGE

FRANCIS
(reluctant)
I . . . She passed away dad. I'm sorry, I assumed you knew?

CEDRIC
(sombre)
No. I didn't. I'd not kept tabs on her. When?

FRANCIS
A few years ago. Cancer.

CEDRIC
Oh.

Beat.

CEDRIC
So he's with his stepdad?

FRANCIS
No. She never married. He lives with her parents now.

CEDRIC
I see.

Beat.

CEDRIC
Good that he has family though.

Francis glares at Cedric.

DAN WEATHERER

ENTER SAUL with a fresh drink.

>FRANCIS
>You OK?

Saul nods.

>SAUL
>Is he?

>CEDRIC
>Yeah, don't worry about me, lad. Just remembering, that's all.

>FRANCIS
>You should have told us sooner.

>SAUL
>Yeah, you shoulda.

Saul takes a large sip of his drink.

>SAUL
>You shoulda trusted us to work things out. Francis, I'm pissed at you too.

>FRANCIS
>I know. I'm sorry. I just needed to think it all through. Get my head around it all.

>SAUL
>And have you?

DEAD STAGE

FRANCIS
No. Not yet. That's why I'm going to see him.

CEDRIC
You are?

SAUL
Do you think that's a good idea?

FRANCIS
I do, yes. If you want to see him, I'll give you his details.

SAUL
I don't. Not yet. I don't know him . . . it'd be weird.

FRANCIS
OK. I understand.

SAUL
But tell him about me, yeah?

FRANCIS
I will.

Francis looks at Cedric.

FRANCIS
And you?

CEDRIC
I . . . I couldn't. It's been too long. I'm sure he's doing fine without me.

FRANCIS
Probably, but at least think about it.

Cedric finishes his drink and stands.

CEDRIC
I made my choice, rightly or wrongly, seventeen years ago. You are my family; you are my boys. Call me when it's all done with. Let me know he's doing OK.

Cedric pats Saul on the shoulder.

CEDRIC
Oh, and regardless of what you think of me, your mother was always the one I loved. We just lost our way. People do sometimes. That's all.

FRANCIS
And Suzanna?

CEDRIC
Suzanna was a remarkable woman, God rest. See you around.

Cedric nods at Francis and pats Saul on the shoulder.

Exit Cedric.

FRANCIS
You OK?

DEAD STAGE

SAUL
I dunno. It's a lot to take in.

FRANCIS
Yes. It is. Why do you think I didn't rush to tell you? I still don't know what to make of it all.

SAUL
Is that why you are going to see him?

FRANCIS
Anthony? Perhaps. I don't know. I feel somebody ought to, even if it's just to acknowledge his existence. Seems like the right thing to do.

SAUL
I suppose. I just can't yet. I will though, one day.

FRANCIS
I know.

SAUL
Is he really OK?

FRANCIS
Who dad? He will be. I just told him that Anthony's mum had passed. I thought he already knew. Regardless of what I think of the man, he obviously felt something for her once. I saw it in his face. She wasn't a one night stand or anything like that. Likely he had his own reasons for doing what he did.

SAUL
Do you think he chose us over them?

FRANCIS
I don't know. I don't think it's ever that simple. At least I hope it wouldn't be. Only he knows for sure. I'm not sure now is the best time to ask.

SAUL
OK.

Beat.

SAUL
You know, I always thought it was just us two, brothers against the world. And now it's not.

FRANCIS
No.

SAUL
D'ya think he'll look like us?

FRANCIS
For his sake, I hope not.

Saul laughs. Francis finishes his drink and stands.

FRANCIS
Come on, I'll give you a lift home.

Saul stands.

DEAD STAGE

SAUL
You still shoulda told me. I'd have been OK.

FRANCIS
I know. Come here.

Saul and Francis hug.

FRANCIS
Promise me if you need to talk, you know where I am right? None of this macho "I'm going it alone" bullshit OK?

SAUL
OK.

Francis and Saul walk towards the exit.

SAUL
I do hope he's doing OK, Anthony, I mean. None of this is his fault. I kinda feel bad for him.

FRANCIS
I know. Me too. He's still just a kid really.

SAUL
Say Hi for me, yeah?

FRANCIS
I will, and I'm sure he's doing great. I'll let you know.

EXIT SAUL and FRANCIS.
BLACKOUT.

SCENE 2

At Rise: Sparsely populated living room with sofa, chair, table and assorted ornaments.
ENTER ANTHONY followed by FRANCIS.
Anthony clears the sofa of magazines etc.

ANTHONY
Grab a seat. You wanna drink or something?

Francis takes a seat.

FRANCIS
No. Thank you, I'm good.

Anthony sits in the armchair. Francis looks around at his surroundings.

FRANCIS
Nice place you have here.

ANTHONY
Thanks. My nan is always on my case to keep it tidy. I do what I can y'know, but she'll always find something I missed.

Francis picks up a picture from the table by the side of the sofa.

FRANCIS
Is this your mum?

DEAD STAGE

ANTHONY
Yeah. When she was well.

FRANCIS
She's pretty.

Francis places the photograph back onto the table.

Beat.

FRANCIS
So, I'm guessing you have questions?

ANTHONY
Some. I dunno. I had a list, but I threw it away. Seemed kinda stupid at the time.

FRANCIS
You can ask anything, no matter how stupid you think it is.

Beat.

ANTHONY
What's he like? Was he a good dad? Did he take you to the football or anything like that?

FRANCIS
Well, that's not an easy question to answer. He hated football. He used to go as a youngster purely to get into fights. When they clamped down on that and made supporters actually watch the game, he quickly lost interest. So no, he didn't take us to the football.

ANTHONY
That's a shame. That's what I wanna do with my kid.

FRANCIS
You have a child?

ANTHONY
No. I meant when I'm older. I've got university to sort first, that and getting a girlfriend. I can't really be bothered with all of that at the moment though. Figure I'll have time for that later.

FRANCIS
You've your head screwed on.
(joking)
You sure Cedric's your dad?

ANTHONY
(matter of fact)
Yes. I'm sure.

Beat.

FRANCIS
So, what do you want to study at University?

ANTHONY
Art. Hopefully, if my grades will get me in.

FRANCIS
Is that what you want to do? Be an artist?

DEAD STAGE

ANTHONY
I dunno. Perhaps. I think there's too much pressure put on people my age to decide though. Who knows what they want to do with the rest of their lives at seventeen?
Most of us don't even know what to do with the rest of the day!

Francis smiles.

FRANCIS
True.

Beat.

ANTHONY
So, tell me about him.

FRANCIS
I'm not sure what to say to be honest. He's old-fashioned, stubborn . . . his heart is in the right place—

ANTHONY
You think?

FRANCIS
Sorry. That must be hard to hear after what he did.

ANTHONY
It is.

Beat.

ANTHONY
He could have looked us up y'know? Mum talked about him from time to time. I got the feeling they never sorted things properly. People are kinda stupid like that.

FRANCIS
He said he thought about you every day.

ANTHONY
That doesn't help.

Beat.

FRANCIS
Saul say's hi.

ANTHONY
He's younger than you, right?

FRANCIS
Yeah, by four years. He'll want to meet you . . . he just needs a bit of time to get used to it all.

ANTHONY
OK. I get that.

FRANCIS
You'll like Saul. He's a bit of a loose cannon sometimes, but he's a good man.

Beat.

DEAD STAGE

ANTHONY
Crazy to think I've two half-brothers. Since mum died I've felt so alone.

FRANCIS
So you've no one else? No other brothers or sisters?

ANTHONY
Not that I know of! Have I?

FRANCIS
No. Just Saul and I.

Beat.

FRANCIS
So, is that why you tried to find your dad?

ANTHONY
I dunno. Maybe. It's not like I needed him or anything. My grandparents are great. I just . . . I just needed to find out where I came from so that I could adjust. Sounds kinda stupid to you, I'm guessing. But for so many years it was just me and mum. Now that she's gone, I need to find my place in the world. I think it's important to know where you come from. I'd have looked to find him at some point. I guess this just hurried things along.

FRANCIS
I understand. As best I can anyway. I'll do what I can to support you. You are family.

ANTHONY
Thanks.

FRANCIS
My kids will want to meet their new uncle too.

ANTHONY
I'm an uncle?

FRANCIS
Yes, you are. To two of Hell's finest!

ANTHONY
I'll bet they aren't that bad!

FRANCIS
No, you're right. They aren't.

ANTHONY
I'd like that, to meet them I mean. Just not yet. That OK?

FRANCIS
Yeah, of course.

Beat.

FRANCIS
There's something I need to inform you of.

ANTHONY
OK, may as well as the revelations keep on coming!

DEAD STAGE

FRANCIS
Cedric... he's not well. He is in the hospital. Massive heart attack. We aren't sure how long he's got.

ANTHONY
Oh.

FRANCIS
It's why I insisted on seeing you so soon. I wouldn't be much of a man if I wasn't straight with you. I know this won't be easy, but if there's anything you want to know from him, you'll need to see him soon.

ANTHONY
OK. I-I don't know. I always thought I'd have time.

FRANCIS
We always think that we do, but we can never be certain of how much.

Beat.

ANTHONY
I'll talk to my grandparents.

FRANCIS
OK. You've got my number. If you want to visit him, and you don't have to... I'm just telling you the situation as it is... then give me a call.

Anthony nods.

> ANTHONY
> OK.

Francis stands.

> FRANCIS
> I'll get out of your way. You gonna be OK?

Anthony stands.

> ANTHONY
> Yeah. Yeah, I'll be OK.

Anthony leads Francis towards the exit.

> ANTHONY
> I'll be in touch. Just let me talk it out with Nan, yeah?

> FRANCIS
> Of course.

The two share an awkward embrace.

> FRANCIS
> Remember, I'll only be a phone call away, brother.

Anthony smiles.

> ANTHONY
> I will. Thanks.

EXIT FRANCIS

DEAD STAGE

Anthony returns to his seat and places his face into his hands.

BLACKOUT.

SCENE 3

At Rise: Cedric is lying in a hospital bed, watching television. The room is sparse. There are no cards or flowers. The steady rhythm of the ECG is audible throughout.

ENTER ANTHONY

CEDRIC
I think you've got the wrong room, fella.

Anthony approaches Cedric's bed and tentatively stands by his side.

Cedric looks closely at the boy.

CEDRIC
You have your mother's eyes.

Cedric clicks the television off.

ANTHONY
She used to say I had your nose. I don't see it.

CEDRIC
No, well you wouldn't, I guess.

Beat.

CEDRIC
Pull up a chair, you are making me nervous hovering

like that. Not sure if you are gonna hug me or smother me.

Anthony sits.

> ANTHONY
> I'm not gonna do either.

> CEDRIC
> OK. I'll rest easy then.

Beat.

> CEDRIC
> Did Francis tell you I was here?

> ANTHONY
> Yeah, he did.

> CEDRIC
> Is he here? I could do with having a word with him. It's not on dropping a surprise like this on a sick man.

> ANTHONY
> I came on my own.

> CEDRIC
> Oh.

Beat.

CEDRIC
Francis said you'd been looking for me?

ANTHONY
I had been, yes.

CEDRIC
Looks like you found me.

ANTHONY
Looks like it. You know, I had an idea, growing up, as to what you'd be like in my head. I think I needed that . . . to give you a face, a job, a personality . . . and now . . .

CEDRIC
I'm guessing this wasn't what you pictured?

ANTHONY
No. You had more hair.

They both smile.

CEDRIC
I don't know what to tell you, kid.

ANTHONY
I don't know what to ask.
Beat.

CEDRIC
Tell me about your mum, did she have a good run? Was she happy?

DEAD STAGE

ANTHONY
She was. I think so anyway. She had a few men come and go. None really stuck around for long. Probably because she had me.

CEDRIC
They treat you OK? Did you ever want for anything?

ANTHONY
I never really got to know any of them. If you mean did we have money, we got by. You could have helped, but she never wanted to bother you about it. I hated that.

CEDRIC
What do you mean?

ANTHONY
She scraped together everything she could so that she could provide for me. She worked two jobs and some days I'd not see her. I wanted to help but I couldn't. The other dads at school, even if they weren't at home, they still helped out. Most of them anyway. You didn't.

CEDRIC
No. I didn't.

ANTHONY
I want to know why?

CEDRIC
I couldn't. Didn't seem right somehow. You weren't mine.

ANTHONY
I'm your son!

CEDRIC
Yes, but, I never saw you. Not even when you were born. Your mum and I, we didn't speak. She was a proud woman and she didn't ask. If I'd turned up with a pocket full of cash she'd have told me to leave and left me with a flea in my ear.

ANTHONY
It's not all about the money. You could have still been there in other ways.

CEDRIC
I couldn't.

ANTHONY
You didn't even try.

CEDRIC
I did.

ANTHONY
No, you didn't. You carried on as though I never existed and expected me to do the same.

CEDRIC
It wasn't like that. I thought about you.

ANTHONY
But you didn't do anything about it. Fact is, I grew up

DEAD STAGE

without a dad and I'm only getting to meet you on your death bed. That's pretty shitty if you ask me.

CEDRIC
Deathbed huh? The docs tell you something I should know?

ANTHONY
Stop changing the subject! Shit . . . I didn't know what to expect, but I didn't expect this! It's not a joking matter.

CEDRIC
Your mum let you talk like that?

ANTHONY
No, but she isn't here.

Beat.

CEDRIC
Look, I know I'm not what you'd hope, and I know I messed up with you, but you seem a bright kid. Trust me, you don't want me in your life ruining things. I messed up with Francis and Saul too, ask them, they'll say so.

ANTHONY
I know you aren't perfect. As a kid, I probably imagined all sorts, like you were a racing driver or a Hollywood stuntman, but I grew up and realized people are fucked up. We all have our faults, I get that. I can't change the past and I don't want an

apology because what is that gonna change? I just wanted to see my dad.

Beat.

CEDRIC
I'm sorry son. I should've done more . . . for you and your mother. I'm an idiot. I made a mess of it all.

ANTHONY
I just said I don't want an apology—

CEDRIC
Well, it needed to be said anyway. Sometimes things just need saying so that you can get past them and onto the real meat of what you wanna say.

ANTHONY
And what's that?

CEDRIC
When I get out of here, when I'm on my feet again, I'll be there. I can't make the past right, and I'll probably still make a mess of things, but I want to get to know my son.

Beat.

CEDRIC
That sound OK?

Anthony nods.

DEAD STAGE

ANTHONY
Yeah. OK. At my pace though.

CEDRIC
Sure. Just don't leave it too long if the doctor did say I was on my way out to you?

Beat.

CEDRIC
You got your mother's chin too.

ANTHONY
Yeah, I know. I hate it.

CEDRIC
Don't.

Beat.

Anthony glances at his watch.

ANTHONY
I better go.

CEDRIC
OK . . . thanks for coming in. I'll let you know when I'm out. Probably get Francis to call you or something?

ANTHONY
OK.

Anthony stands.

> ANTHONY
> Get well soon, yeah?

> CEDRIC
> I will.

Anthony extends his hand. Cedric shakes it.

> ANTHONY
> Catch up with you soon.

Cedric nods.

EXIT ANTHONY

Cedric settles back to watch television. He is smiling.

The volume of the ECG rises as the stage slowly begins to darken.

Once the stage is completely dark the ECG flat lines.

> FADE TO BLACK.
> END.

THE RELEASE OF THEODORE MARLOW

Genre: Drama
Length: Approx. 80 minutes
Acts: Three
Cast: 6 x male 2 x female

Synopsis: Victorian England. A gothic chiller which details the complicated relationships between troubled dreamer Theodore, his estranged wife Elsie, and their respective lovers.

Author's note: This was the first full-length piece that I wrote. I originally began with the ending, intending it to be a short piece. However, after much feedback, I then worked backwards and produced a fuller piece, further detailing the story of Theo's journey. It was the only piece I wrote in such a manner, not through choice, but necessity!

The piece was performed and recorded in full by *Shoestring Theatre*, San Francisco, and was broadcast in two parts across the USA during January, 2016.

The Release of Theodore Marlow is published by *Off The Wall Plays*.

It has been described as a complex piece to stage, due to its many short scenes and a high number of locations. I still hold out that one day I shall see it performed on stage.

DAN WEATHERER

Cast of Characters
Theodore Marlow
Rebecca Evans
Oliver Hampford
Bailey Jameson
Elsie Marlow
Percival Harding
Dr Forster
Constable Lowry

ACT 1

ACT 1-1

The Dining Room—Evening.

At Rise: A dimly lit dining room. THEODORE MARLOW (mid-thirties and well dressed in Victorian attire) sits to the left of a long dining table and ELSIE MARLOW (late twenties, pretty, well dressed) sits to the right. A meal is set before them as is an assortment of cutlery. Each has a small hand bell easily within reach. A decanter of wine sits in the middle of the table.

Elsie and Theo are eating.

ELSIE
Heavens, I swear I have not had the time to draw breath today. I took tea with Lady Green and we spent the afternoon discussing the antics of her younger sister. Honestly, she is positively dreadful in her behaviour, a lady she is most certainly not!

Theodore does not respond.

ELSIE
May I inquire as to your day?

THEODORE
You may, but you will no doubt find my exploits tiresome.

DAN WEATHERER

ELSIE
Why do you say that?

THEODORE
Because my dear it did not involve lewdness or laughter at the expense of others.

ELSIE
Oh come now, it is human nature to have an interest in the activities of others.

THEODORE
Yes, I am all too aware of your interest in others and to where it may lead.

Elsie slams her cutlery down.

ELSIE
Meaning what exactly?

Theodore does not answer. Elsie resumes eating.

ELSIE
I forgot what a joy dining with you had become. Do you not remember how we would set the world to rights over a fine meal back when we were courting?

THEODORE
(sighing)
I am afraid I must not, I recall no such conversation, intellectual or otherwise whilst you have a full plate under your nose.

DEAD STAGE

ELSIE
(ignoring his insult)
Have I not told you about Lady Forshaw's latest misdemeanour? Oh, it's positively ghastly! How Lord Forshaw is able to live with that woman, I shall never understand!

THEODORE
No, you have not and I beg that you go no further. I have no time for the sordid details of Lady Forshaw's latest affairs and in answer to your question— assuming it was not rhetorical, Lord Forshaw is able to live with that vile woman because he is unaware of the majority of her exploits.

Elsie places her cutlery neatly onto her plate and reaches for her glass of wine. She finishes it in one gulp.

ELSIE
Well, that may be so but I was merely trying to partake in the art of casual conversation. Apparently, it's the done thing at dinner? Trying to engage you further is becoming a frightful bore!

THEODORE
Apologies. My thoughts are elsewhere for I have much to ponder.

ELSIE
Oh, not this again! Theodore, you always were a dreamer, but that is all you shall ever be! How many times must we discuss this? Now is the time of the

achiever and I for one am glad! If we did little but look to the stars, our days would be spent with crooked necks!

Elsie places her empty glass onto the table.

ELSIE
(shouting)
Boy! Boy! My glass is empty. Boy!

THEODORE
(sighing)
His name is Bailey, this much I have told you many times and for the sake of both of our ears, please use the bell to call for his attention.

ELSIE
I have no time to learn the names of our help and that you well know!

Elsie picks up the bell and begins to ring it.

THEODORE
He has been with us for many years.

ELSIE
Well, he won't be with us for much longer if he keeps me waiting! Has he got lead in his shoes?

BAILEY enters.

BAILEY
Yes, my lady?

DEAD STAGE

Elsie points to her empty glass.

ELSIE
It's about time!

Bailey fills Elsie's glass.

Bailey places the wine decanter back onto the table and awaits his next order.

THEODORE
Thank you, Bailey, that will be all.

Bailey nods and leaves the room.

ELSIE
You do know that you don't need to thank the help? Payment is thanks enough for the likes of them.

THEODORE
That is where you and I differ in our view of the world, my dear. I know that I am not required to thank Bailey but I feel it only right to do so.

Elsie drinks her wine.

ELSIE
I do wonder what I ever saw in you, we are worlds apart you and I.

THEODORE
You mean aside from my wealth, good standing and

promising career? Come now, you saw exactly what you wished to see.

ELSIE
I also saw a man, kind and noble . . . at least I thought that I had.

THEODORE
You did. Once.

Theodore continues his meal in silence.

Bailey knocks on the door and enters the room.

BAILEY
Begging your pardon sir, Mr Hampford is here to see you.

Theodore places his cutlery to one side and wipes his mouth with a napkin.

THEODORE
Ah, excellent. I was beginning to worry that Oli had dropped off the face of the earth! Send him to my quarters, I shall follow in a moment.

BAILEY
Yes, sir.

Bailey exits the room. Theodore stands in readiness to leave.

DEAD STAGE

ELSIE
Are you not going to invite him to join us?

THEODORE
Not tonight.

ELSIE
Oh, I had wished to say hello; Oli is such a dear.

THEODORE
I have business to discuss and I would prefer to get right to the heart of the matter in private.

ELSIE
I see. So you are just going to leave your darling wife to drink alone?

THEODORE
That seems to be the sum of it, yes. You do tend to enjoy your drink more when I am not amongst your company.

ELSIE
Meaning?

THEODORE
I had Bailey update me on our wine stock. It has depleted rapidly these past few months.

ELSIE
Humph. What else would you have me do? A girl needs to entertain herself!

THEODORE
Yes, so I keep hearing. Excuse me, I shall not keep Oliver waiting.

Theodore leaves the room. Elsie helps herself to another glass of wine.

ELSIE
(shouting)
Boy! Boy!

Bailey enters the room.

BAILEY
Yes, my lady?

ELSIE
Fetch another bottle. My good husband has taken it upon himself to leave me to my own amusement, I fear I shall be here a while.

BAILEY
Yes, my lady.

Bailey turns to leave.

ELSIE
Oh-boy?

BAILEY
Yes?

DEAD STAGE

ELSIE
Better if you bring a few.

Bailey leaves the room. Elsie continues to drink alone. She empties her glass and holds it up to the light. She catches her reflection in the glass.

ELSIE
Ah, there you are. Whatever happened to your spirit? Your vigour? You look so tired now . . . so very tired. It's because he knows, and though I shall never admit it, not even in my dying breath, I cannot lie to myself. What was I to do? Drown amongst the misery of a loveless marriage? Whilst it is true that he has extended every kindness to me I see that my infidelity although unspoken, erodes our union.

Bailey enters the room. He sees that Elsie is talking and holds his position in the shadows.

ELSIE
He hurts because of me but he can never know. I have standing, I have influence and these things mean more to me than a wounded ego. He could have me again if he so wished, I'd lay with him and all would be forgotten. Oh, how I am angry at that cursed man! If only he reached out now and again if only he would trust enough to let me in! Perhaps then my eye would never have wandered . . .

Elsie notices Bailey standing in the shadows.

ELSIE
(angry)
You! Boy! How much did you hear just now?

BAILEY
(panicked)
Not a word my lady—not a word a swear!

ELSIE
Liar!

Elsie throws the empty wine glass at Bailey.

ELSIE
Begone with you boy! Speak not of this to my husband or I shall have you flogged to within an inch of your life!

Bailey places the wine on the table and quickly leaves.

Elsie rises from her seat and fetches Theo's glass for herself.

ELSIE
Insolent boy, I'd have him out was it my decision to make.

Elsie takes her seat and resumes her drinking.

FADE TO BLACK.

ACT 1-2

Theodore's Chambers—evening.

MASTER BEDROOM. OLIVER is standing and looking out of the window. There is a table with two chairs to the right of a grand four-poster bed. A decanter of Scotch sits upon the table with two empty glasses.

Enter Theodore.

THEODORE
Dreadfully sorry for the wait, I made haste my escape as best I could.

Oliver turns to face his friend.

OLIVER
Not at all, I was quite content here watching two crows have at it over a worm. I find amusement in the most trite of situations. I must ask, why are we reduced to meeting in your chambers? I much prefer the library myself, for the ease of access to your Scotch as much as any book, mind!

THEODORE
I fear this to be the one room in which she dares not tread.

Theodore motions towards the table.

THEODORE
As you can see, I took the liberty.

OLIVER
Are things between you so bad?

THEODORE
On the contrary! I am glad that she avoids my chambers! I sleep more soundly knowing that she is residing in another wing.

OLIVER
I really do not understand you, dear friend. You have wealth beyond measure, status that is unparalleled and a darling wife who is blessed with both youth and beauty.

THEODORE
It would seem that I have much to be envious of I imagine, especially regarding Elsie. Yet she is both beautiful and terrible in equal measure and I am rapidly becoming disillusioned with my place beside her.

Oliver takes a seat

OLIVER
Really? I have always thought of you as happily in love!

Theodore joins Oliver and pours him a drink

DEAD STAGE

THEODORE
Not so. With every passing day, my outlook darkens. The future for Elsie and I is uncertain. I know not how to describe my temperament other than I feel that a good portion of myself is missing. Did I ever feel complete? That I cannot say. I believe that as a man grows to know himself, he faces stark truths that he either acknowledges and makes an effort to address, or buries deep in some forgotten part of his mind in the vain hope that they will one-day fade to nothing. I have buried mine for too long and yet they trouble me still. I must admit that change needs to be made and soon. Alas, I suspect Elsie has already acted upon her unhappiness.

OLIVER
How do you mean and what changes are you contemplating? I must say this is all news to me!

Theodore gets up from the table and walks towards the window.

THEODORE
The very gravest. As for Elsie, though I cannot say for certain . . . I fear she has bedded with another.

Oliver joins Theodore.

OLIVER
You suspect?

THEODORE
I do, though it may well be my predicament which

clouds my judgment so I shall discount it. I believe that I must act on what I know for certain.

OLIVER
Promise me that you will not make any decision in haste? There is your standing to consider—your fall from grace will be sharp and painful should you decide to—

Theodore shakes his head.

THEODORE
I care not for the wagging of tongues. Let them fill their engagements with talk of my fortunes if they must. Whatever course of action I shall decide upon will be the one which suits Elsie and I. Of course, she may not see it that way but I shall endeavour to ease her pain the best I can.

OLIVER
Well, at least permit me to take your mind away from such troublesome thoughts. Sir Gathwell is holding a small gathering tonight, of which I am invited. You shall also join me. It will do you the world of good to be away from this place and amongst the company of decent people for a change. What say you?

THEODORE
I am in no mood to socialize. I would be poor company.

OLIVER
Then that is settled. Be sure to bring your current

DEAD STAGE

humour, you shall make me appear all the more charming and desirable! I shall see you at eight.

Oliver leaves the room. Theodore finishes his drink by the window.

THEODORE
Very well, eight it shall be.

FADE TO BLACK.

ACT 1-3

Gathwell's Super—evening.

Dining room: Theodore and Oliver sit around a crowded table.

OLIVER
Tell me you feel much better drinking wine that has cost you nothing, in the splendour of Gathwell's gaudy mansion?

Theodore takes a sip of his wine.

THEODORE
It will take more than a few glasses of second-rate wine to lift my spirits tonight friend.

OLIVER
Remind me why I insisted on your company again?

THEODORE
I am at a loss as to an answer.

PERCIVAL HARDING and REBECCA EVANS enter the room Percival notices Oliver and catches his eye. Percival approaches Theodore and Oliver with Rebecca following behind.

OLIVER
Oh, good lord, I curse my wandering eye! Brace yourself for we are about to be joined by an insufferable simpleton!

DEAD STAGE

PERCIVAL
Ah, good evening gentlemen, such a pleasant evening wouldn't you say?

Percival and Oliver stand and shake hands.

OLIVER
Indeed it is, Percy, isn't it? How wonderful to see you again.

PERCIVAL
Lord Harding if you would, only my mother calls me by my Christian name. I shall be glad when the witch finally gives up the ghost so that I will no longer have to suffer that cursed word ever again!

REBECCA
I find it a lovely name, my Lord.

Upon hearing Rebecca's voice, Theodore's attention is drawn from his wine glass and onto her.

PERCIVAL
Yes, well, the things that you find appealing could fill an entire library, my dear! I pay your opinion little attention.

OLIVER
And who is this delightful young lady? I have not yet had the pleasure.

PERCIVAL
(laughing)

Nor shall you! This is Lady Rebecca Evans. She and I are to be wed in the autumn. Her father owns a lavish estate beyond the border, has a few mountains dotted about the place but beggars can't be choosers!

REBECCA

(sheepish)

No, my Lord.

OLIVER

Lovely to meet you, Miss Evans.

Theodore approaches Rebecca, his eyes are locked with hers. He takes her by the hand before planting a small, delicate kiss upon it.

THEODORE

My lady, permit me to introduce myself, I am Theodore Marlow and it is an honour to make your acquaintance.

REBECCA

(blushes)

Why, thank you, Sir.

THEODORE

Theodore. Please.

PERCIVAL

(interrupting)

Yes, well, please excuse us, we have drinks with Sir Gathwell waiting.

DEAD STAGE

Rebecca and Theodore's eyes are locked together.

REBECCA
Must I attend? You do know that I find Sir Gathwell a frightful bore!

PERCIVAL
(angry)
You shall do as you are bid woman.

THEODORE
Permit me if I may, I would be happy to entertain the good lady whilst you talk business with Sir Gathwell. After all, a man's affairs should be his and his alone.

PERCIVAL
(cautiously)
Well . . . I suppose you have a point. Rebecca, you are to remain here with . . .

THEODORE
Theodore.

PERCIVAL
Yes, you are to remain here with him. I will not hasten my business but I shall not be absent for long either.

Percival nods at Theodore and Oliver before disappearing off stage.

OLIVER
What a complete and utter Oaf—apologies my lady, I meant no offence.

REBECCA
None taken. His manner can be overbearing at times but his heart is . . . well, there are worse men than he in this world.

THEODORE
I don't doubt that at all. However, as you are in my care and it is my duty to entertain you. Oliver, if you would excuse us?

Rebecca smiles. Oliver nods politely and exits the stage.

Theodore takes Rebecca's hand and seats her next to him.

THEODORE
I have something to confess.

REBECCA
Oh? We have only just met; you are either awfully trusting or you are carrying around an abundance of guilt!

Theodore laughs.

THEODORE
Trusting perhaps, but I must say this for I know not if I shall see you again. When our eyes first met I felt

DEAD STAGE

a warmth within my chest that I have never felt before.
It feels almost like the explosion of a thousand suns.
It remains still.

REBECCA
You did? What do you suppose it could mean? Did you eat the shellfish? I hear they can lead to an all manner of sensations if not adequately prepared!

Theodore laughs again.

THEODORE
No, my dear, though I know that you tease. I don't know how to describe it other than you seem awfully familiar to me, your eyes—I have gazed into them before.

Rebecca looks away. She is embarrassed.

THEODORE
What is it? Have I said too much? I apologize, my emotions run deep and at times can get the better of me.

REBECCA
No, it's not that. I thought I would feel foolish admitting this but I too have that same sensation in my bosom. It is almost as though a hundred butterflies decided to take flight all at once.

THEODORE
It is.

REBECCA
I have a confession too. I never intended to attend drinks with Percy and Gathwell. I was hoping that I could arrange further time in your company. Thank you for speaking up for me.

THEODORE
Not at all, there was something within me that was not ready to let you disappear, I almost felt as though my actions were not my own! Tell me, have we met before? I must know!

REBECCA
We have not, yet your touch, your voice, your eyes, I know you but from where I cannot say.

The music ends and the dancers stop and applaud. Percival enters the stage.

REBECCA
I'm afraid that I must go, it looks as though his business is complete. Trust his return to mark the onset of another of my painful heads. Thank you for your company.

Rebecca takes a tablet from her purse and stands as to leave.

THEODORE
Please, give me one more moment of your time for if I do not speak now, regret shall haunt me for the remainder of my days. I must see you again, I must.

DEAD STAGE

REBECCA
How? I-I cannot, I am arranged to marry Percy.

THEODORE
Do you love him?

Rebecca shies away from this question.

REBECCA
It matters not, the date is set.

THEODORE
Of that, I am aware but hear me out. Do you know Thistlewood Grove? It is located on the northern edge of the city?

REBECCA
I do?

THEODORE
There is a lake situated within it, I shall be there every day for the next two weeks at one o'clock in the afternoon. If you wish to pursue this meeting further, if you feel that fate has placed us together this night for a reason, then please . . . meet me there.

PERCIVAL
(shouting)
Rebecca! Come now, I require your presence!

REBECCA
I-I must go, I'm sorry.

THEODORE
Please. One o'clock by the lake in Thistlewood Grove.

Rebecca goes to join Percival on the edge of the dance floor. Theodore remains alone. Rebecca gives him one last longing look before disappearing off stage with Percival. Oliver joins Theodore in the centre of the dance floor.

OLIVER
Oh don't look so fearful, I'm not here to ask for the next dance! I do however want to know what the devil you are playing at?

THEODORE
(absently)
How do you mean?

OLIVER
How do I—what you just did was most out of character. I would blame the wine but you have hardly touched a drop!

THEODORE
Oli, do you believe in true love?

OLIVER
Do I what?

THEODORE
I know it sounds completely preposterous but Rebecca, I know her and I have loved her, I am sure of it.

DEAD STAGE

OLIVER
Well, one brunette looks much the same as another if you ask me.

THEODORE
Oh, Oli dear boy, you really have no idea what I am talking about, do you?

OLIVER
I am beginning to have my doubts as to what that good lady wife of yours has done to your sanity . . . but, tonight was the first time that I have seen you smile in an age and I cannot begrudge you that no matter how absurd your reasoning. By the way, what did you say to her when she left? Percival looked most aggrieved.

THEODORE
I asked if she would consider meeting me again.

OLIVER
You asked the fiancé of Percival Harding whether she would be prepared to meet you in secret? My word, you really have gone up in my estimation tonight old chap!

THEODORE
I felt compelled to for I am not convinced fate is yet finished with she and I.

FADE TO BLACK.

ACT 1-4

Theodore's Chambers—afternoon

Theodore is gazing out of the window whilst Bailey busies himself making the bed etc.

BAILEY
Forgive my intrusion Sir but are you feeling well?

THEODORE
(After a pause)
I am, Bailey.

BAILEY
If I may be so bold I do not agree. I have served you for many years and one grows attuned to the mood of the house and its occupants. Lately, you appear most distant, more so than usual. So if I may ask again, are you feeling well?

Theodore turns towards Bailey.

THEODORE
I am sorry, you deserve an honest answer and I feel compelled to give it. I am not sick but I am missing something, missing someone in my life. I had the merest taste of happiness several nights ago and it has left an enduring impression upon my soul.

BAILEY
Who was she, Sir?

DEAD STAGE

THEODORE
(laughing)
You are right not to assume it was Lady Marlow!

BAILEY
I have seen the cruel way with which her words cut you. I could not pardon her words quite so easily.

THEODORE
It is true that at one time her remarks would wound my spirit, but as the years have passed I gradually became numb to her venomous outbursts. Really, you need not worry.

BAILEY
So who is she? Who is the lady that has captured your thoughts?

THEODORE
It matters not. She is betrothed to another.

BAILEY
Is she the reason for your daily excursions?

THEODORE
Bailey, my boy, in any other house your curious tongue would lead you to a sound scolding!

BAILEY
I'm sorry sir.

Theodore turns back to the window.

THEODORE
No, Bailey, I am sorry. You were merely showing concern for my well-being, and I have few others around me that do. Her name is Rebecca Evans and she is to wed Percival Harding. The reason for my frequent absence is I requested she meet me in Thistlewood Grove should she have any desire to pursue our connection further.

BAILEY
Connection? It was my understanding that you had only met her the once?

THEODORE
You understand correctly yet the bond between us was almost tangible.

Bailey stops what he is doing. Theodore turns to face him and ushers him to take a seat upon the bed.

BAILEY
Please, go on.

THEODORE
When our eyes met, it was as though every doubt that I had about myself and the direction that my life was taking, every worry that I ever had, they all vanished and everything made complete sense. It was a moment of absolute clarity.

BAILEY
I see. No wonder your heart hangs heavy.

DEAD STAGE

THEODORE
Indeed.

BAILEY
Do you think that you will see her again?

THEODORE
I fear not. The window in which I set to meet has expired. It is clear to me that she has made her choice.

BAILEY
Permit me if I may, but I have something that I need to discuss with you?

THEODORE
Is that so?

BAILEY
Indeed, though am not sure as to whether now is the time—

THEODORE
Out with it boy! You know that you and I can discuss all but the most personal of matters. When your father trusted me with your care you became far more than a manservant, you know I look upon you as a son.

Bailey looks to the floor.

BAILEY
Thank you, you have extended every kindness to me

but I'm afraid this would be considered a personal matter.

THEODORE
I can see the weight upon your shoulders. Out with it.

BAILEY
Several nights back I interrupted Lady Marlow as she was thinking aloud. She was speaking of an act that she had committed—

THEODORE
(interrupting)
There is no need to continue.

Theodore and Bailey are silent for a moment.

THEODORE
I suspected as such. It seems that the stars have aligned dear boy.

BAILEY
How do you mean?

THEODORE
One encounters many signs upon his journey, it is up to he whether he chooses to follow them.

BAILEY
So what will you do now?

THEODORE
I do so hope that is the last of your questions today?

DEAD STAGE

Bailey nods.

THEODORE
Good—As for now . . . I feel that a change of direction is in order. Bailey, do you happen to know with whom she has lay?

Bailey looks to the floor and shakes his head.

THEODORE
No matter, my mind is set.

FADE TO BLACK.

ACT 1-5

Dining Room—evening.

Lady Marlow is sitting at the dining table, eating her evening meal alone. Theodore enters the room with Bailey trailing behind.

ELSIE
Well, it's about bloody time! I was beginning to think that my wish had come true and I had, at last, become a widow! I have seen barely hide nor hair of you these past few weeks!

THEODORE
I see you have made your customary early start on the wine?

ELSIE
(ignoring his comment)
Honestly now, I don't know whether to rejoice or despair!

THEODORE
(annoyed)
Enough of your jibes Elsie! I have reached a conclusion regarding our marriage, in fact, I reached it many months ago yet much to my discredit, dithered over carrying out my intentions.

Elsie places her wine on the table and turns in her chair to face Theodore.

DEAD STAGE

ELSIE
Oh, a little entertainment to go with dinner, this shall be fun!

THEODORE
I shall not mix my words. I am leaving you, Elsie, I want a divorce.

ELSIE
(shocked)
You wish to leave me?

THEODORE
Do not even attempt to act as though this is not what you truly desire.

Elsie turns her attention to Bailey.

ELSIE
(spiteful)
He told you didn't he! That blasted boy opened his mouth when I told him not to!

THEODORE
Bailey has not uttered a word regarding your adultery, I am no fool, I suspected as such.

ELSIE
You know that should you ever air this in public I shall deny it. I have many who would rally around to defend my character. You, on the other hand, do not. Your solitude counts against you. It would be so much easier to besmirch the good name of Theodore Marlow.

THEODORE
Worry not for I intend never to discuss the matter beyond tonight.

Elsie claps her hands.

ELSIE
Good! I am glad that you can at least see the sense in my argument. I will take what's mine and more you know.

THEODORE
Have it. Have it all. Tis nothing but trinkets and furniture, it means nothing to me. The house too, it is yours. After all, it is filled with nought but stale air and bitter memories.

ELSIE
You mean you are just going to hand it all over to me and walk away? Your fortune . . . this house . . . everything?

THEODORE
Yes, it is all that you ever wanted anyway. It was never me; it was always what I had.

ELSIE
What about your name? What of your honour?

THEODORE
Do what you will. You shall either tarnish my name or you shall not.

DEAD STAGE

Elsie returns her attention to her meal.

ELSIE
(coldly)
Then I accept your decision. If you would kindly leave first thing in the morning.

THEODORE
I shall, Bailey—if you would accompany me to my chambers we shall make a start now.

Bailey leans close to his master.

BAILEY
(whispering)
Sir, I beg of you, take me with you. Don't leave me here to serve her.

Theodore acknowledges Bailey's request.

THEODORE
Bailey has requested that he remain with me.

ELSIE
That's fine so long as he prefers working for bread and water!

THEODORE
(To Bailey)
Fear not, I have enough set aside for us to start a humble house, though I cannot pay you what I once did.

BAILEY
Have no worries sir, If I remain here I will be out on the street within a week, of that I am certain!

ELSIE
Are you two still here?

THEODORE
I wish you well Elsie, I am sure you will be happy here now that I shall no longer be.

Theodore and Bailey leave the stage.

FADE TO BLACK.

ACT 1-6

Dining room—night

Oliver and Elsie enter the dining room.

OLIVER
Pardon my late intrusion, I just came by in order to—

ELSIE
He's not here.

OLIVER
I beg your pardon?

ELSIE
He's packed his things and gone. Taken that damned boy with him too.

OLIVER
I see, do you have any idea—

ELSIE
He knows, Oliver.

OLIVER
What do you mean? Did you tell him?

ELSIE
Of course I didn't tell him, that bloody boy did!

DAN WEATHERER

OLIVER
Does he know specifically?

ELSIE
You mean does he know that I lay with you? No, I think not. Though it may only be a matter of time.

OLIVER
This . . . this changes things. No one must know, you understand?

ELSIE
Of course, no one must know! I'll not have my name dragged through the mud! This estate, it belongs to me, to us if you wish it.

OLIVER
Now is not the time to dwell upon such details, we need to assure silence and I have an idea as to how.

FADE TO BLACK.

ACT 1-7

Living room, (Morning)—Theo's new home

There is a knocking upon the door. Bailey answers.

BAILEY
Yes?

REBECCA
I . . . well, I came to see if Theodore was at home?

BAILEY
And who might I say is calling?

REBECCA
Lady Rebecca Evans.

BAILEY
Ah—in that case, I must inform you that Sir Marlow is not in the best of minds at this time.

REBECCA
Oh . . . I do not wish to add to his woes. He requested to see me and only now have I managed to escape the attention of my wretched Fiancé.

BAILEY
Wretched you say? Do come in.

Bailey welcomes Rebecca into the Hallway and hurries to fetch Theodore.

THEODORE
(surprised)
Rebecca—what are you doing here?

REBECCA
I'm sorry, I feel that I must apologise. I couldn't get away before tonight and I feared it was too late? Your friend Oliver informed me of your current situation.

THEODORE
How kind of him. Too late for what?

REBECCA
Ever since we spoke I have thought of no-one but you. I feel foolish allowing myself to be swept up by my emotions but I know in my heart that marrying Percival is not what I truly desire.

THEODORE
(smiling)
Are you saying that you want to explore this connection further? I must warn you that I have left my wife and all of my worldly possessions behind. I have little to offer but the man I am.

REBECCA
That is more than I would ever need. I thought that I would be afraid leaving Percival and coming here, but in your presence, those fears turn to ash. I know

DEAD STAGE

not what the future holds but I want to experience it with you.

THEODORE
As do I with you.

Theodore takes Rebecca into his arms and they kiss.

FADE TO BLACK.

ACT 1-8

Theodore and Rebecca's home. Morning.

Living room: Theodore and Rebecca sit at the table as Bailey busies himself at the sink.

THEODORE
That will be all for now Bailey. Take the rest of the morning off but be sure to meet me in town at the agreed time.

Bailey finishes up at the sink.

BAILEY
Of course. Thank you, sir, M'lady. Good day to you both.

Bailey exits the kitchen.

REBECCA
He is a good man.

THEODORE
That he is, in service and in companionship.

REBECCA
You think highly of him?

THEODORE
I do. Though I pay him to aid us I consider him a friend. I would be honoured if he thought of I in the same way.

DEAD STAGE

REBECCA
I am sure that he does.

Rebecca leans across and kisses Theodore. Theodore holds her hand in his and rests them on the table.

THEODORE
I know this is not what you pictured when you came to me that night.

REBECCA
It matters not, I had no clear picture as such, only that I wanted to be with you. Nothing else mattered.

THEODORE
Even so, your happiness matters to me above all else.

REBECCA
Worry not for I am as happy as I can ever remember. It has been many years since I felt so at peace with the world.

THEODORE
Does it trouble you?

REBECCA
Does what trouble me?

THEODORE
What they say?

REBECCA
I don't listen. They cannot even begin to understand the love that we share. Emotions like these are to be savoured. I'll wager that none who felt this way would ever wish us to suffer apart.

THEODORE
This warms me.

REBECCA
Do their words trouble you, my love?

THEODORE
Not with you by my side. We have committed no sin. Our love is blessed and pure. I imagine that their tongues will grow weary and their attention shall shift soon enough. There shall come a time of tolerance and understanding, though it shall not be within our lifetime, this much I know to be true.

Rebecca kisses Theodore again.

REBECCA
The way you look at the world, the way you look at people . . . I find you intriguing.

THEODORE
I am glad that you do. Now If you will excuse me, I must prepare myself for the afternoons business.

Rebecca and Theodore rise from their seats and embrace.

DEAD STAGE

REBECCA
Of course. I do hope all goes well.

THEODORE
Worry not, my sweet.

They kiss one last time and Theodore leaves the kitchen.

FADE TO BLACK.

ACT 1-9

Living room: Rebecca is busying herself unseen off stage.

There is knock on the front door. Rebecca hurries onstage and answers.

REBECCA
Yes?

Elsie Marlow is standing in the doorway. She looks at Rebecca with distaste.

ELSIE
I take it that you are Theo's latest love?

REBECCA
And what business is it of yours?

Elsie pushes past Rebecca and enters the house. She takes a seat and waits for Rebecca to join her. Taken aback, Rebecca closes the door and takes the seat opposite Elsie.

ELSIE
It is my business whom my soon to be ex-husband decides to invite into his bed. Lest you forget that we are still married!

REBECCA
I am aware of that fact. Tell me, why are you here?

DEAD STAGE

ELSIE
(nervously)
To bring him this.

Elsie produces a small vial and places it on the table.

REBECCA
I shall make sure he receives it, thank you.

Rebecca stands up and prepares to show Elsie out.

ELSIE
Don't you want to know what it is?

REBECCA
I take it upon myself never to trouble in Theo's affairs. I'm sure that he will know what to do with it.

ELSIE
(laughing)
I find that highly doubtful, once he finds out it is from me I imagine he will throw it into the gutter! It is a medicinal formula, one concocted to treat the most severe of head pains. Has he told you about his head pains?

Rebecca does not reply.

ELSIE
Ah, I see. You still have much to learn of Theo, my dear. I pity you, your future is paved with much misery.

REBECCA
I hardly think so. Theo and I are very much in love.

ELSIE
Ha! As were he and I many years ago. How quickly he distanced himself from me, how often he left me wanting nothing more than a kind word and an acknowledgement of my existence!

Rebecca motions towards the door.

REBECCA
It will not be that way with us, now if you will excuse me, I have much to be getting on with.

ELSIE
Where is he anyway? And what of that cumbersome boy servant?

REBECCA
He and Bailey are in town attending to a business matter.

Elsie stands up and smiles.

ELSIE
Is that so? Likely you will find them both in the whorehouse, drunk as Lords!

REBECCA
(angry)
You have said your piece now if you would please excuse me.

DEAD STAGE

Elsie passes Rebecca and is about to leave.

ELSIE
You would be wise to get out whilst you still can. He will not have two pennies to rub together when I have finished with him . . . Oh yes, I know he has a small fortune which he imagines is out of my reach, but I have the very best counsel and I shall see all three of you in the gutter where you belong!

REBECCA
(shaken)
Good day to you Lady Marlow.

Rebecca slams the door on Elsie and begins to weep.

REBECCA
What an irksome woman! My head is spinning.

Rebecca sits and takes the vial.

REBECCA
I'm sure Theo won't mind If I take a little to soothe my aching head. Under the circumstances, I am positive that he will understand.

Rebecca takes a sip from the vial and pulls away in disgust.

REBECCA
Ugh! That is most unpleasant.

She places the vial back on the table and falls quickly ill.

FADE TO BLACK.

ACT 1-10

Living room: Theo and Bailey return from their business and find Rebecca lying on the floor.

THEODORE
I'd say that my finances are looking a great degree more secure than they were after that, wouldn't you agree, Bailey?

BAILEY
Indeed, I would, it was a most . . . Oh, my!

Theodore sees Rebecca on the floor and rushes to her aid.

THEODORE
(panicked)
Rebecca, my darling speak to me!

Theodore helps her to her feet but she is so weak that her legs buckle beneath her.

THEODORE
(angry)
Bailey! Help me support her.

Bailey assists and the two of them help Rebecca to her feet.

REBECCA
(confused)
Father? I'm sorry that I have not finished my chores.

THEODORE
Tell me what has happened my sweet?

Rebecca looks at Theodore. She is confused.

REBECCA
I couldn't find the dog, I'm sorry, I only turned my back for a moment, please don't beat me.

Theodore takes Rebecca into his arms. She begins to convulse.

THEODORE
Dammit! Bailey, fetch a Doctor. NOW!

Bailey exits the stage.

THEODORE
(upset)
I will take care of you my sweet. The Doctor is on his way. I know that you can hear me, he will be able to help.

Theodore carries Rebecca off stage.

FADE TO BLACK.

ACT 1-11

Dimly lit bedroom: DR FORSTER is taking Rebecca's pulse at her bedside. Theodore watches from the opposite side of the bed.

THEODORE
Doctor, do you have any idea what ails her?

Dr Forster shakes his head and packs his instruments into his bag.

DR. FORSTER.
A word if you please, away from the patient.

Dr Forster and Theodore move towards the bedroom door.

DR. FORSTER
I am gravely concerned. Her symptoms are unusual, Memory loss, extreme fatigue and convulsions . . . it pains me to say this but I suspect foul play?

THEODORE
(shocked)
What? How can this be so?

DR. FORSTER
Forgive me, perhaps misadventure then?

THEODORE
Damn it, man, get to the point—can you help her?

DR. FORSTER
I have given her the appropriate treatment but I confess that we may well have found her far too late. You see, I suspect that she has ingested the seeds of the Datura plant—her symptoms suggest as such.

THEODORE
How can this be so?

DR. FORSTER
I am not at liberty to say but I saw several such cases of symptoms the likes of these when I practised in the city. It was often used by whores to dull the senses of their customers before robbing them. In small doses, it results in fatigue and memory loss, however in larger doses . . .

THEODORE
(cautiously)
Go on . . . please

DR. FORSTER
I'm afraid it can lead to death.

THEODORE
(distraught)
Oh God no. Please tell me that is not so!

DR. FORSTER
I'm sorry, I have done all that I can. All we can do now is pray for her. Of course, the relevant authorities will need to be notified of my suspicions. I shall see myself out. Once again, I am deeply sorry.

DEAD STAGE

Dr Forster leaves the room. Theodore crosses to Rebecca's bedside and falls to his knees.

THEODORE
How? How can this be so? Darling, if you can hear me please, tell me how this happened!

REBECCA
(laboured)
I-I cannot say. Everything is so distant. I am tired now. So tired.

Rebecca passes out. Theodore buries his head in the bedsheets and begins to cry.

FADE TO BLACK.

ACT 1-12

Theodore is sitting by Rebecca's bedside. Bailey enters the room.

BAILEY
Sir, if I could just disturb you for a moment.

Theodore does not turn to acknowledge him.

THEODORE
What is it?

BAILEY
There is a young constable here to see you, he wishes to discuss Miss Rebecca's condition.

THEODORE
Tell him to leave. I shall not desert my beloved when she requires my attention the most—not even for a second.

BAILEY
Sir, he was quite insistent.

THEODORE
(angry)
As am I. Tell him to leave.

BAILEY
As you wish, sir.

DEAD STAGE

Bailey leaves the room. Theodore brushes a wisp of hair from Rebecca's forehead.

FADE TO BLACK.

ACT 1-13

Front room: CONSTABLE LOWRY stands waiting to question Theodore.

Bailey enters the room.

BAILEY
Forgive my master, he is torn in duty but decided that he shall not leave the side of his beloved.

CONSTABLE LOWRY
Not at all, it is to be expected under the circumstances. Perhaps you might be able to shed light upon this unpleasantness?

BAILEY
I can certainly try, though I was with Sir Marlow when he found Miss Evans and before that we were in town together.

CONSTABLE LOWRY
Yes, on business I presume.

BAILEY
Yes.

CONSTABLE LOWRY
Would you care to elaborate?

BAILEY
I'm not sure Sir Marlow would permit—

DEAD STAGE

CONSTABLE LOWRY
(interrupting)
Under the circumstances, I am sure that he would have little objection. Please.

BAILEY
Well, Sir Marlow was to be involved in a divorce. He had already passed the house and its contents to Lady Marlow alongside a good portion of his fortune might I add, all in order to smooth the separation process. Not wishing to leave himself destitute he had an amount of coin set aside for such an eventuality.

CONSTABLE LOWRY
I see. I imagine the business of separation is a costly one, both in terms of coin and dignity?

BAILEY
I couldn't possibly say having neither married nor divorced sir.

CONSTABLE LOWRY
Of course. How would you say Sir Marlow has handled the stress of the situation?

BAILEY
I'd say well. Very well in fact. He and Lady Evans are very happy together.

CONSTABLE LOWRY
I see, and how about Lady Marlow?

BAILEY
It would be hard to say. She is a very proud woman who fiercely guards her standing.

CONSTABLE LOWRY
Meaning what exactly? Would she feel it was threatened by Theodore's decision to leave her?

BAILEY
It is possible, however . . .

CONSTABLE LOWRY
Go on.

BAILEY
Well . . . before he left, Sir Marlow found out that Lady Elsie had committed adultery.

CONSTABLE LOWRY
Ah.

BAILEY
I must explain that he had suspected as much and the revelation seemed to hurt him little. Perhaps he felt that her admission justified his choice of action. However, Lady Elsie made him swear to never discuss the matter beyond that night.

CONSTABLE LOWRY
I see, I shall make a note of that. Thank you. Now onto more pressing matters. I have reason to believe that Miss Evans was poisoned. Would you have any idea how this could have occurred?

DEAD STAGE

Bailey reaches into his pocket.

BAILEY
I didn't mention this to Sir Marlow for fear of his reaction.

Bailey produces the vial that held the poison and was given to Rebecca by Elsie.

BAILEY
I found this shortly after Miss Evans was taken ill.

Bailey passes the vial to the Constable.

BAILEY
I have seen vials similar to this in Lady Marlow's quarters. Aside from her love of wine, she is fond of other substances that alter her state of mind. Sir Marlow was not aware of this fact, at least I think not.

CONSTABLE LOWRY
I see. You suspect that this came from Lady Marlow?

BAILEY
All I can say is that I have seen similar items in her possession. I can point you to her collection if you like?

CONSTABLE LOWRY
Thank you, you have been most helpful. Send my best regards to Sir Marlow and add that I hope Miss Rebecca makes a hasty recovery.

BAILEY
Of course.

Bailey shows the Constable out.

FADE TO BLACK.

ACT 1-14

Theodore is sitting by Rebecca's bedside. He is unshaven, dishevelled and visibly exhausted. His hand holds Rebecca's.

THEODORE
My love, I chanced upon you only recently, please do not leave me so soon. We have much to share together, you and I. I could not stand to be without you, you who have shown me so much about the nature of true love and of myself. I have little in the way of coin or even prospects, yet with you by my side I count myself as amongst the richest men alive!

Theodore begins to sob.

THEODORE
Oh God, show mercy upon her. She is too pure to suffer such an untimely fate.

Rebecca stirs. She opens her eyes and looks to Theodore.

REBECCA
My darling . . . you are with me still . . . I shall wait for you in the next life . . . I love—

Rebecca starts to convulse. Theodore tries to calm her.

                    THEODORE
(panicked)
          Rebecca! Darling no! Please!

(Shouting)
                    Bailey! Bailey!

Bailey hurriedly enters the room.

                    BAILEY
                  Yes, sir—oh!

                    THEODORE
              Fetch help at once! Go!

                    BAILEY
                  Of course!

Bailey leaves the room. Theodore continues to try to calm Rebecca but her convulsions continue.

                 FADE TO BLACK.

ACT 1-15

Hallway (Lady Marlow's residence). There is a knock on the door. Lady Marlow takes her time answering. The knocks grow more persistent.

CONSTABLE LOWRY
Good evening, my lady, I am awfully sorry to disturb you.

ELSIE
(shocked)
Constable! Well, I should think so! Unsettling a lady with such a violent knocking! To what do I owe this visit?

CONSTABLE LOWRY
May I come in?

ELSIE
(flustered)
Of course, please do.

Constable Lowry steps into the hallway. Elsie closes the door behind him and leads him into the sitting room. Lowry takes a seat.

ELSIE
May I pour you a drink?

CONSTABLE LOWRY
No, my lady, that won't be necessary.

ELSIE
I hope you will excuse me if I indulge? I have had the most troublesome of days.

Elsie pours herself a drink with her back to the constable.

CONSTABLE LOWRY
I can imagine that news of your husband's partner falling ill under suspicion of foul play could prove to be quite troublesome?

Elsie pauses in pouring her drink.

ELSIE
Really? Oh-I hadn't heard.

Elsie takes her half-filled glass and sits opposite the Constable.

CONSTABLE LOWRY
Tis a shady business. The attending physician is almost certain that Miss Evans was the victim of a poisoning.

ELSIE
(uneasy)
You-you, don't say. Well, that is just awful, isn't it?

Constable Lowry produces the vial from his pocket and places it upon the table.

DEAD STAGE

CONSTABLE LOWRY
It certainly is, especially when the poison was never meant for her in the first instance.

ELSIE
Wh-what. How could you know, that is an awfully large assumption!

CONSTABLE LOWRY
Does this look familiar to you Lady Marlow?

ELSIE
(flustered)
No-why should it?

Constable Lory rises from his seat and begins to pace around the room.

CONSTABLE LOWRY
Allow me if you will to explain the basic requirements for a successful investigation. You see a criminal act is very much a puzzle, and in order to solve a puzzle, you need to be able to understand its mechanics.

ELSIE
I-I don't follow.

CONSTABLE LOWRY
You will Lady Marlow. I have developed a theory . . . well a string of theories actually, and so far, they have never failed me in my work. Each criminal act contains four key components. The Motive, The

DAN WEATHERER

Means, The Execution and The Outcome. Understand these and you will understand not only the crime, but the criminal himself.

ELSIE
If you say so, I find all of this hard to follow.

CONSTABLE LOWRY
Of course you do, but the key to the success is to work backwards. So for example, in this particular case we have the poisoning and subsequent death of Rebecca Evans, a tragic turn of events indeed.

Constable Lowry fixes his attention upon Elsie.

Elsie takes a large sip of wine.

ELSIE
Death? Oh . . . how truly awful.

CONSTABLE LOWRY
Which leads me to my first deduction. The poison was never intended for Miss Evans.

ELSIE
What makes you say that?

CONSTABLE LOWRY
Simple, I start by examining the outcome. Firstly, Rebecca was well liked and of humble standing. She had no debts nor grievance save for her former Fiancé. I spoke to him earlier and he assured me that he was out of the country and only arrived back this

DEAD STAGE

morn. Of course, I checked his story and all seemed correct. Sir Marlow, on the other hand, had recently split from yourself. With the emotional burden aside, the financial aspects of such a decision must be vast. I began to think that perhaps Sir Marlow had fallen foul of a bad debt and that his failure to pay on time led to an attempt on his life?

ELSIE
Yes . . . yes that would make sense, he was always spending beyond his—

CONSTABLE LOWRY
Only that isn't the case now is it Lady Marlow? Your husband's financial affairs are in good order. I checked for myself.

ELSIE
Oh. I see. Well, that is good to know.

CONSTABLE LOWRY
Isn't it? So, if one can rule out money as a motive, one must assume the attempt on his life to be a crime of passion . . . Seeing as how Miss Evans and Sir Marlow were so much in love, the eyes of suspicion fall upon you . . . but we shall get to that shortly. If I may draw your attention back to this vial. I have it on good authority that if I were to search your quarters I'd find vials similar to this, vials containing an all manner of hallucinogenic substances. Therefore, not only do you have the ability to pass a harmful substance to your former husband granted by forced opportunity . . . let's say by visiting him at his home,

in this case, the execution . . . you have the means in which to acquire the poison. After all, it takes a specialist knowledge to concoct a potion of this ilk and I know that you already had the contacts in place. I am well aware of your fondness for peculiar medicines, even if your former husband was not.

ELSIE
I-I don't know what you mean. What are you implying?

CONSTABLE LOWRY
Come now, let us not drag this out. I can be back in the afternoon with several of my colleagues.

ELSIE
I can assure you that won't be necessary—

CONSTABLE LOWRY
(interrupting)
Good. Because that means you will tell me now that you meant the poison for your husband. How do I know this to be true? It's all about the motive, which in this case is simple. If you didn't wish him dead for financial gain, then what for? This leads me to believe that Sir Marlow knew of your infidelity and that you were afraid he would speak freely of it. You valued your position in high society enough to kill. You figured that his sudden death would quash the incessant interest in the breakup of your marriage and it would also guarantee that nobody outside of Sir Marlow, Bailey and yourself would ever know about your adultery. Bailey was never a threat, after

DEAD STAGE

all, who would believe the word of a servant boy? Public knowledge of your adultery would destroy your standing and shame you beyond measure. Poorly executed though it was, this was a crime of passion.

ELSIE
I-I did no such thing, I swear!

CONSTABLE LOWRY
Did you act alone or did your lover assist?

ELSIE
I shall never tell you his name.

CONSTABLE LOWRY
That is not what I asked.

ELSIE
I acted alone. There is no need to mention his name, he is innocent in all of this.

Constable Lowry stands up and gestures her to leave the house with him.

CONSTABLE LOWRY
Lady Marlow, if you please. We shall continue this discussion with my colleague in attendance.

Elsie places her glass on the table, straightens her dress and composes herself before leaving with the Constable.

FADE TO BLACK.

ACT 1-16

A dimly lit bedroom. evening. Torn curtains struggle to keep out the morning sun.

Theodore sits in a high backed chair next to a fireplace that burns with a blue flame. He appears dishevelled and distant. Rebecca is dressed in white and watches from the fringe of the stage, appearing and disappearing at random. Theo reacts to her presence throughout.

There is a knock on the door. The flame in the fireplace changes from blue to orange and the library lightens. Theodore turns his head away from the sound of the knocking and continues his brooding. The knocking intensifies.

THEODORE
(weary)
Leave me be.

BAILEY
(OFF)
But sir you must eat something!

THEODORE
I have no need for sustenance. Go, leave me to my misery.

Bailey enters the room carrying a tray of food and places it onto a small table that is littered with open books.

DEAD STAGE

BAILEY
I shall just leave this here for when you change your mind.

THEODORE
(angry)
Did you not hear me, boy? I asked that I be left alone, I have no desire for food, not now, not anytime. Take it and leave . . . leave for a while. Take a trip to see your sister but go and go now.

Bailey leaves the food on the table and exits the library. The flame in the fireplace changes back to blue and the library darkens a little.

THEODORE
Blasted boy! Why do I even pay him when he insists upon disobeying me at every turn? I really should look for a more compliant butler.

There is another knock on the library door. Again the flame in the fireplace switches from blue to orange and the room lightens a little once more.

THEODORE
(angry)
What is it now? You defied me before, can you not leave me to my grief?

The door opens and Oliver enters the room.

OLIVER
I must say I don't know how poor Bailey puts up with

your frightful temper, I can only assume you pay him a handsome wage!

THEODORE
That I do—more fool me. I pay him to keep the likes of you away from my door. I am not good company at present and he of all people knows this to be true.

Oliver takes a small stool and positions it near to where Theodore is sitting.

OLIVER
He is worried about you, as am I in fact. It's been three weeks since you set foot outside of this room.

THEODORE
(absently)
Has it? Only three? I feel like I have spent most of my life mourning within these four walls.

OLIVER
It's not healthy old chap. You need to find your feet and get back into the swing of things.

THEODORE
How can I without her? Without her, I am but a shadow of the man I once was.

OLIVER
Come now . . .

DEAD STAGE

THEODORE
(interrupting)
Come now what? Rebecca shall not be brushed aside and forgotten as one might care so easily. She was taken too soon, we had much to enjoy together. I curse that idiotic doctor and his ineffective treatments. He should have saved her . . . yet, cold in the ground though she is, I feel her with me still.

OLIVER
Of course she is, you shall never forget her, she will always be a part of you. When you love somebody . . . well, they stay with you.

Theodore turns his attention to the fireplace

THEODORE
(quietly)
She is with me even now. I see her, one moment she is there, the next she is not.

OLIVER
I see. I assume that you have heard what fate has befallen Elsie?

THEODORE
I have. I never knew that her hatred ran so deep.

OLIVER
She suffers.

THEODORE
So she must.

> OLIVER
> It is a sorry affair, none of which was meant to occur.

Theodore turns towards Oliver.

> THEODORE
> How do you mean?

> OLIVER
> The estate is yours as Elsie will likely hang.

> THEODORE
> I care not for money!

> OLIVER
> It was supposed to be you, Theo.

> THEODORE
> *(angry)*
> What?

> OLIVER
> You were supposed to take the vial; Rebecca was never meant to die. With you gone and only the word of your boy servant, Elsie and I could have lived in happiness. You never loved her.

Oliver unsheathes a dagger.

> THEODORE
> You lay with Elsie?

DEAD STAGE

OLIVER
Many times . . . and I love her. Loved her. Now, it is all gone . . . and you get to keep it all!

THEODORE
You treacherous swine!

Theodore reaches for a fire poke but Oliver lunges towards him. Theodore is able to evade him and the two fight. Theodore is able to grab the fire poke in the struggle and strikes Oliver in the head, killing him instantly.

THEODORE
Why Oli? Why did you not just say? Why the need for bloodshed?

Theodore breaks down and begins to sob.

FADE TO BLACK.

ACT 1-17

Bedroom. Night. Theodore is alone. The fireplace burns blue and the drapes are drawn. An eerie blue light illuminates Theo as he sits on his bed. The corpse of Oliver lies still.

THEODORE

I know that you are here Rebecca yet by lingering, you prolong my grief. I cannot close this chapter of my life when your scent fills my nostrils and your laughter dances on the wind. I will not forget you—cannot forget you but my suffering must end for I fear that I shan't be able to handle my sorrow for much longer.
(weeping)

Please, Rebecca, heaven beckons to you, leave me now or so help me I will end my life and condemn myself to hell for no longer can I take to be without you!

Rebecca appears behind Theodore. She is bathed in a radiant light. Her glow attracts his attention and he falls to his knees before her. She begins to speak to him but no sounds are heard. She is trying to comfort him.

THEODORE
(Sobbing harder)
I see you—I see you and you are beautiful, but these hands of mine can never touch you again and your

DEAD STAGE

words fall upon useless ears. I am tormented by your presence; you are as far from me now as you can ever possibly be. I sense you but cannot have you. I do not wish to live in this purgatory!

Theodore grabs a knife from the floor and places it across his throat. Rebecca shakes her head.

THEODORE
I want to be with you, I am meant to be with you even in death . . . I have killed tonight. I have lost my true love and my only friend, I cannot remain here so utterly alone. Take me with you.

Theodore drops the knife onto the floor and begins to cry. Rebecca reaches down for the knife and picks it up. She gestures for her husband to stand.

THEODORE
I-I don't understand. I want to be with you yes, but . . . is this how it is meant to be? Yes. I think that it must be. I want to spend eternity in your arms. I place my life in your hands. Release me from my misery and into your arms once more!

Rebecca slides one hand onto the back of her husband's head and places the point of the knife over his heart.

THEODORE
I love you, Rebecca.

Rebecca leans in and kisses Theodore and plunges

the blade into his heart. He falls to the floor dead and Rebecca vanishes. The blue flame in the fireplace extinguishes.

> BLACKOUT.
> CURTAIN FALL.
> END.

TUESDAY OF THE DEAD

Genre: Comedy
Length: Approx. 15 minutes
Cast: 2 x female

Synopsis: Two thirty-something women catch up on the events of the apocalypse over a mug of tea.

Cast of Characters:
    Megan
    Zoe

ACT I

SCENE 1

At Rise: ZOE is sitting at a small kitchen table with a mug of tea. A teapot and a spare mug are on the table.

ENTER MEGAN spattered in blood. She is carrying a bloodied cricket bat in one hand, and a blood-spattered plastic bag in the other. She has a handbag over her shoulder.

ZOE
(nonchalant)
Hiya. Tea's in the pot.

Megan places her cricket bat onto the table and takes a seat. The bag and handbag are placed onto the floor.

MEGAN
Sorry I'm late. Bloody manic out there this morning!

Megan pours herself a cup of tea.

ZOE
Yeah, I'm trying to put off going out myself.

MEGAN
I would. I only popped in for a loaf, seemed like half the town had the same idea. Wasn't much to choose from.

DEAD STAGE

ZOE
What did you end up with?

Megan lifts the blood-spattered carrier bag from the floor and produces a loaf.

MEGAN
Wholemeal.

ZOE
Ugh! I hate whole meal.

Megan places the loaf back into the bag and puts it on the floor.

MEGAN
It's all they had left. I asked when they were next due a delivery, but I don't think the poor bloke could hear me?

ZOE
Why's that then?

MEGAN
Oh, some other fella was disembowelling him.

ZOE
In the bread aisle?

MEGAN
Yep. Plain as day.

ZOE
You'd have thought that security would do something? After all, keeping their staff from getting murdered must be in their job description?

MEGAN
You'd think so wouldn't you? They were far too interested in fetching a cleaner instead of trying to save the poor bloke. He must have been a temp or something.

ZOE
Oh.

Beat.

ZOE
That reminds me, what do you make of this Armageddon business then? I think it's just the media hyping things up, y'know . . . as they do.

MEGAN
Well if it's not one thing, it's another. There aren't enough hours in the day as it is, never mind having time to deal with a zombie apocalypse!

ZOE
I know! I was supposed to be going away this week.

MEGAN
Were you?

DEAD STAGE

ZOE
Yeah, I told you. Malta. That's out of the window now that they closed the airports and dropped those bombs.

MEGAN
Oh, I wouldn't wanna go after that. I imagine it's in a bit of a mess.

ZOE
Yeah. You are probably right. Still a bit of a pain though. Cost me five hundred quid all inclusive. I won't see a penny of that again. And I was looking forward to topping up my tan. What do you reckon so far?

Zoe shows Megan her arm.

MEGAN
That's coming on great!

ZOE
Yeah, it was until her next door jumped the fence and savaged that stray cat I was telling you about.

MEGAN
The one with the manky eye?

ZOE
The cat or my neighbour?

MEGAN
The cat.

ZOE
Yeah, that one. Well, ever since she ate it, it kinda put me off wanting to sunbathe. Honestly, is it too much to ask for a bit of peace now and then? Dizzy cow.

MEGAN
That reminds me, there was a right to-do at the top of your street just now.

ZOE
Up by Maureen's you mean?

MEGAN
Yeah. In fact, Maureen seemed to be causing it. Seems she'd gotten loose again. I told her boys the last time I was down that the chain needs to be properly anchored. Anyway, she was out again, throwing herself at anyone and everyone, dressing gown billowing in the wind, and her with no shame. The whore.

ZOE
Where is she now? Tied back up?

MEGAN
No. She came at me, and after she nearly had my arm off last time, I wasn't bloody having it. So I whacked her with this.

Megan toys with the cricket bat on the table.

DEAD STAGE

ZOE
I was wondering what all the blood was about? Just didn't want to say. You know I don't like to pry.

MEGAN
Oh, it's not all hers. A bunch of Jehovah's witnesses were prowling the street when I left this morning.

ZOE
Zombie Jehovah's witnesses?

Megan shrugs

MEGAN
I dunno. Maybe.

They both sip their tea and sit deep in thought for a moment.

MEGAN
How are you faring in all of this anyway? I don't like the thought of you here on your own.

ZOE
Oh, I'm OK. You know me, same old same old. I'm not sure how, but the end of days has somehow prompted my ironing pile to grow.

MEGAN
What are you still ironing for?

ZOE
I dunno, really. To keep up appearances I guess. If I

go out, I wanna go out in clean, crease-free clothing. Paramedics can be a judgmental sort y'know? I heard that if they think you've a bit of money behind you, they put their foot down. If they think you are skint, they don't even bother with the siren!

>MEGAN
>Really?

Zoe nods.

>ZOE
>So Mary Whister was saying.

>MEGAN
>Them of all people! What a bunch of bastards.

>ZOE
>Yep.

Beat.

>ZOE
>How's your Nigel? I haven't seen him about for a while.

>MEGAN
>You won't have.

>ZOE
>Has he been ill?

>MEGAN

DEAD STAGE

In a manner of speaking. Dozy git only went and turned on me didn't he!

ZOE

(Shock)

He never!

MEGAN

He did. He comes in from work last Tuesday, and I said to him, "you are looking a little peaky, you probably should go to the doctor and get yourself one of those injections they keep banging on about on the news."

ZOE

And did he?

MEGAN

Did he bollox! Next morning, I threw back the duvet, and he's lying there, blood and all sorts seeping out of his mouth, with this pleading look on his face. And I say to him "I bloody told you so!" Then I caved his head in with the radio alarm clock, y'know . . . just to be sure.

ZOE

The dizzy sod.

MEGAN

I know. As if I didn't have enough to do that day as well as clean up after him! It was Josh's sports day and I had a mountain of errands to run!

ZOE
How'd Josh do?

MEGAN
(proudly)
Second in the 100 meters . . . which was lucky for him, because the young boy who came third got caught and eaten by the headmistress. I tell you, for sixty-three she can really move. They called the rest of the day off after that.

ZOE
Probably for the best.

Megan finishes her tea and stands.

MEGAN
Anyway, this is just a flying visit. I said I'd go and visit my mum later.

ZOE
How's she finding that home?

MEGAN
Alright. I think. It's me that struggles. Never know which of them are dead and which are alive. I got myself into a right spot of bother last week when I clubbed to death the old fella next door. He came at me as I went past his room and grabbed hold of my coat. Well, instinct kicked in as you might well imagine, and I swung my handbag at his head. That put him down. Then, to make sure, I followed up with another five or six good swings. You can't be too

DEAD STAGE

careful these days I'm telling you. Better to be safe than end up getting bitten!

ZOE
You killed him with your handbag? What on earth have you got in there?

Megan roots in her handbag.

MEGAN
Oh the usual . . . purse, tissues, a few carrier bags . . .

She produces a house brick

MEGAN
Oh, and this. To give it more weight.

ZOE
(impressed)
That's a good idea! Mind if I steal it?

MEGAN
I thought so too. Sure, go ahead. Saw it on This Morning the other day. Holly was demonstrating several takedown techniques for the discerning handbag carrier. Anyway, must dash. You still on for Sully's this Thursday?

ZOE
If you think it'll be alright? Sounds a bit frantic out?

Megan shoulders her cricket bat.

MEGAN
Don't worry. I'll have your back. Can't let those undead zombie bastards ruin Metal Night for us eh? I mean, what else is there to look forward to these days? I'll line up the Jager Bombs.

Megan opens the door to leave.

MEGAN
Looks like him across the street has turned now.

ZOE
Oh. Who?

MEGAN
Him who's always working on that dirty van.

ZOE
You mean Keith?

MEGAN
That's him. Crap, he's seen me . . . and he's coming over.

ZOE
Great. You'll never get rid of that one even if he has turned. He just keeps talking nonsense to anyone who will listen. Half the time I haven't a clue what he's blabbering on about.

MEGAN
Don't worry, I've something to shut him up for good.

DEAD STAGE

Megan begins twirling her handbag.

                MEGAN
          See you Thursday, Zo!

                 ZOE
        Too right! Ta-ra a bit!

Exit Megan

          FADE TO BLACK.
              END.

THE HAUL

Genre: Drama
Length: Approx 12 minutes
Cast: 2 x male

Synopsis: Two highwaymen work through the night to uncover the grave of an accomplice while discussing a recent job-gone-bad.

The Haul is published by Heartland Plays, USA.

The Haul was performed in full as part of the finals of The Congleton Players International One-Act Festival, 2016.

Cast of Characters:
    Albert
    Jim

ACT I

SCENE 1

Curtain up: Night. A moonlit graveyard. JIM is waist deep in an open grave. ALBERT stands at the grave's edge a lamp.

ALBERT
(agitated)
C'mon man, put your back into it!

JIM
I'm trying! Tis hard work this . . . and why can't you lend a hand anyway?

ALBERT
Told you before, someone's gotta keep lookout ain't they! We get caught digging up Ol' Casey here and questions is gonna follow.

JIM
But it's the middle of the night, ain't nobody gonna be about.

ALBERT
Sure there are . . . folk like us who are up to no good, folk who will start asking questions, folk who will need paying off . . . Do you wanna buy their silence cuz it sure as hell ain't comin' outta my half!

JIM
(solemnly)
No.

ALBERT
Thought as much . . . so shut yer bellyaching and get digging!

Jim digs in silence.

ALBERT
Soon be sun up dammit!

JIM
How far down d'ya reckon he'll be?

ALBERT
Six feet or so, but the fella that digs here, he's an idol sort. Don't reckon it will be much further than four.

Jim stabs his spade into the ground and takes a moment to rest.

JIM
Reckon I'm at that now.

Albert peers into the hole.

ALBERT
Reckon so.

Jim wipes his brow.

DEAD STAGE

> JIM
> It was a good haul, wasn't it?

> ALBERT
> Aye. Told you Bagshot Heath was a good spot.

> JIM
> An' the lockbox is safe?

> ALBERT
> Course it is . . . we just gotta divvy up and go our separate ways. Too much interest round 'ere, we need to get gone.

> JIM
> Sets us up for life more or less?

> ALBERT
> That it will.

Jim picks up the spade and resumes his work.

> JIM
> No more killing 'n that?

> ALBERT
> No.

Jim continues to dig in silence. Albert maintains his vigil looking out across the graveyard.

Jim stops digging and looks up at Albert who has his back towards him.

                    JIM
           Why'd you have to kill her, Al?

Albert remains still for a moment.

                  ALBERT
        To make sure they knew we was serious.

Jim continues his digging.

                    JIM
    I think they knew we was serious . . . they looked
                 scared to me.

                  ALBERT
        Scared is good. Brave people don't pay up.

                    JIM
           You didn't need to kill that one.

Albert turns towards Jim.

                  ALBERT
(angry)
              And how do you know that?

Jim stops digging.

                    JIM
           We got everything, didn't we?

DEAD STAGE

ALBERT
Yes, we did, but do you know for sure we'd have gotten the lot had I not stabbed that girl?

JIM
I think we would have.

ALBERT
Ah . . . you think so, but you don't know so.

JIM
No. I suppose not.

ALBERT
My way may not be pretty but I get the job done. No point robbing a coach if half the goods get away! I'm not risking my neck for half a haul, not never and God save me I won't start now!

JIM

(reluctantly)

I suppose.

ALBERT
Ain't no suppose about it now get on with yer diggin'

Jim continues his digging. Albert resumes his watch. Jim pauses again.

JIM
Why'd you make her tell you her name before you stuck her?

ALBERT
(angry)
Jim, I swear to God if you don't stop with these bloody questions it's gonna get light and we will both be swinging before dusk!

Jim resumes his digging in silence.

After a short time, his shovel strikes wood.

Albert turns his attention to the grave.

ALBERT
That's him! Clear the lid, c'mon hurry!

Jim scrapes the dirt clear allowing access to the coffin lid. Once clear, Albert and Jim regard the coffin.

JIM
Now what?

ALBERT
What d'ya mean now what? Get it open!

JIM
(reluctant)
How long has he been down here?

ALBERT
Since the morn, he'll not be rotted or anything yet . . . takes months or more.

DEAD STAGE

Jim begins to feel for the edge of the lid.

JIM
How'd it happen again?

ALBERT
What? Casey ending up here you mean?

JIM
Aye.

ALBERT
Heard he got his throat slit . . . ear to ear, whilst he slept.

JIM
Bloody 'ell! Who'd do such a thing to a man in his own bed?

ALBERT
Someone with good reason I reckon. He had his debts. Word must've got out that he didn't intend to pay up. Those types don't take kindly to non-payment.

JIM
Guess not.

Jim pries open the coffin lid, places the shovel to one side and takes a step back from the sight before him.

> JIM
> Sure don't look like Casey.

> ALBERT
> Sure don't smell like him neither, that's what death'll do to a man, bloat him and make him food for the worms. C'mon then . . . get it off him.

Jim turns to Albert who is crouched on the edge of the grave.

> JIM
> Do I have to?

Albert fixes Jim with a stern look.

> JIM
> I don't even know where it will be . . . I'm not going through his pockets . . . don't seem right.

> ALBERT
> Where's yours?

> JIM
> Round ma neck . . . where you told me to keep it.

> ALBERT
> Try there then, I told him to do the same.

Jim reaches into the coffin and searches around the throat of Casey. Albert places his lantern onto the ground and picks up the shovel.

DEAD STAGE

> JIM
> It ain't here, he ain't wearing it.

> ALBERT
> I know he ain't.

Jim turns to Albert and Albert brings the shovel down onto the top of Jim's head. Jim collapses into the open coffin.

Albert tosses the spade aside and jumps into the grave. He removes a cord and a small key from Jim's neck.

Albert climbs back out of the coffin and removes a similar cord from his own neck. It has two keys on it. He threads the third onto it.

> ALBERT
> I know he ain't.

Albert picks up the spade and begins to fill in the grave, burying both Jim and Casey.

END.

THE HOLDING

Genre: Drama
Length: Approx 30 minutes
Cast: 1 x male 2 x female

Synopsis: Three strangers awake to find themselves locked in a cell together. They are informed that only one of them will be allowed to leave, and are drip fed snippets of one another's past. Tensions mount as the group tries to facilitate a means of escape where everybody gets out alive.

The Holding is published by Heartland Plays, USA. *The Holding* was performed in full as part of the Norths Staffordshire One-Act Festival, by Bold As Brass Theatre Company. It also received several rehearsed readings at Bath University.

Cast of Characters:
　Tony
　Anna
　Sophia
　Facility Director -Voice (either male/female)

ACT I

SCENE 1

Lights up (halfway): Three figures are laid on the ground. The stage is shrouded in darkness. ANNA (well dressed) is the first to wake. She sits up. She is afraid and disorientated. She begins to grope around in the darkness.

ANNA
(upset)
Oh . . . oh . . .

Her hand brushes against TONY'S foot. He mutters something unintelligible, startling Anna who retreats into a corner. Tony slowly gets to his feet.

ANNA
(sobbing)
What's happening? Where am I? Where's David?

TONY
Who's David?

Anna stops sobbing.

ANNA
My husband, I was with him and . . .

Tony regards Anna for a moment before turning

his attention to SOPHIA (Fashionably attired, pretty) who is still unconscious on the floor.

TONY
And now you ain't.

Tony gestures towards their surroundings.

ANNA
Well . . . where is he? Where am I?

TONY
Where are we don't you mean? I don't see him here, just you, me and this 'un on the floor. As for where we are, your guess is as good as mine.

Tony checks Sophia for a pulse.

ANNA
Is she . . .

TONY
Dead? No.

ANNA
I wasn't going to say dead! I was going to ask if she's alright!

TONY
I dunno about that. Perhaps you should ask her.

Sophia sits up. Tony backs away to give her space.

DEAD STAGE

SOPHIA
Christ! My head is killing me!

Tony checks his pockets.

TONY
Good morning, miss sunshine, I'd offer you an aspirin but as you can see, I'm all out.

Anna stands and approaches Sophia.

ANNA
Are you OK, sweetie?

Sophia frantically checks her pockets.

SOPHIA
(angry)
Ah shit! They took my smokes! Fuckers took my smokes, the hell is up with that?

TONY
I'd say she's about as fine as the rest of us lady.

Sophia begins to pace the stage. Anna watches whilst Tony takes a seat on the floor.

SOPHIA
So, what shit did I do now? Why did I wake up in a place I don't recognize with people I don't know?

TONY
I'm sure it's not the first time.

SOPHIA
(angry)
The hell is that supposed to mean?

TONY
Nothing as such, you just don't strike me as the type tucked up in bed at nine with a glass of warm milk and a chocolate chip cookie.

SOPHIA
Don't be acting like you know a damn thing about me! Where'd they drag you in from? A park bench?

TONY
Ha! Says the real tramp in the room!

Sophia covers her arm.

SOPHIA
You don't know a thing about me!

ANNA
(nervous)
Please, this isn't getting us anywhere. I don't do well with conflict.

TONY
She's right. We need to cool it and figure out where we are.
(To Sophia)
Sorry, toots.
(To Anna)
You, what was the last thing that you remember?

DEAD STAGE

ANNA
I-I don't know, one minute I was with David, the next . . .

SOPHIA
The next what?

ANNA
I don't know, it's all a blur.

TONY
(interrupting)
Same here. Reckon we are in some kind government holding facility or something. Probably ruffled the wrong feathers somewhere along the way and ended up here.

SOPHIA
That's a pretty outlandish statement to make—you read about that whilst hawking copies of the Big Issue?

Tony laughs

ANNA
I haven't done anything wrong . . .

TONY
(interrupting)
Ladies, I don't know spit. Just throwing an idea out there, You wanna venture yours? C'mon, let's hear it?

Anna shakes her head and retreats to a corner.

SOPHIA
Last thing I remember is leaving the deli at lunch. Now I'm here with you two. How about you shoot me your names at least?

ANNA
I'm Anna, Anna Caudlow, I'm from Buckinghamshire, I work in . . .

SOPHIA
OK Anna, I don't need your life story. I'm Sophia Redman. You?

TONY
Tony.

SOPHIA
Tony what?

TONY
Just Tony.

SOPHIA
Ah right, so that's how you wanna play it then? Tony, it is.

Tony stands

TONY
I'm not playing anything anyway. I don't know you people and at this point, I don't see what good it's gonna make getting to. We gotta figure out where we are. Agreed?

DEAD STAGE

Anna nods.

SOPHIA
(To Tony)
Suppose so. Time wasted talking is time I gotta spend in your company. I'm all for getting outta here.

The lights suddenly switch fully on. The Facility Director begins to speak over a PA.

FACILITY DIRECTOR *(OFFSTAGE)*
Your reluctance in regards to knowing your cellmates will be your downfall.

SOPHIA
(angry)
Cellmates? I knew it! Just what the hell is going on? You can't just lock us up for no reason!

TONY
They can hear us.

ANNA
Does that mean they can see us?

SOPHIA
Probably.

Anna begins to sob.

FACILITY DIRECTOR
Who we portray ourselves as to the outside world is not who we are at heart. Three strangers, thrown

together, trying to understand a situation that they cannot possibly comprehend. One of you is an aid worker who has given much time and money in order to safeguard the welfare of others. Selfless and dedicated, a latter-day saint, you are traumatized by your experiences. One of you is a swindler and a thief, a master of misdirection with an unrelenting ruthless streak. You have taken much from the vulnerable and given nothing in return. Though you lay blame elsewhere, it is you who smiles as you watch the gullible sign away their savings. One of you has bloodied hands and no matter how many times you wash them; the taint of death remains upon you. At first, you killed for necessity, pushed beyond breaking point by a world oblivious to your hardship, you were a product of your suffering. Now you kill for sport. Broken though you are, insane you are not.
This is your day of reckoning.

Silence

TONY
And?

FACILITY DIRECTOR
One of you shall leave this place. It is up to you to decide who.

The lights dim to half-light.

ANNA
What? Just one of us? Why? I want to go home! What have I done to deserve this?

DEAD STAGE

TONY

(To Anna)

What indeed?

SOPHIA

And what's that supposed to mean?

TONY

You heard him! You heard who we are amongst!

SOPHIA

Yeah! And what if he is wrong? What if all that is a load of bullshit?

TONY

And what if it ain't?

Tony begins to pace the stage.

ANNA

I've never done anything wrong, I've cared for others all of my life . . . I shouldn't be here.

TONY

Well, that's a load of B.S already!

ANNA

What? How do you know?

TONY

Look at your fancy clothes and your expensive jewellery! Only one of us is the aid worker and it sure as shit ain't you! You are far too well off to give a shit about anybody else.

ANNA
So just because it appears that I have money that means I couldn't possibly be an aid worker? How insulting! I know my own life! I'm the one who shouldn't be here! I have nothing in common with you two!

TONY
That right?

Anna regards Tony with a look of fear.

ANNA
Yes.

TONY
Care to elaborate?

Anna moves closer to Sophia and further from Tony.

ANNA
Because you two are criminals.

TONY
And you figure Paris Hilton over there is the lesser of two evils?

Anna looks at Sophia

ANNA
(whispers)
Look, Sophie, I don't know what you've done and I

don't care, but I don't trust him . . . I mean look at the state of him. Look at how he's pacing. He's spent time locked up, I can tell . . . he's like a caged animal. I think we should be careful?

Sophia looks at Tony, then at Anna.

SOPHIA
You saying I'm the con artist and he's the killer?

ANNA
Con artist sounds so harsh, I'm not labelling you but look at him, look at how hostile he's being? Plus, he wouldn't give us his name, that's suspicious, right? Maybe he is worried we'd remember it from the newspapers?

TONY
(assertive)
My names Tony. I already told you.

SOPHIA
Why not give us your full name?

TONY
Would it make a huge difference if I gave it now? Of course not. You'd not believe me even if I did. It changes nothing, not after the seeds of suspicion have been sown by our captors . . . that's right, our captors! Seems to me they—whoever they are, they are the only ones that we can be one hundred percent sure are guilty of any wrongdoing.

ANNA
But they said . . .

TONY
Exactly, they said! Are you going to trust the words of your faceless kidnappers on this? It's only their say so! Who are they to label us?

SOPHIA
I'd expect a murderer to say something like that.

TONY
And I'd expect a murderer to pick up on someone saying that and make a point of it. Look, we can deflect accusations as to who we all are till the cows come home but it ain't gonna get us out of here. We need to figure out where we are and who is behind all of this.

ANNA
You're right. Suspicion isn't going to get us anywhere; we will just play right into their hands.

SOPHIA
Any idea who put us here?

TONY
I dunno. Some rich guy with a hard-on for fly on the wall drama? A secret government experiment . . .

SOPHIA
Oh, I've heard it all now! You are one of those conspiracy nuts, aren't you! Those sort come undone all the time!

DEAD STAGE

TONY
That's what the governments want you to think, that all those horrible stories of social manipulation and chemical testing are just that! Stories! I'm telling you now, we are caught up in one of those black book studies now . . . the types that are kept hidden from the public eye.

SOPHIA
Bullshit! We live in a free country! A fucked up country maybe but shit like that only happens in the movies.

TONY
Does it now? Look around you! Do you think that you did something which warrants putting you into a situation like this? You think you deserve this? Is that what you are saying? Seems to me like you got something to hide!

SOPHIA
Rubbish, you are deflecting onto me! Hiding behind your conspiracy theories to conceal your true nature—sure, I belong here if hearing that helps you sleep at night, but you aren't fooling me!

ANNA
What are you saying?

SOPHIA
Isn't it obvious? He's trying to build a reality where he isn't here because he's a murderer! Your mask isn't fooling me.

TONY
I think I'm the only one who isn't wearing a mask in here! I'm not playing up for the cameras or pretending to be someone I'm not. Wouldn't you agree Anna?

ANNA
I-I don't know! I don't know anymore, I want to go home, I want to see my David!

TONY
None of us are going home.

SOPHIA
(Threatening)
Shut up! Yes, we are, maybe not you—I know who you are.

TONY
You really think so? Blinded by your captors will already? Tell me, do you even see a way out of this room?

Sophia and Anna look around the room.

TONY
Thought not.

ANNA
We-we have to do what they say, then they will show us the way out. David would say the same.

DEAD STAGE

TONY
You do that.

Anna and Sophia retreat into the corner opposite Tony.

Pause.

The lights flicker onto full beam. A door is heard unlocking and a small box slides into the middle of the room. The door quickly closes and is locked again.

The lights dim to half-light again.

Anna and Sophia look at the box and then look to Tony.

TONY
I see the age-old assumption of the male taking all of the risk in order to protect the female is alive and well.

ANNA
Surely you can't expect either of us to open it . . . it could be a bomb!

TONY
If it's a bomb and I trigger it, we'll all feel it. Hiding in the corner of the room won't spare you.

Tony approaches the box and kneels before it. The lid opens towards the audience. Tony looks at the contents.

Pause.

                    SOPHIA
                    What is it?

Tony stands up and produces a gun from the box

                    ANNA
(shocked)
                    A gun?

                    TONY
Revolver. Colt 45 . . . quite a nice example too.

                    SOPHIA
              They gave you a gun?

Tony turns towards the girls and opens the gun with practised ease.

                    TONY
No, they gave us a gun with two bullets. You starting to get a clearer picture of what's required here?

                    ANNA
Oh my God! They can't expect us to—

                    SOPHIA
            Is there something else?

Tony turns his attention back to the box and crouches alongside it.

DEAD STAGE

Tony sifts through the contents of the box with his free hand.

TONY
A bracelet, several bank statements and a newspaper clipping.

SOPHIA
Let me see!

Sophia pushes past Tony and takes the box to a corner of the room. She produces the bracelet first.

ANNA
What does it all mean?

TONY
(To Sophia—winks)
If I was to take a stab in the dark I'd say that these relate to us in some way. Sort of like a prop from our past.

SOPHIA
This bracelet is handmade, some kind of leather . . . looks ethnic to me.

ANNA
That's mine, it was given to me in—

TONY
(interrupting)
What about the other stuff?

Sophia produces the bank statements.

SOPHIA
Just a load of bank statements for a company called easistair? Lot of money going in . . . huge sums in fact, nothing going out.

TONY
Any names on there?

SOPHIA
Nope. All blacked out.

TONY
Perhaps the accounts of our con artist . . . and the newspaper clipping, what's that about?

SOPHIA
Hold on . . . a lot of it is blacked out . . . male . . . found dead in front room . . . stab wounds to the head and chest . . . investigation ongoing. It's dated last week.

Sophia places the items back into the box.

TONY
And there's the prop for our murderer.

ANNA
You don't know that for sure! It's just their word against ours.

DEAD STAGE

TONY
This entire situation is based on their word against ours. Maybe it's about time we showed one another who we really are?

Tony crosses the room and takes the box from Sophia. He places the gun back into it and lays the box in the middle of the room.

TONY
Anyone wanna lay claim to any of this?

ANNA
I already told you that the bracelet is mine—

TONY
(interrupting)
Yet I don't believe it is. Let's look at what we have, two bullets, a box of evidence that relates to us all . . . I knew this is what we were here for!

SOPHIA
How could you possibly know they want one of us to kill the others?

TONY
You heard what the voice said. One of us leaves, we decide who. Only this isn't to be a discussion where we debate self-worth, this is a test of morals, or more to the point, to see if we have any.

ANNA
I-I really shouldn't be here . . .

TONY
(interrupting)
None of us should, that's the whole point! We should be standing together, refusing to play this sick game, not actively looking for ways in which to fuck the others over. We should all be looking to get out of here alive!

SOPHIA
That's what you want us to think that you believe.

TONY
I'm getting real tired of your reverse psychology bullshit.

ANNA
You can't think that I'm a criminal?

TONY
(agitated)
I don't care if you are! The only criminals I know for sure are the ones who put us in here.

SOPHIA
(To Anna)
He's got a point. What does it matter what happened before we wound up here? That's not for us to judge, despite what those fuckers said over the speaker.

TONY
That's right. It's who we are now—the choices that we make in the moment—that's what is important. Are we the sum of our past choices? Labelled and judged

without a chance of reprieve? I don't believe so. If that were true nobody could ever change. Perhaps that's what our captors want to see? I don't know. Forget the past, its who we are in the present that really counts.

ANNA
I-I guess so. How do we get out then?

TONY
I-I don't know yet. We need to take time to think about this, all of this. Forget the gun, that's not an option. Agreed?

Anna nods. Tony turns his attention to Sophia who is looking at the box.

TONY
Agreed?

Sophia turns towards Tony.

SOPHIA
(reluctantly)
Agreed.

Tony takes a seat on the floor. Sophia begins to pace the room. Anna takes a seat on the floor.

Lights out.

Pause.

Lights on half.

Tony is pacing the room. Sophia and Anna are sitting together. Anna is asleep on Sophia's shoulder. Sophia is staring at the box.

Lights out.

Pause.

Lights on half.

Tony and Anna are asleep. Sophia slowly creeps towards the box but is startled by Tony stirring.

Lights out.

Pause.

Lights on half.

Tony is seated away from Anna and Sophia who are sat together. The box remains in the centre of the room.

ANNA
David will be wondering where I am. We are supposed to fly out to Niger tomorrow . . . or today, I don't know how long we've even been in here. The Red Cross will be wondering where I am . . . I shouldn't be here.

DEAD STAGE

TONY
So you keep saying.

ANNA
I remember one visit. We were in the Sudan. There was a war going on between rival tribes at the time. We were called into this village, I forget the name now. When we got there the place was ablaze. Every hut had been set alight, all the crops too. It took us hours to get the blaze under control. The only men left in the village were too sick to help us and the women, they were all in despair. It was only when the fires were out that we noticed the absence of children. I spoke to one of the women. She was inconsolable, I'd never seen anyone so upset before. Apparently, one of the warlords had come to the village that day demanding the children go with him and join his army. When the elders refused, citing that the able-bodied men had already surrendered to their cause, they set the village alight and took the children anyway.

SOPHIA
That's awful.

TONY
So what did you do? Colour me curious.

Anna begins to fumble in her pockets.

ANNA
The best we could. What else could we do?

Sophia hugs Anna who begins to break into tears.

TONY
That's a nice story by the way. Those extra touches really help sell it. You don't seem awfully traumatized by it all though?

SOPHIA
Can't you give it a rest?

TONY
Come on now, we all know that story was a pack of lies. I thought we'd agreed to stop trying to play the game?

Anna stops crying and turns towards Tony. Sophia lets Anna go.

ANNA
Wh-what do you mean, of course it wasn't a lie, I'm not playing any game, I'm just telling it how it is!

TONY
So you are trying to tell us that you are an aid worker and you don't belong here because your life is spent doing good for others right?

ANNA
I am an aid worker, yes.

TONY
Seems to me you are trying to convince yourself more than us, why else would you keep banging on about it.

DEAD STAGE

ANNA
What? I should be going to Niger with David tomorrow, I'm offering relief—

TONY
And what of David. Will he go without you do you think? I mean there are always people needing help—where do you think you lie in terms of his priorities?

ANNA
I . . . he will wait for me. We will go together after all of this.

Tony turns his attention towards Sophia

TONY
(interrupting)
So, if we are back to playing the game, where do you stand on this then? You buying that bullshit?

Anna turns towards Sophia

ANNA
Sophie, he's starting to scare me.

Sophia looks at Anna then looks at the box. After a short pause she strolls over to the box and opens it.

SOPHIA
It's not here!

ANNA
Wh-what do you mean? The gun?

Sophia turns towards Tony

SOPHIA
Damn right I mean the gun, where is it you son of a bitch?

Tony takes the gun from his pocket and places it on the floor next to where he is seated.

TONY
With me. Where it will be safe.

Anna approaches Sophia's side.

SOPHIA
Safe? Safe for who?

TONY
Safe for me.

Tony gestures towards Anna

TONY
Safe for her.

ANNA
(To Sophia)
What does he mean?

DEAD STAGE

TONY
(To Anna)
I saw her going for the gun while we slept. I startled her enough for her to back off. Figured I'd keep it with me. Didn't fancy waking up to a gun being waved in my face. So much for us standing together.

SOPHIA
Liar!

ANNA
(To Sophia)
Why would you go for the gun? I thought we agreed that wasn't an option?

TONY
Because she's a junkie and she's getting desperate. I saw those marks on your arm!

Sophia covers her arms.

SOPHIA
I didn't make a play for the gun, he's lying . . . trying to paint me as dishonest, trying to divert suspicion from himself. I'm a diabetic and I need my insulin, without it, I'm going to die!

TONY
Bullshit. Diabetics don't inject into the vein. You are an addict, I should know, I've seen enough of them.

SOPHIA
And how do you know about how diabetics take their

meds? Maybe I take mine that way, what the hell has it to do with you?

TONY
I know a lot of things, and you are a junkie liar and can't be trusted. Funny you never mentioned this earlier. Your mask is starting to slip.

ANNA
Her mask?

SOPHIA
Don't listen to him, I have a serious medical condition and I need my medication. It's been hours since my last shot.

TONY
Don't you mean fix?

SOPHIA
(to Anna)
We need to get out of here. You were right, he's gotta be the killer. Look at him with that gun. Did you see how easily he opened that thing earlier?

TONY
Oh, so because I know how to load a pistol that automatically makes me a killer right?

SOPHIA
You seem awfully at ease with it, like it's not the first time you've handled a gun.

DEAD STAGE

TONY
It isn't, but that doesn't make me a killer. I've been around guns. That's all.

SOPHIA
I'm not buying it—I think you should put the gun back in the box before this gets ugly.

Tony picks up the gun, stands, and aims it towards Sophia and Anna.

TONY
I think you should both sit down and shut up.

Sophia moves towards Tony.

SOPHIA
Or else what asshole? You haven't got the stones!

Tony cocks the trigger.

TONY
Sit. Down.

Anna pulls Sophia back and they sit opposite Tony. Tony takes a seat and rests the gun on his lap.

TONY
That's better.

ANNA
(To Sophia)

I knew it was him all along, you can see death in his eyes, trust me.

TONY
Lady, you don't know shit.

SOPHIA
(To Tony)
As I guess you are calling the shots, what now?

TONY
Same as before, we try an' figure out a way outta here.

SOPHIA
Only you are keeping the gun. Sort of shortens our odds of getting out alive a little, don't you think?

TONY
So long as the gun stays with me, we've all got a chance to get out of this alive.

Lights out.

Pause.

Lights on half.

Tony is pacing the room. Sophia and Anna are sitting together.

Lights out.

DEAD STAGE

Pause.

Lights on half.

Tony, Anna and Sophia are asleep.

Lights out.

Pause.

Lights on half.

Tony is stood with his back to Anna and Sophia who are sat together on the opposite side of the room. Tony is fidgeting with the gun.

SOPHIA
Any ideas yet?

TONY
Shut up—I'm trying to think.

SOPHIA
It's been hours now . . .

ANNA
Days even—I've missed my flight; David will be so worried. I'm so thirsty . . . Someone will come for us soon. They have to!

TONY
Really? You think that they will? You think that they know where we are?

ANNA
It's just a matter of—

Tony turns towards Anna and Sophia

TONY
Don't you get it? Nobody is coming because nobody knows we are here!

ANNA
But—

TONY
But nothing. We stay here till we starve or until someone makes a decision. That's the only way.

Sophia stands up. Anna follows.

SOPHIA
Wait . . . I thought you wanted us all to get out of here together?

TONY
I did . . . I do, dammit I do! There's no way though, not until we choose! I've seen this sort of thing before governments playing with their people. In the end, you have to play by the rules or everybody loses.

ANNA
What are you saying? Are you going along with what they want?

DEAD STAGE

               TONY
I'm sorry—I don't know you. I don't know what
you've done, but I can make up for all this if I get out,
I'm well positioned to help others and I don't believe
              that you are.

Tony raises the gun and fires twice in quick succession.

Anna and Sophia scream and react but are not hit.

               TONY
            (angry)
Fuck! They gave us blanks! They gave us fucking
              blanks!

Tony throws the gun into the middle of the floor and turns his attention to the ceiling.

Anna and Sophia are in a state of shock.

               TONY
You assholes have your answer! I chose! I made the
fucking call, rightly or wrongly! We played your game
            now let us go!

               ANNA
          (To Sophia)
         He-he tried to kill us!

Sophia nods.

ANNA
(shocked)
That maniac actually tried to kill us!

Anna picks up the gun and holds it by the barrel. She approaches Tony from behind.

TONY
(breaking down)
Open the damn door! You won! You won . . .

ANNA
You tried to kill us you bastard!

Anna strikes Tony on the back of the head and he falls to the ground. She attempts a follow-up blow but Sophia catches her arm.

SOPHIA
No!

ANNA
But I have to be sure!

Sophia bends down to check for a pulse. Her fingers come away bloody.

SOPHIA
He's dead.

Anna drops the gun onto the floor and begins to shake.

DEAD STAGE

ANNA
Oh . . . Oh . . . he tried to kill us . . . you saw right? He shot at us!

SOPHIA
He did yes.

ANNA
It was him or us, right?

Sophia extends her arms to welcome Anna into a comforting embrace. Anna accepts.

SOPHIA
It would have been, yes.

Anna pulls away from the embrace slightly, Sophia rests her hands on Anna's shoulders.

SOPHIA
You did good Anna.

ANNA
I did?

Sophia nods.

ANNA
I never killed anyone before, Sophie.

SOPHIA
I know. It's not easy to kill somebody. When the situation demands it, that's when you find out if you

have it in you. If you think I was gonna let some drunken piece of shit fuck me and leave me for dead, well you'd be mistaken.

ANNA
You killed a man?

SOPHIA
Several. I forget how many. First one when I was fourteen. It's rough on the streets. Saw too many girls beaten or worse. I seemed to attract the fucked up types. I make sure they don't hurt anybody else. As for now—I want out of this hole.

Anna tries to pull away. Sophia wraps her hands around Anna's throat and begins to strangle her. After a brief struggle, Anna slumps to the floor. After a few moments more, Sophia releases her grip.

SOPHIA
And it's Sophia you stupid bitch.

Sophia stands and regards the two bodies beside her. The sounds of a door unlocking are heard and a doorway is illuminated.

Sophia exits the room.

CURTAIN FALL.
THE END.

FRIENDS LIKE US

Genre: Drama
Length: Approx 30 mins

Synopsis: A Halloween party takes a disastrous turn.

Cast:
    Chad
    Becky
    Izzy
    Jack

ACT I

SCENE 1

At Rise: apartment living room adorned with tacky Halloween decorations.

CHAD (dressed as a skeleton) is busy setting the table (four chairs set at each side—centre stage) with a Ouija Board/Glass in the middle. He adjusts it so that the angle sits "just so."

Enter BECKY dressed as a zombie nurse. She is carrying a bowl of crisps and sets them alongside a row of drinks on a small table located next to the sofa (left centre).

BECKY
What time did you tell them again?

CHAD
You don't "tell" Jack a time, he arrives whenever he feels like it, it's one of his many quirks.

BECKY
But you told him eight, right?

CHAD
Yes.

BECKY
It's almost nine.

DEAD STAGE

CHAD
So they will be here in a minute. Or not. What's the hurry? The night is still young!

BECKY
I just don't like waiting. I want a drink and the blood is starting to itch.

Becky scratches the dried blood on her throat.

CHAD
Then get a drink! We've plenty. I'll join you. Toss me a can.

BECKY
I can't . . . it's rude . . . I'll wait.

Chad indicates he still wants a drink.

CHAD
I won't. Beer me.

Becky tosses him a can.

BECKY
Try and save some for our guests . . . should they ever show.

Chad opens his can.

CHAD
Cheers.

DAN WEATHERER

Chad takes a sip of his can and eyes the Ouija Board. Becky notices and follows his gaze.

BECKY
I'm telling you now, Izzy won't be happy with the night you've got planned.

CHAD
Why not?

Becky picks up the Ouija Board and scrutinizes it.

BECKY
She's not into Halloween—she doesn't approve. She's deeply religious; I did warn you about getting one.

Chad snatches it from her.

CHAD
She'll come around when she hears the history behind this particular board.

BECKY
I kinda doubt that . . . but humour me.

CHAD
This isn't just any talking board . . .

BECKY
Here we go . . .

CHAD
This board came from an old, mental asylum that

DEAD STAGE

specialized in the treatment of violently disturbed orphans . . .

BECKY
(sarcastic)
Did it now?

CHAD
One of whom escaped on Halloween, fifty years to the day. This lunatic, this madman, not content with a mere escape, set the place alight and burnt it to the ground.

BECKY
Of course he did . . .

CHAD
The only survivor of that night . . .

Chad pauses and gazes at the Ouija Board

CHAD
. . . was this very board.

Beat.

BECKY
That's the best you can do?

CHAD
What do you mean? That is an awesome back-story!

BECKY
I think Stephen King can rest easy. So, where did you really get it from? Amazon?

CHAD
(sheepishly)
Yeah. Do you think it looks a bit too new?

BECKY
Does that matter?

CHAD
No. I suppose not. I mean, it's just for fun—I don't expect it to actually work.

BECKY
If ever there was a time, tonight would be it! Anyway, I hope you don't expect me to play along with this charade? Izzy is beside herself with worry over Jack. Tonight was supposed to be a laid-back affair, one where they could possibly reconnect. How are they going to do that with you playing Derek Acorah?

CHAD
Relax! This is just to break the tension! Once the drinks are flowing I'm sure they will be fine. They can have their relationship breakthrough, but don't deny me a laugh or two, first? I've been planning this for weeks!

BECKY
(sighs)
Fine.

DEAD STAGE

Becky checks her phone.

> BECKY
> Fuck it—I'm having a drink.

The doorbell rings.

> BECKY
> Finally!

> CHAD
> Showtime!

Becky moves to exit stage left

> CHAD
> Hang on!

Becky pauses while Chad resets the Ouija Board. The doorbell chimes insistently.

> CHAD
> How's that?

> BECKY
> Fine! It looks fine—can I get the door now?

Chad nods without taking his eyes off the board.

Becky opens the door

Enter JACK and IZZY. They appear to be dressed normally.

CHAD
Where the hell are your costumes? I told you I wanted you to make an effort!

JACK
And a pleasant evening to you, too.

BECKY
Ignore him. He's just hyped up on sugar. Honestly, I've never known such a big kid.

Jack nods to Becky.

JACK
We did come in costume, didn't we darling?

IZZY
Yes. I'm Wendy Torrance y'know—played by Shelley Duvall in The Shining. See?

Izzy pulls a "silent scream" type face.

JACK
And I'm Paul Sheldon. Misery.

CHAD
How's that then?

Jack rolls his jeans up to reveal a cast around his ankle.

JACK
That do for you?

DEAD STAGE

CHAD
That looks convincing?

IZZY
Yeah, unfortunately it's the real thing.

JACK
Car accident. I hit a tree a couple of weeks back.

BECKY
My God! Are you OK? Chad, why didn't you tell me?

CHAD
He's fine! He's standing in front of you now, isn't he?

JACK
Aside from the foot and the written off Merc . . .
yeah.

BECKY
Oh, how awful!

IZZY
He's been milking it for all its worth.

JACK
Hey! I'm walking wounded.

CHAD
Pfft! Whatever. If you went trick or treating dressed like that you'd get nothing.

JACK
(snappy)
But we aren't going to go trick or treating because we aren't ten anymore, are we Chad?

CHAD
(dejected)
No. I guess we aren't.

Beat.

(awkward silence)

BECKY
Well, I love your costumes! And don't just stand there—come on in, grab a drink and a seat.

Becky hugs Izzy as Jack moves towards Chad.

BECKY
It's really good to see you. How are you?

Izzy glances towards Jack to make sure he is out of earshot. Jack is talking to Chad over by the drinks.

IZZY
I don't know. OK, I guess.

BECKY
Any change with him?

Izzy shakes her head.

DEAD STAGE

IZZY
No.

BECKY
I know it's not easy, but have you thought about telling him outright?

IZZY
I can't.

BECKY
Why?

IZZY
I'm not ready. I don't understand it all myself. You get that, right?

BECKY
I guess.

Izzy shrugs.

IZZY
Thank you.

BECKY
Oh, hun.

Becky hugs Izzy.

JACK
So, what's the plan? Beers and a film?

CHAD
Yeah, yeah, we'll get to that. I've plans before then, mate. Big plans.

Jack opens a can of beer.

JACK
Why do I not like the sound of that?

CHAD
You will. It'll be fun. You'll see. So, how are things with you and your lady?

JACK
Really? You want to go into that now? I thought tonight was going to be "fun?"

CHAD
It will be. I'm just asking as a mate. Becky thinks you are knobbin' someone else.

JACK
(scoffs)
Does she? Chance would be a fine thing. Likely Izzy gave her that idea.

CHAD
You know how they get when they talk.

JACK
You set her straight?

DEAD STAGE

CHAD
C'mon, mate. I don't get involved, you know that. I'm just asking how you are man to man. You've been outta sorts of late. Anything you wanna voice?

JACK
Not really. It's just work, y'know?

CHAD
No, it's not. Don't bullshit me, man. Level with me. It might help to offload.

JACK
Jeez . . . when did you become so caring?

CHAD
I don't. Not really. Be an ass then. Fuck you and your problems.

Jack laughs

JACK
OK. I'll level. Izzy is being full on . . . like settle down, have a family, two point four kids and all that bollox, full on.

CHAD
And you aren't keen?

JACK
Would you be?

CHAD
Fuck no!

JACK
I've so much more I want to do with my life before all of that.

CHAD
You mean there's many more to fuck before you are ready to settle?

JACK
Well . . . yeah. Why the rush into a commitment like marriage?

Chad/Jack take a sip of their drinks.

CHAD
I get that.

BECKY
So, listen. Don't freak out or anything, but Chad has got something lined up tonight you might not approve of.

IZZY
Oh, you do surprise me.

Becky steers Izzy towards the table.

BECKY
I thought it better to warn you now, and you don't have to take part in it if you don't want to.

DEAD STAGE

Becky nods towards the Ouija Board.

IZZY
You are kidding, right?

BECKY
Sorry. If I'd have known I'd have talked him out of it.

IZZY
I can't believe . . . after what I . . .

CHAD
Bex! Why'd you have to spoil the big surprise?

Becky
I was merely warning Izzy what you had in mind.

Jack puts down his drink and picks up the board.

JACK
What is it? A board game or something? You should have said you were having a games night, I'd have dug out my old Monopoly set.

Chad snatches the board from Jack and gingerly places it back onto the table.

CHAD
You need to be careful with that, for this is a portal into another realm.

IZZY
It's evil is what it is.

BECKY
Izzy, come on now.

JACK
What?

IZZY
You shouldn't be messing around with things like that. You've no idea what you are meddling with. Jack, we are going.

BECKY
Don't be silly, Izz. It's not like it's going to work or anything!

CHAD
What do you mean? Of course it will! Tonight's the night when the divide between our world and theirs is at its narrowest. Even a complete novice like you could contact the dead on Halloween.

JACK
You want to contact the dead? That's your idea of fun?

BECKY
Oh, and you're some kind of expert now? You are just spouting what you read online!

CHAD
Only because I understand it. Izzy, you don't have to be involved, but trust me, I know what I'm doing.

DEAD STAGE

IZZY
No, you don't.

JACK
We are staying. You heard him—you don't have to take part. Besides, you have been harping on about tonight for weeks, saying it is important for us to go out and spend some time together. Well, here we are.

IZZY
I know I did, but I didn't know Chad was going to attempt something like this!

JACK
Like what? Nothing's going to happen. I've seen this shit in films—it's all fake. Besides, I've got a drink now. I'm staying.

IZZY
I'll call myself a taxi.

JACK
Fine. Do that.

BECKY
Izz!

Izzy sits on the sofa and takes out her phone. She begins to dial.

CHAD
Let her go if she wants to. She'd just kill the mood anyway.

> BECKY
> Chad! Shut up!

> JACK
> *(whispers)*
> She won't really go. Watch.

Izzy clicks off her phone.

Beat.

> JACK
> Are they on their way?

> IZZY
> It was engaged.

> CHAD
> Bound to be if you think about it. Busy night in town, tonight.

> BECKY
> So you'll stay?

> IZZY
> I'm not joining you. I'll try again in a bit.

Izzy plugs her headphones into her phone, and listens to music

> CHAD
> *(To Becky)*
> What the hell was that about?

DEAD STAGE

			BECKY
		I did warn you.

			JACK
	She's like that a lot. Y'know . . . argumentative.

			BECKY
		(whispered)
		She has reason to be in regards to this . . .

Becky gestures towards the board

			BECKY
	She did one before, years ago . . . she was just a kid.
			Scared the shit out of her.

			CHAD
		So, it worked?

			BECKY
		That's not really my point.

Chad claps his hands together.

			CHAD
		Well then, let's get started!

Chad closes his eyes and places his palms onto the table. After a moment, he opens his eyes and gestures for Jack/Becky to do the same.

When they close their eyes, Chad reaches for a book and discreetly opens it, and places it on to his lap.

Chad begins to read aloud, but disguises the fact.

CHAD
I call upon the white light for protection.

JACK
I recommend Durex, mate. Much more reliable.

Becky stifles a laugh.

Chad glares at Jack, and continues.

CHAD
Tormented spirits of the netherworld . . .

JACK
Oh, dear God.

BECKY
Do they have to be tormented? Why can't they be content? I'd much prefer to share my evening with a content ghost.

Chad opens his eyes.

CHAD
(irritated)
They are not Ghosts, they are spirit entities. Stop being deadist! We won't get anyone willing to communicate if you carry on with language like that.

Becky bows her head, hurt.

DEAD STAGE

Chad continues

CHAD
Heed not her words, for she is uneducated in the matters of the deceased. Come forwards, use our strength to make yourself known to us.

Chad places his finger on to the top of the glass, and gestures that Jack and Becky do likewise.

Beat.

JACK
Well, this is a fun way to spend an evening.

CHAD
Shush!

JACK
At least this particular finger is getting plenty of rest . . .

The glass jerks towards Jack. Jack and Becky withdraw their hands.

BECKY
Shit!

JACK
Oh, ha-ha, Chad. Very funny.

CHAD
It wasn't me! Come on, back on.

Chad, Jack and Becky place their fingers back onto the glass.

CHAD
Is there somebody with us? So to speak.

Beat.

The glass moves again, further this time.

Becky and Jack withdraw their hands again.

JACK
For fuck sake . . .

CHAD
It wasn't me!

BECKY
Enough now, Chad. You've had your fun.

CHAD
I haven't yet, and it's not me moving the glass!

JACK
Yes, it is. And it's not funny.

IZZY
(without looking around)
You're such a prick, Chad.

DEAD STAGE

CHAD
Guilty, but where's your sense of adventure? We are on to something here. Let's see it through, OK?

Becky and Jack exchange looks and reluctantly place their fingers back on to the glass.

CHAD
Do you have a message for us?

The glass moves smoothly to YES.

BECKY
Yes.

JACK
Of course it does, eh, Chad?

CHAD
For the love of . . . it's not me! I never expected anything to happen, but . . . I'm telling you, I'm not fixing this . . . I was gonna, but I'm not. I didn't get chance to move the glass, it moved before I could try!

BECKY
Bull crap.

CHAD
I'm serious. You know I was planning to set them up, but now this has happened . . . I'm curious . . .

JACK
And scared?

CHAD
A little, yes. But I wanna know what it has to say. So, please, can we continue?

JACK
Becky?

BECKY
He was going to bullshit you, but look at him . . . he's not that good an actor. I think this is real.

JACK
Fuck it, let's see where this goes.

Jack places his finger back on to the glass.

BECKY
If you are sure?

Becky places her finger back on to the glass.

CHAD
Spirit, we welcome you among our number. This message, whom is it for?

The glass moves in Izzy's direction.

BECKY
Chad? She's not playing, remember?

CHAD
I know, I know. I'll ask again.

DEAD STAGE

Chad centres the glass. All three put their fingers back on base of the upturned glass.

CHAD
For whom . . .

The glass slides towards Izzy, again.

CHAD
Erm . . . Izzy?

Izzy unplugs her headphones and looks up.

IZZY
Yes?

CHAD
The board . . . it wants to talk to you.

IZZY
You're an asshole, Chad. This isn't funny anymore.

She turns to Becky.

IZZY
Your man is an asshole. I'm calling a taxi.

Izzy dials a number on her phone.

JACK
Just come and sit with us, I'll be here. I wanna know what this message is about?

> IZZY
> No. I'm calling it a . . . Yes, hello? Can I get a taxi please?

Becky rises and snatches Izzy's phone from her hands.

> IZZY
> Hey!

> BECKY
> You need to hear this.

> IZZY
> Give me back my phone!

> BECKY
> The message, it will be important. We have to finish this properly.

Becky glances at Jack, then Chad.

She sits.

> IZZY
> Fine, do what you gotta do.
> *(To Jack)*
> We are leaving afterward, OK?

> JACK
> Yeah, sure. Whatever.

The three of them place their fingers back onto the upturned glass.

DEAD STAGE

> CHAD
> You ready?

Becky nods. Jack glances nervously at Izzy, who is standing away from the table, watching intently.

> CHAD
> Spirit, we are listening. Speak.

The glass begins to move around the board

> CHAD
> It's spelling out something—get a pen and paper, I can't keep up!

Izzy looks at Becky, Jack, then Chad.

> CHAD
> Quickly!

> IZZY
> Fine.

Izzy fetches a pen and paper. The glass continues to move at a frantic pace. The lights begin to flicker.

> CHAD
> L,Y,I . . . fuck, it's moving too fast!

> JACK
> This better be a joke.

Chad continues to scribble until the glass comes to an abrupt halt.

Chad stares at the note, mouth ajar.

>>JACK
Well?

>>CHAD
Erm . . . I . . .

>>IZZY
(tentatively)
What does it say?

>>CHAD
It says, and I quote, "Lying Jack."

>>IZZY
What does that mean?

Izzy looks at Jack.

>>IZZY
Is this some kind of joke?

Jack glares at Becky.

>>JACK
It had better be.

>>IZZY
Then what's so funny, because I'm not laughing?

DEAD STAGE

CHAD
Shall we ask the board more questions?

JACK
No.

BECKY
Yes.

IZZY
Why not, Jack? Something to hide?

JACK
No, of course not. This is all Chad's idea of fun.

CHAD
Seeing my best friends falling out, erm . . . no, not really.

BECKY
I'll ask it more.

Becky places her finger on the glass.

Jack stands and turns to Izzy.

JACK
This is stupid, you were right. C'mon, let's go.

BECKY
Spirit, has Jack been unfaithful to Izzy?

Jack freezes.

All eyes watch as the glass moves across the board.

>   CHAD
> Yes.

>   JACK
> The fuck?

>   IZZY
> What is this? You bring me here tonight to be humiliated? Was that your idea?

>   JACK
> Babe, no . . . listen.

>   BECKY
> Is the person Jack has been unfaithful with, sat at this table?

The glass slides to Yes.

>   CHAD
> Becky? You are joking, right?

Izzy stands.

>   BECKY
> You said it yourself, this is the real deal.

She looks at Jack.

DEAD STAGE

BECKY
Right?

IZZY
(To Becky)
Why are you doing this?

BECKY
You had to see the truth.

IZZY
And this is how you show me? By sleeping with my boyfriend?

BECKY
I did it for you . . . for us. I didn't need to give him much of a hint, he was well up for it with me. That could have been any other girl in town, and you'd still sleep with him, maybe even marry him, never knowing what a liar he is.

Izzy gathers her things.

BECKY
Don't go. There's nothing between him and me, I just wanted you to see his true colours.

IZZY
And what of your true colours?
(To Jack, but not looking at him)
You asshole, you total asshole.
(To Becky)
And you . . . to think I said I loved you . . .

Izzy storms out.

CHAD
What the hell just happened?

JACK
(To Becky)
You stupid bitch.

IZZY
Over or not, they had a right to know.

JACK
Yes, but not like this? Couldn't you have written them both an email?

CHAD
(To Becky)
You were sleeping with my best friend?

BECKY
One time, Chad. One time. An email? That's a little cold, don't you think?

CHAD
And you were sleeping with Izzy?

BECKY
Yes, we are together.

JACK
Correction—were together. This little piece of theatre has put paid to that!

DEAD STAGE

CHAD
(To Jack)
You were sleeping with my girlfriend?

Beat.

JACK
I'm sorry, mate. It just sorta happened.

CHAD
And you were having an affair with his girlfriend?

BECKY
Yeah.

CHAD
(To Jack)
And you are ok with this?

JACK
Yes. No . . . I dunno. It's kinda hot if you think about it.

BECKY
Pig!

CHAD
So you were all sleeping with one another, meantime nobody was sleeping with me?

Beat.

CHAD
Go.

JACK
Yeah, I probably should.

CHAD
I mean both of you.

BECKY
I am sorry, Chad. It's not you . . . I wanted to tell you, I just didn't know how.

CHAD
I'm no expert on relationship break-ups, but I'm fairly confident staging a mock-seance to tell your boyfriend you are cheating on him with his best friend, and his best friend's partner, is not one of the more *tried and tested* methods.

BECKY
I know . . . but I am who I am.

CHAD
Yes, yes. Dumped. Goodbye.

Becky leaves. Jack picks up his coat, moves past Chad, head bowed, turns to say something but decides against it.

Chad stands, taking in his surroundings, and realizes he is dressed as a skeleton. Resigned, he exits.

DEAD STAGE

The glass in the middle of the board moves on its own.

END.

A FINAL NOTE

THE QUESTION I am asked most as a playwright is: how do you write dialogue that doesn't sound artificial?

Without meaning to over-simplify, the answer is to listen to how people speak. For example, your primetime newsreader will not relay a story in the same way as the grizzled old drunk, who shouts insults at passers-by at the end of your street.

Think about your character's background, where they are from, where they were educated, and build from there.

I often overhear conversations around me and take mental notes of them. Dialogue is like music, and if you can portray an array of different rhythms, tones, structures and sounds on the page, you will have written something that once spoken aloud, sounds altogether natural.

Break a leg . . . or, in this instance, place that stageplay!

Dan.
9/4/2018

THE END?

The end?

Not quite . . .

Dive into more Tales from the Darkest Depths:

Novels:
House of Sighs (with sequel novella) by Aaron Dries
Beyond Night by Eric S. Brown and Steven L. Shrewsbury
The Third Twin: A Dark Psychological Thriller by Darren Speegle
Aletheia: A Supernatural Thriller by J.S. Breukelaar
Beatrice Beecham's Cryptic Crypt: A Supernatural Adventure/Mystery Novel by Dave Jeffery
Where the Dead Go to Die by Mark Allan Gunnells and Aaron Dries
Sarah Killian: Serial Killer (For Hire!) by Mark Sheldon
The Final Cut by Jasper Bark
Blackwater Val by William Gorman
Pretty Little Dead Girls: A Novel of Murder and Whimsy by Mercedes M. Yardley
Nameless: The Darkness Comes by Mercedes M. Yardley

Novellas:
A Season in Hell by Kenneth W. Cain
Quiet Places: A Novella of Cosmic Folk Horror by Jasper Bark
The Final Reconciliation by Todd Keisling
Run to Ground by Jasper Bark
Apocalyptic Montessa and Nuclear Lulu: A Tale of Atomic Love by Mercedes M. Yardley
Wind Chill by Patrick Rutigliano
Little Dead Red by Mercedes M. Yardley
Sleeper(s) by Paul Kane
Stuck On You by Jasper Bark

Anthologies:
Welcome to The Show, edited by Doug Murano
Lost Highways: Dark Fictions From the Road, edited by D. Alexander Ward
C.H.U.D. Lives!—A Tribute Anthology
Tales from The Lake Vol.4: The Horror Anthology, edited by Ben Eads
Behold! Oddities, Curiosities and Undefinable Wonders, edited by Doug Murano
Twice Upon an Apocalypse: Lovecraftian Fairy Tales, edited by Rachel Kenley and Scott T. Goudsward
Tales from The Lake Vol.3, edited by Monique Snyman
Gutted: Beautiful Horror Stories, edited by Doug Murano and D. Alexander Ward
Tales from The Lake Vol.2, edited by Joe Mynhardt, Emma Audsley, and RJ Cavender
Children of the Grave
The Outsiders

Tales from The Lake Vol.1, edited by Joe Mynhardt
Fear the Reaper, edited by Joe Mynhardt
For the Night is Dark, edited by Ross Warren

Short story collections:
Frozen Shadows and Other Chilling Stories by Gene O'Neill
Varying Distances by Darren Speegle
The Ghost Club: Newly Found Tales of Victorian Terror by William Meikle
Ugly Little Things: Collected Horrors by Todd Keisling
Whispered Echoes by Paul F. Olson
Embers: A Collection of Dark Fiction by Kenneth W. Cain
Visions of the Mutant Rain Forest, by Bruce Boston and Robert Frazier
Tribulations by Richard Thomas
Eidolon Avenue: The First Feast by Jonathan Winn
Flowers in a Dumpster by Mark Allan Gunnells
The Dark at the End of the Tunnel by Taylor Grant
Where You Live by Gary McMahon
Tricks, Mischief and Mayhem by Daniel I. Russell
Samurai and Other Stories by William Meikle
Stuck On You and Other Prime Cuts by Jasper Bark

Poetry collections:
WAR by Alessandro Manzetti and Marge Simon
Brief Encounters with My Third Eye by Bruce Boston
No Mercy: Dark Poems by Alessandro Manzetti
Eden Underground: Poetry of Darkness by Alessandro Manzetti

If you've ever thought of becoming an author, we'd also like to recommend these non-fiction titles:

Where Nightmares Come From: The Art of Storytelling in the Horror Genre, edited by Joe Mynhardt and Eugene Johnson

Horror 101: The Way Forward, edited by Joe Mynhardt and Emma Audsley

Horror 201: The Silver Scream Vol.1 and *Vol.2*, edited by Joe Mynhardt and Emma Audsley

Modern Mythmakers: 35 interviews with Horror and Science Fiction Writers and Filmmakers by Michael McCarty

Writers On Writing: An Author's Guide Volumes 1,2,3, and 4, edited by Joe Mynhardt. Now also available in a Kindle and paperback omnibus.

Or check out other Crystal Lake Publishing books for more Tales from the Darkest Depths.

ABOUT THE AUTHOR

www.fatherdarkness.com

Dan Weatherer is represented by The Cherry Weiner Literary Agency.

Award-winning author, Dan Weatherer, was first published by Haunted Magazine in Spring, 2013. 'The Legend of the Chained Oak' was an immediate success and was made into a short film which won the award for **'Best Horror'** at the **Portobello Independent Film Festival (2014)**, **'Best Short'** at The **Bram Stoker International Film Festival (2014)** and also the **'Best UK Short Film'** award at the **Stoke Your Fires Film Festival** 2014. The film featured at numerous film festivals around the world during 2014. The premiere screening took place in his hometown of Cheadle.

In 2015, Dan was shortlisted for the prestigious position of Staffordshire Poet Laureate 2016-2018.

Aside from the publication of numerous short stories with a multitude of presses, his next major project was a solo collection of short stories titled 'The Soul That Screamed' (Winner of the Preditors & Editors™ Readers' Poll 'Best Anthology 2013).

A further two collections Only the Good Burn Bright (Spring 2015, James Ward Kirk Fiction) and

Neverlight (Spring 2016, Spectral Press) quickly followed. In 2017, Neverlight was shortlisted for the first annual Arnold Bennett Literary Prize. His fourth, Just Eventide, was released in August 2017.

2017 saw the release of Dan's historical novella, 'Crippen', courtesy again of Spectral Press.

His first non-fiction book titled 'What Dwells Within' was released in the Autumn of 2015 and details the life's work of paranormal investigator Jayne Harris.

An accomplished playwright, Dan was a winner of the 2017 Soundwork—UK play completion, a finalist in the Blackshaw Showcase Award 2016 and a two-time finalist of the Congleton Players One Act Festival, 2016. Dan has had several of his plays appear at festivals and fringe events.

Completed novels The Underclass, and English Gothic, are currently with his agent. Expect to see The Dead Stage, a book detailing Dan's experiences as a novice playwright appear via Crystal Lake Publishing in 2018.

Continuing on from the success of 'Legend of the Chained Oak', 2017 has seen Dan's short film Beige, added to The British Comedy Guide, and it continues to appear at film festivals nationwide.

Dan currently writes for FoundFootageCritic.Com.

Dan lives in Staffordshire, where is married to his wife Jenni and is a (proud) full-time dad to his daughter Bethany, and his son Nathan.

Visit www.fatherdarkness.com for more information

Awards:
Neverlight—shortlisted for the Arnold Bennett Literary Prize, 2017.

A Brother Born—Winner of the Soundwork-UK Play competition, 2017.
Beige—Finalist in the Bottle Smoke Film Competition, 2017.
Beige—Shortlisted for Best Drama at the Portobello International Film Awards, 2017.
Two Time finalist in the **Congleton Players One Act Festival, June 11th 2016.** (*Killing Gary* and *The Haul.*)
Parents—Shortlisted finalist in the **Blackshaw Showcase Award 2017.**
Shortlisted for Staffordshire Poet Laureate 2016-2018.
The Soul That Screamed—**Winner of the Critters Writers Workshop 'Best Anthology of 2013.'**
Ta Skoulikia—**Finished in the Top 3 in the 2013 Screen-con Horror Writing Competition.**
Only The Good Burn Bright—**Sep 2014, Winner Autumn Flash Contest, Massacre Magazine.**
One and Free—**March 2014, Runner-up in Spring Flash Contest, Massacre Magazine.**
Legend of the Chained Oak—**Winner of the 'Best Horror' award at the Portobello Film Festival 2014.**
Legend of the Chained Oak—**Winner of Best Short award at Bram Stoker International Film Festival 2014.**
Legend of the Chained Oak—**'Best UK Short Film' award at the Stoke Your Fires Film Festival 2014.**

Published Books:
Just Eventide—2017 (Ghostley Books)
The Dead Stage—2018 (Crystal Lake Publishing)

Crippen—May 2017 (Spectral Press)
Neverlight—March 31st 2016 (Spectral Press)
Only The Good Burn Bright—February 2015 (James Ward Kirk Fiction)
The Soul That Screamed—October 2013 (Horrified Press)
What Dwells Within: A Study of Spirit Attachment—June 2015, (6th Books)

Published Stage Plays:
A Brother Born—Spring, 2018 (Heartland Plays)
Tuesday of the Dead—Autumn, 2017 (Heartland Plays)
Beige—Summer, 2016 (Heartland Plays)
The Holding—Summer, 2016 (Heartland Plays)
The Haul—Summer, 2016 (Heartland Plays)
The Release of Theodore Marlow—Autumn, 2016 (Off The Wall Plays)

Performed Works:
A Brother Born—Winner of the Soundwork-UK Play competition, 2017. (Produced as an audio play.)
The Holding—Two performances by Taylorsville High School, Taylorsville, Utah, May 2017.
Beige performed as part of the Roses and Thorns night, One Night Stand Theatre, Aroura, Colorado, February 2017.
Points performed as part of the Speak Out Scratch Night, Stoke on Trent, July 4th, 2016.
The Haul performed as finalist in the Congleton Players One Act Festival, June 11th 2016.
Killing Gary performed as finalist in the Congleton Players One Act Festival, June 11th 2016.
Parents—Performed as finalist for the Blackshaw Showcase Award 2017 @ Horse and Stables, Waterloo, March 2016.

The Release of Theodore Marlow—Produced/aired by Shoestring Radio Theatre, San Francisco, 2016.
The Holding—performed by Bold As Brass productions as part of the North Staffordshire One Act contest, March 2016.
The Holding—performed as part of Wordplay by Theatrelab and Bath Spa University, January 30th, 2016.
Penkhull Paranormal—performed as part of Leytonstone Itch Blind Readings @ All You Read Is Love, Leytonstone, 9th January, 2016.
Beige—Performed at Left Coast Theatre, San Francisco, May, 2015.
Beige—Performed as part of the Blackshaw Theatre New Writers Night and the Wandsworth Arts Festival, May 2015.

Audiobooks:
Neverlight—Spectral Press (August, 2016)

Song and Music:
Maude by The Dead Certs. October 26th 2015.

Art:
Provided supporting poetry for the Exposed Exhibition by Holly Madew, at the One One Six Gallery, Stoke on Trent, August 12th—24th, 2016.

Articles/Essays:
Writer at www.foundfootagecritic.com
Behind the Legend of the Chained Oak—The Way We Were, September, 2017.
Growing up as a child in the 1980's—The Way We Were, June, 2017.

Christmas: Then and Now featured in The Sentinel, December 2016, as part of a Christmas Supplement.

Place The Play was published on the Horror Writers Association website as part of their permanent Writing Tips section. (September, 2016)

Kiln featured in the Autumn edition of Looky Bags, a quarterly bagzine that went out across Staffordshire. The issue was a City Of Culture Special. (September, 2016)

We Are A City of Creativity And Culture was published in the Autumn issue of Pubzine. (September, 2016)

Published Short Stories:

Signed, The Raven and the Wolf, My First Horror Story, The Withered Touch, Abarath and *Six Feet*—Mammoth Book of Spectral Horror, Spectral Press, Autumn 2018.

Just Eventide—Trapped Within, Eyecue Productions, June 2017.

The Journal Of Tiffany Poulter—Autumn 2017, The Spectral Book of Horror vol 5 (Spectral Press)

Cotton Face—October 2016, The Spectral Book of Horror Vol 3 (Spectral Press)

Girl, Soiled,—April 2016, Infernal Ink

The Raven and The Wolf—March 1st 2016, Reginald and Friends Vol 2 (Whimsical Press)

A Quest For Noah—March 1st 2016, Reginald and Friends Vol 2 (Whimsical Press)

Kleevar—The Prophets of Profanity, April 2015, HorrorMetalSounds.com

Kleevar—The Prophets of Profanity—November 2014, Axes of Evil Vol 2—Rise of the Metal Gods (Morbid Books)

Birth Of The Blackguard—Autumn 2014, The Black Hand Supremacy (Horrified Press.)
Falworth Manor—October 2014, Flashesinthedark.com
Only The Good Burn Brightly—September 2014, Massacre Magazine (Massacre Publishing)
Gyll's Whel—June 2014, Silent Scream (Blood Reigns Anthology)
Agnes—May 2014, Serial Killers Quattuor (James Ward Kirk Fiction)
Kleevar—The Prophets of Profanity—July 2014, Torched (Nocturnal Press Publishing.)
Gilbert's Well—February 2014, Reginald and Friends (Colin Evans Press—In aid of Acorns Children's Hospice)
Florian—August 2013, Haunted Magazine
The Legend of the Chained Oak—May 2013, Haunted magazine
The Lazarus Stratum—September 2013, Suffer Eternal vol 3 (Horrified Press)
The Fall of Silas Galloway—September 2013, Suffer Eternal Vol 3 (Horrified Press)
The Fall of Silas Galloway—October 2013, Daylight Dims (Stealth Fiction)
The Fall of Silas Galloway—(Chilling Tales for Dark Nights)
The Curse of Colyton—September 2013, Suffer Eternal vol 3 (Horrified Press)
Pride and PowerPoint—via Kindle Self-Publishing (13/3/13)
One and Free—March 2014, Massacre Magazine
Once a Butcher's Wife—June 22nd, 2013, Hell Whores Volume 2 (Horrified Press)
Gyll's Whel—Schlock bi-monthly/Nightmare Illustrated (Horrified Press)

Published Poems:
The One Five Six—Pitman Tales, Tickety Boo Press, Autumn 2018
The One Five Six—Helmer End Exhibition, April 23rd, 2017 (as part of the Minnie Pit Disaster memorial).
Huenco Mundo (Hollow World)—October 2016, The Spectral Book of Horror Vol 3
Mortem Praeteriti (Death of the Past)—Spring 2017, The Spectral Book of Horror Vol 4
Mo Jikangai (Outside the time)—Autumn 2017, The Spectral Book of Horror Vol 5

Film work:
Writer—*Strings* (Monkeelistens LTD, 2017)
Writer—*Beige* (Monkeelistens LTD, 2016)
Writer and co-producer of the movie *The Legend of the Chained Oak (Weatherer/Maynard Productions)* **Winner of the Best Horror at Portobello Film Festival, Best Short at The Bram Stoker International Film Festival and Best UK Short Film at Stoke Your Fires Film Festival 2014.**

Screenings:
Beige
Listed in The British Comedy Guide
Shortlisted for Best Drama at the Portobello International Film Festival, September 11th 2017
Finalist—The Bottle Smoke Film Festival, September 2nd 2017
Shown as part of the Cardiff Mini Film Festival, June 2017
Shown by The London Horror Society, May 27th, 2017
Shown as part of Made in Stoke on Trent, Stoke Your Fires Film Festival, 2017

Shown as part of the Birmingham Horror Convention, October 28th/29th 2017

LA Cinefest International Film Festival Semi-Finalist, February 2017

Shown as part of the Beeston Film Festival, Nottingham, March 2017

Shown as part of the Feel The Reel International Film Festival, Glasgow, January 2017

Shown as part of the Five Lamps Film Festival, Derby, November 2016

Legend of the Chained Oak

Shown before the screening of 'Pan's Labyrinth', as part of the Scalarama Festival, Nottingham, September 23rd 2017

Shown as part of the Birmingham Horror Convention, October 28th/29th 2017

Shown on 19th April 2014 @ Lulworth House, Cheadle, Staffordshire. £474 raised for the Cheadle and District Food-Bank/Cheadle Discovery Centre

Shown as part of the Ozark Shorts Film Festival, Missouri, USA, 2016

Shown as part of the Tri-Cities International Fantastic Film Festival, USA, 2015

Shown as part of the Phnom Penh international film festival, Cambodia, 2014

Shown as part of the Molise Cinema Film Festival, Italy, 2015

Shown as part of the First International Film Festival, China, 2015

Shown as part of the Fanter Film Festival, Spain, 2015

Shown as part of the Bram Stoker International Film Festival, October 2014

Shown as part of the 'Novella Showcase' Television show, Michigan, 2014

Shown as Battle Creek's, Access Vision, Comcast Channel 16 and

Lansing's Public Media Center, Comcast Channel 16
Both air at 11:00 PM, Fridays.

Comcast Channel 21 is in Haslett, Okemos, and East Lansing. And is also seen on AT&T U-Verse Channel 99 in 17 communities.

Shown as part of the 2014, Portobello Film Festival, London.

Legend of the Chained Oak—A voice from the past Shown as part of the Five Lamps Film Festival, March 2015

Radio and Podcasts:

A Brother Born—Winner of the Soundwork-UK Play competition, 2017

Numerous interviews on BBC Radio Stoke regarding my work

The Release of Theodore Marlow—Shoestring Theatre, San Francisco USA

The Dolly Who Is My Friend—aired as part of Signal One's Halloween Breakfast Broadcast, Oct 30th 2015.

Exit—Dark Dreams Podcast (Oct 2013)

Education and Public appearances:

St. Giles Primary School (November, 2016)—Script Workshop

St Thomas' Primary School (June, 2016)—Vocation Day Talk

Cheadle Library (February 2016)—Script Workshop

Sledge-Lit Derby (November 2015)—Script workshop/Horror Panelist

Scribe Middlewich Literary Festival (October 2015)—Meet the Author
City Central Library (October 2015)—Meet the Author
Excel Academy, Stoke on Trent (July 2015)—5 Creative writing workshops

Panels:
Sledge-lit—*Is Horror ready for a new golden age?* With Charles Stross, Simon Marshall Jones, Thana Niveau and Marie O' Regan
Scribefest—*Writers in the real world* with Catherine Green, Paula Manely and Gill Hoffs.

Influence:
Instigator of the Arnold Bennett Award for Literacy.
A Poet Laureate for Stoke on Trent
The Potteries Anthem

Hi readers,

It makes our day to know you reached the end of our book. Thank you so much. This is why we do what we do every single day.

Whether you found the book good or great, we'd love to hear what you thought. Please take a moment to leave a review on Amazon, Goodreads, or anywhere else readers visit. Reviews go a long way to helping a book sell, and will help us to continue publishing quality books. You can also share a photo of yourself holding this book with the hashtag #IGotMyCLPBook!

Thank you again for taking the time to journey with Crystal Lake Publishing.

We are also on . . .

Website:
www.crystallakepub.com

Be sure to sign up for our newsletter and receive two free eBooks: http://eepurl.com/xfuKP

Books:
http://www.crystallakepub.com/book-table/

Twitter:
https://twitter.com/crystallakepub

Facebook:
https://www.facebook.com/Crystallakepublishing/

Instagram:
https://www.instagram.com/crystal_lake_publishing/

Patreon:
https://www.patreon.com/CLP

Or check out other Crystal Lake Publishing books for more Tales from the Darkest Depths. You can also subscribe to Crystal Lake Classics where you'll receive fortnightly info on all our books, starting all the way back at the beginning, with personal notes on every release. Or follow us on Patreon for behind the scenes access.

With unmatched success since 2012, Crystal Lake Publishing has quickly become one of the world's leading indie publishers of Mystery, Thriller, and Suspense books with a Dark Fiction edge.

Crystal Lake Publishing puts integrity, honor, and respect at the forefront of our operations.

We strive for each book and outreach program that's launched to not only entertain and touch or comment on issues that affect our readers, but also to strengthen and support the Dark Fiction field and its authors.

Not only do we publish authors who are legends in the field and as hardworking as us, but we look for men and women who care about their readers and fellow human beings. We only publish the very best Dark Fiction, and look forward to launching many new careers.

We strive to know each and every one of our

readers while building personal relationships with our authors, reviewers, bloggers, podcasters, bookstores, and libraries.

Crystal Lake Publishing is and will always be a beacon of what passion and dedication, combined with overwhelming teamwork and respect, can accomplish: unique fiction you can't find anywhere else.

We do not just publish books, we present you worlds within your world, doors within your mind from talented authors who sacrifice so much for a moment of your time.

This is what we believe in. What we stand for. This will be our legacy.

Welcome to Crystal Lake Publishing.

THANK YOU FOR PURCHASING THIS BOOK

www.ingramcontent.com/pod-product-compliance
Lightning Source LLC
Chambersburg PA
CBHW071143070526
44584CB00019B/2645